CHRISTOPHER ANDERSEN

The #1 New York Times bestselling author who has reported on the Rolling Stones since Altamont

MICK

The international bestseller that tells the full, uncensored story of the legend who has rocked five decades like no one else

SEX: jaw-dropping new details about Jagger's thousands of conquests—who, what, when, and where . . . and the sexy star who had Mick pleading ("Angelina, it's Mick. Call me!")

DRUGS: cocaine, LSD, hashish, and speed—the truth about Jagger's substance abuse, and how long it really went on

ROCK: the scandal, mayhem, madness, and genius that made the Rolling Stones the world's greatest rock band

ROYALTY: the backstage drama of Mick's knighthood, as well as Mick's ties to Prince William and Kate Middleton

RICHES: a rare glimpse into his business dealings and the killer instinct that produced a $400 million personal fortune

FAME: his no-holds-barred takes on today's superstars, from Lady Gaga and Britney Spears to Beyoncé, Justin Timberlake, Kanye West, and Justin Bieber

FRIENDS: behind-the-scenes accounts of his often turbulent relationships—from Keith Richards, whose searing comments almost ran the bandmates' "marriage" aground, to such celebrated intimates as Andy Warhol, John Lennon, Eric Clapton, Jackie Onassis, David Bowie, Bill Clinton, and others

FANS: how the fit, athletic Jagger deals with ravenous groupies and rabid fans.

MICK

ALSO BY CHRISTOPHER ANDERSEN

William and Kate: A Royal Love Story

Barack and Michelle: Portrait of an American Marriage

*Somewhere in Heaven: The Remarkable Love Story of
Dana and Christopher Reeve*

After Diana: William, Harry, Charles, and the Royal House of Windsor

Barbra: The Way She Is

American Evita: Hillary Clinton's Path to Power

Sweet Caroline: Last Child of Camelot

George and Laura: Portrait of an American Marriage

Diana's Boys: William and Harry and the Mother They Loved

The Day John Died

Bill and Hillary: The Marriage

The Day Diana Died

Jackie After Jack: Portrait of the Lady

*An Affair to Remember: The Remarkable Love Story of
Katharine Hepburn and Spencer Tracy*

Jack and Jackie: Portrait of an American Marriage

Michael Jackson Unauthorized

Madonna: Unauthorized

Citizen Jane

The Best of Everything (with John Marion)

Young Kate

The Serpent's Tooth

Father

The Name Game

MICK

◆ ◆ ◆

THE WILD LIFE AND
MAD GENIUS OF
JAGGER

◆ ◆ ◆

Christopher Andersen

GALLERY BOOKS

New York ◆ London ◆ Toronto ◆ Sydney ◆ New Delhi

Gallery Books
A Division of Simon & Schuster, Inc.
1230 Avenue of the Americas
New York, NY 10020

First Gallery Books paperback edition March 2013

GALLERY BOOKS and colophon are registered trademarks of Simon & Schuster, Inc.

For information about special discounts for bulk purchases, please contact Simon & Schuster Special Sales at 1-866-506-1949 or business@simonandschuster.com.

The Simon & Schuster Speakers Bureau can bring authors to your live event. For more information or to book an event, contact the Simon & Schuster Speakers Bureau at 1-866-248-3049 or visit our website at www.simonspeakers.com.

Designed by Jaime Putorti

Manufactured in the United States of America

10 9 8 7 6 5 4 3 2 1

The Library of Congress has cataloged the hardcover edition as follows:

Mick : the wild life and mad genius of Jagger / Christopher Andersen.
p. cm.
Includes bibliographical references and index.
1. Jagger, Mick. 2. Rock musicians—England—Biography. I. Title.
ML420.J22A74 2012
782.42166092—dc23
[B]
2012003741

ISBN 978-1-4516-6144-6
ISBN 978-1-4516-6145-3 (pbk)
ISBN 978-1-4516-6146-0 (ebook)

Photo Insert Credits:
IPOL-Globe Photos: 1; Alpha/Globe Photos: 3, 37; Dezo Hoffmann/Rex USA/BEImages: 4, 5, 7, 8, 12; Rex USA/BEImages: 6, 15, 16, 34; Popperfoto/Getty Images: 9; Richard Polak-Globe Photos: 10; Everett Collection/Rex USA/BEImages: 11, 13, 14; Retna: 17; AFP/Getty Images: 18; Getty Images: 19, 22, 24, 39, 40; Adam Scull/Globe Photos: 20; Richard Young/Rex USA/BEImages: 21; WireImage: 23; News Ltd./Newspix/Rex USA/BEImages: 25; Time & Life Pictures/Getty Images: 26; Dave Lewis/Rex USA/BEImages: 27; Adam Hollingsworth/Newspix/Rex USA/BEImages: 28; Richard Young/Rex USA/BEImages: 29; Bernadette Lou/Rex USA/BEImages: 30; Omedias-Globe Photos: 31; PIXPLANETE/Globe Photos: 32; Pazzazz.GB.com/Globe Photos: 33; Dave Benett/Globe Photos: 35; MURRAY/MCKAY/Rex USA/BEImages: 36; Mark Large/Daily Mail/Rex/Rex USA/BEImages: 38; Richfoto.com/Globe Photos: 41; Back Page Images/Rex/Rex USA/BEImages: 42; FilmMagic, Inc.: 43; Ken Babolcsay-Globe Photos: 44; Sonia Moskowitz-Globe Photos: 45; Anthony Harvey-Allstar-Globe Photos: 46.

For my wife, Valerie,
who was there when

Obviously I can't do this forever!

—MICK JAGGER,

NOVEMBER 1969

CONTENTS

✦ ✦ ✦

PREFACE

◆   ◆   ◆

*W*hen Justin Timberlake chronicled his painful breakup with Britney Spears in 2002's "Cry Me a River," Lizzy Jagger showed the autobiographical video to her father. "You see the scene in the video?" she asked. "That actually happened, Dad." Mick Jagger knew instinctively that the rules that applied to other stars did not necessarily apply to him. "If I wrote about what my life is really about, directly and on the money," Mick said, "people would cringe."

No matter to the millions of fans who spanned the generations, and for whom the term "Jagger swagger" defines what it means to be truly hip and cutting edge—not just fifty years ago when Mick first stepped onto a stage with the Rolling Stones, but today. As the Stones approach their half-century milestone, such contemporary artists as Ke$ha, Kanye West, and the Black Eyed Peas pay musical homage to Jagger—none more memorably than Maroon 5's Adam Levine and Christina Aguilera, who added their voices to the mounting crescendo of musical tributes with "Moves Like Jagger." First performed on the hit NBC reality TV show *The Voice* in June 2011, "Moves Like Jagger" zoomed to number one. With the aid of a hit video featuring the lanky, tattooed Levine, a seductive Christina, and riveting archive footage of a fleet-footed Mick—the true star of the production—"Moves Like Jagger" dominated the musical landscape for the rest of the year.

Is he Jumpin' Jack Flash? A Street Fighting Man? The Midnight Rambler? A Man of Wealth and Taste? All this, it turns out, and far, far more. By any definition, Mick Jagger is an original, one of the dominant cultural figures of our time. Swaggering, strutting, sometimes sinister, always mesmerizing, he grabbed us by our collective throat a half century ago and—unlike so many of his gifted peers—never let go.

Jagger is arguably the last of the rock titans, although even that description sells him short. Over the past half century—from the tumultuous sixties and hedonistic seventies to the booming eighties and no-holds-barred nineties to hardscrabble 2012—Mick seeped into the pores of the culture in a way few others have.

To baby boomers and subsequent generations, Mick was a funhouse mirror reflection of every phase, fad, movement, and trend. Once the Beatles paved the way with their squeaky-clean brand of youthful rebellion, the Stones gloried in being dirty, scruffy, raunchy, and rude. Students took to the streets to protest the war in Vietnam, and Mick supplied them with rage-filled anthems.

No group epitomized the sex, drugs, and rock-and-roll ethos of the psychedelic era more than the Stones. And when the occult was added to the mix, Mick wrapped himself not in some mystic's robes but in Lucifer's crimson cloak.

His macho street fighter image behind him, Mick became an avatar of androgynous chic, wearing mascara and lipstick and exploring his bisexual side. This, in turn, morphed seamlessly into the disco era, when Mick slipped his bony frame into white satin jumpsuits, bathed himself in glitter, and belted out dance hits between hits of cocaine.

The "Just Say No" eighties of Ronald Reagan brought another shape-shift for Jagger. Now Mick was a family man, and staunchly antidrug. "Why," he now claimed with a straight face, as if the previous thirty years hadn't happened, "I never really did any of those things."

As it turned out, more than Mick's lips were larger than life. Everything he did both on and off stage seemed to be bigger, faster, louder. As the lead singer of the Rolling Stones, he sang, pranced, strutted, vamped, and yes, swaggered, before more people than anyone in history. By 2010, of the ten highest-grossing concert tours of all time, the Rolling Stones occupied spots one, three, four, five, and nine.

Then, of course, there were the records—an astounding 250 million albums sold—and the annual polls never failing to rank the Rolling Stones as the greatest rock-and-roll band of all time. Which, logically, made Mick the number one rock vocalist of all time.

Offstage Mick did not disappoint, living the sybaritic life of an arrogant, self-obsessed, seemingly out-of-control rock star to the hilt. The public dramas and private heartaches were detailed meticulously by a ravenous press, along with the wretched excesses of Mick's private life: the lavish homes and limousines, the private jets and yachts, the drugs, the women—and sometimes the men. But especially the women.

Along the way, Mick used skills he learned as a student at the London School of Economics to help the band earn billions and make its members all absurdly rich—in Mick's case, to the tune of $400 million. He also slavishly pursued his dream of being accepted into the highest circles of British society—a quest that, in time, earned him a knighthood.

For essentially his entire adult life, this vocal enemy of the Establishment has also been cozy with England's aristocracy—just one in the mind-spinning tangle of contradictions that make up Jagger the man.

Mick is the suburban English schoolboy who exploded on the scene singing blues from America's heartland; the gym teacher's son who became the poster boy for unfettered hedonism; the street tough with the refined tastes of a proper English gentleman; the androgynous dabbler in bisexual love with boundless heterosexual appetites; the knight of the realm who for fifty years has reveled in his worldwide image as rock's rebel emeritus, the legendary Lothario whose most important and enduring human relationship is with another man who claims not to understand him at all: Keith Richards.

As the Rolling Stones celebrated their fiftieth anniversary, Jagger remained one of the most written about, talked about, and speculated about people on the planet. Yet, incredibly, he succeeded in cultivating the one thing that all true icons have in common: a powerful mystique.

It is, in the end, that singular, galvanic force of nature—a charismatic creature who would have achieved stardom with or without the Rolling Stones—who continues to mesmerize, excite, and enthrall us after a half century. Scandal, money, drama, music, fame, drugs, sex, and genius—all this and more are embodied in the man whose very name defines an era. That man is *Jagger*. That man is Mick.

MICK

I'm one of the best things England's got. Me and the Queen.

—MICK

♦   ♦   ♦

Please allow me to introduce myself.
I'm a man of wealth and taste.

—"SYMPATHY FOR THE DEVIL"

♦   ♦   ♦

He's a smart little motherfucker, I'll give him that.

—KEITH RICHARDS

1

"Tell Them to Stick It Up Their Arse"

BUCKINGHAM PALACE
FRIDAY, DECEMBER 12, 2003

*P*rince Charles adjusted the braided cuff of his rear admiral's dress uniform and cleared his throat as he ran down the list of names. He was searching for one in particular. "Ah," he said, his finger stopping halfway down the single sheet. "'Sir Michael Jagger.' So he'll be here this time, I see."

"Yes, sir," answered the Lord Chamberlain, whose job it was to see that the day's investiture ceremonies went off without a hitch. "I can't imagine he'd miss it."

Mick had shown an attitude toward being knighted that verged on the cavalier. He had postponed the date no fewer than ten times, most recently opting out of an invitation to be knighted just two days earlier, on December 10. On that day, one of the few people who could upstage him—rugby superstar Jonny "Wilko" Wilkinson, who had just led England to victory in the World Cup—was also to be honored, and sixty-year-old Mick had no intention of competing for the spotlight with a twentysomething sports hero.

"It's really quite difficult to believe," the Prince of Wales said, shaking his head. "Mick Jagger. A *knighthood*. Just incredible." Then, turning to the Queen's chief usher, he added, "My mother did not have the stomach for it."

It was not unusual for Charles to stand in for his mother at such ceremonies—particularly if she was ill or otherwise indisposed. In this case, she surprised her son and even her staff when she suddenly decided to have elective surgery on her left knee on December 12—an operation that could have been performed anytime over the previous year and for which there was no pressing need. Indeed, that same week, she appeared hale and hearty when she welcomed Wilkinson and his teammates to Buckingham Palace following the World Cup victory parade through central London.

"The Queen looked at Mick Jagger's name on that list," a senior courtier observed later, "and there was absolutely no way in the world that she was going to take part in that. So she simply arranged to be elsewhere."

The Queen had, in fact, privately opposed Prime Minister Tony Blair's efforts to include Jagger among the parade of humanitarians, scientists, diplomats, artists, academics, civil servants, sports figures, and business and labor leaders who made up her twice-annual honors list. The vast majority received an MBE (Member of the Most Excellent Order of the British Empire), OBE (Officer of the Most Excellent Order of the British Empire), or perhaps a CBE (Commander of the Most Excellent Order of the British Empire). As many as 2,500 such royal honors were announced each year, and while the monarch's approval is technically required, she seldom gave an individual recipient her personal attention.

Knighthoods were another matter. Next to a peerage, this was the highest honor the Queen could bestow, and she paid special attention to those few men and women she was being asked to make Sirs and Dames. Still, it was rare for the monarch to ever voice an objection—not even in private—once the government had drawn up its list of honorees.

Jagger was such an exception. Shortly after taking office as prime minister in 1997, Tony Blair had proposed Jagger for a knighthood. An unabashed rock fan and self-proclaimed master of the air guitar, Blair was still a young member of parliament when he first met Jagger at a dinner party hosted by Lord Mandelson. "Tony summoned up his courage," Lord Mandelson recalled, "and went up to Mick. Looking him straight in the eye, he said, 'I just want to say how much you've always meant to me.' He looked wistful," Lord Mandelson added. "For a moment, I thought Tony might ask for an autograph."

Unfortunately, Blair's request that Mick be knighted was immediately met by stern opposition from the Queen. Over the next five years, Blair repeatedly submitted Jagger's name for a knighthood, only to have the Queen make it known each time that she believed he was "not suitable."

Jagger's profession had nothing to do with it. The Queen had taken great satisfaction in knighting other pop stars, most notably Paul McCartney and Elton John. But Jagger was different. Unlike most of those to receive such honors, he appeared to have embraced few charitable causes despite having accumulated a massive personal fortune. Nor could he remotely be regarded as patriotic. While other British rock stars had remained in England and paid dearly for the privilege in the form of exorbitant income tax rates, Jagger had been technically living abroad to legally escape paying those taxes since the early 1970s.

To be sure, opposition was grounded in a deep-seated personal dislike of Jagger and all that he stood for since the 1960s. More than any other figure, Mick embodied the hedonistic sex, drugs, and rock-and-roll ethos of the era. His early public persona—scruffy, surly, obscene, resolutely antiestablishment—was calculated to offend, and who more than the woman who sat at the very pinnacle of the social heap?

As for his private life, Mick had fathered seven children by four different women, but everyone knew that this was barely the tip of what amounted to an Everest-sized sexual iceberg. As for the drugs, there were arrests, two convictions—even a brief stint in jail. For a time, Jagger appeared to embrace the dark side, singing Satan's praises in "Sympathy for the Devil" and hiring the appropriately named Hell's Angels motorcycle gang to provide security at the notorious Altamont Rock Festival in California—a decision that would result in mayhem, and in bloody murder.

It certainly did not help that over the years Jagger had routinely mocked the royal family and that he repeatedly referred to the Queen specifically as England's "Chief Witch." He also made a habit of calling for a full-scale revolution. With no hint of irony or self-consciousness, he once actually proclaimed that "anarchy is the only slight glimmer of hope. There should be no such thing as private property."

For all Jagger's posturing and hyperbole, something more personal was at the core of the Queen's anger toward him: she had always been concerned about the curiously intimate and potentially explosive relationship between Jagger and her late sister, the famously free-spirited Princess Margaret. Time and again, the Queen had intervened to cover up one scandalous revelation after another regarding Jagger and Princess Margaret—including one sex-and-drugs party that might have taken the government, if not the monarchy, down with it.

Equally galling for Her Majesty was the fact that Mick, despite his rebel pose, had blatant social ambitions of his own. "Mick always wanted to be one of them," his friend and longtime publicist Keith Altham said. "He aspired to be an aristo from the very beginning. A knight? He wants to be a prince of the realm!"

Far worse, in the eyes of the Queen, was that he sought to use her emotionally fragile sister to climb the social ladder. "The Queen loved her sister and worried about her. Jagger was a friend of Princess Margaret's for over forty years, and all that time the Queen thought he was a corrupting influence."

So now, the very morning that Mick was scheduled to receive his knighthood, the Queen slipped quietly into King Edward VII Hospital. Once there, doctors would also remove cancerous lesions from her face. The operation to remove cartilage from the monarch's knee went smoothly, but the procedure on her face left the Queen with deep scars above and below her left eye and along her nose. When she hobbled out of the hospital two days later with the help of a cane, onlookers were shocked by her appearance. "All at once, it seems," wrote a reporter for the *Daily Mail,* "the Queen has become a frail, vulnerable old lady."

No matter. "I would much rather be here," she'd told one of the attending physicians, "than at Buckingham Palace knighting a certain party."

In the meantime, it fell to Prince Charles to perform the deed. Years earlier, during a gala to benefit his own charity, the Prince's Trust, the prince had told Jagger that he "couldn't believe" Mick had never been on the Queen's biannual Honors List. But he later told an aide that he was not remotely suggesting a knighthood—"a CBE, perhaps."

Prince Charles had his own axe to grind with Jagger. Princess Diana was an ardent fan of the Stones and Mick in particular. Shortly after her marriage to Charles in 1981, Diana, then just twenty years old, planned to invite Jagger to tea at Kensington Palace. Charles, despite being distracted by his own affair with Camilla Parker Bowles, had ample time to be jealous. He was well aware of Jagger's reputation as a womanizer with a particularly keen interest in long-stemmed blondes in Diana's age bracket and insisted she cancel the meeting with Mick. An angry row ensued, but in the end, Diana grudgingly accepted a compromise offered by her husband: by way of consolation, the princess was allowed to invite a pop star Charles found less threatening than Mick Jagger to tea at Kensington Palace—the then happily married, slightly paunchy, prematurely balding Phil Collins.

Charles may have been even more offended by what he saw as Jagger's overt lack of manners. At another Prince's Trust dinner, this time at Windsor Castle in June 1991, Mick was photographed keeping one hand in his pocket as he shook Prince Charles's hand with the other—a flagrant breach of royal etiquette that the next day's papers blasted as "especially insulting to the royal family." Painfully aware of every slight both real and imagined, the Queen and Charles both recalled the incident and the photo that was picked up by papers around the world. "Charles was really appalled by that," Diana once said of the Jagger hand-in-pocket faux pas. "It's the kind of silly thing they never forget."

The one person whose opinion mattered most to Mick made no secret of how he felt about the knighthood controversy. Two years earlier, Jagger had called Keith Richards to break the news.

"Keef," Mick began, "I've got to tell you this now: Tony Blair is insisting that I accept a knighthood."

"Oh, come on man," Richards groaned. "Just fucking ridiculous. A knighthood? What the fuck would you want with *that*? That's not you, is it? That's not what we're about."

"I mean, Paul has one, and Elton," Mick replied meekly. "It's not really the kind of thing you turn down, is it?"

There was a pause. Not long before, Mick had opened the Mick Jagger Centre at Dartford Grammar, the suburban prep school where in the late 1950s he got into serious trouble for wearing his hair too long and his jeans too tight. Had Keith's old friend changed? After forty years as a convention-smashing iconoclast, was Mick now craving bourgeois respectability?

"You can turn down anything you like, pal," replied Keith, incredulous. "Tell them to stick it up their arse."

◆

The black Bentley made its way along Birdcage Walk, turned onto Buckingham Gate, and then, once waved past the gate, pulled up to the porticoed ambassadors' entrance. A palace aide dashed to open the near passenger door, but the familiar lithe figure emerged from the far side, and without saying a word, bounded up the red-carpeted steps and into the palace.

Once inside, he walked up the horseshoe-shaped Grand Staircase and was led into an anteroom to wait for his group of honorees to be called. As he passed the time, Mick surveyed the works of Rembrandt, Vermeer, Van Dyck, and Rubens that lined the walls. He also noticed that several of his fellow honorees chose to wear their national garb: Scots in plaid kilts, saffron-robed Buddhists, and several women in brightly colored silk saris. There was the occasional military uniform and more than a smattering of men in morning coats, but the vast majority wore formal dark suits. Most of the ladies present were attired in chic suits or cocktail dresses—nearly all worn with that staple of old-school British fashion, the hat.

Much to the relief of palace aides, Jagger shed his leather trench coat and six-foot-long red cashmere scarf to reveal a striped suit—albeit one with leather lapels—and tie. They were less than delighted with his choice of footwear: $55 Adidas sneakers.

The investiture itself would take place inside the cavernous white and gold ballroom, built by Queen Victoria in 1854 and easily the largest space in the palace. Several hundred guests—each of the one hundred honorees was permitted to invite three—sat with their programs in their laps, waiting anxiously for the name of their friend or family member to be called. Mick had invited his father, Joe, then ninety-two, and two of his children: thirty-three-year-old Karis and Elizabeth, nineteen. "They would all have loved to come," Mick said, "but we were limited to three. I chose them in order of seniority and availability."

At precisely eleven o'clock, musicians seated in the balcony began playing, and five members of the Queen's Body Guard of the Yeomen of the Guard—the elite detail created by Henry VII in 1485 and better known as Beefeaters—marched up the center aisle to the front of the room.

Prince Charles then made his entrance accompanied by two Gurkha orderly officers, a tradition started in 1876 by Queen Victoria. As the band played "God Save the Queen," Charles stood at attention before twin thrones on the dais beneath the Durbar Shamiana, a towering, domed velvet canopy that was used when George V was crowned emperor of India in 1911.

"Please be seated," Charles told the crowd and then, with his equerry at his side to whisper in his ear details about each recipient, waited for the Lord Chamberlain to announce the first honoree.

Mick stood impatiently in the anteroom, chewing gum and jangling the change in his pants pocket. Once one of the Queen's "Gentlemen Ushers"—in this case, a rear admiral in the Royal

Navy—informed Mick that he was to join the next group of ten to file into the ballroom, Mick hastily disposed of the gum and fell into line behind a priest and an elderly man being honored for his services to the sheep industry. Of the scores of men and women being honored that day, Jagger was the only person being knighted.

"Sir Michael Philip Jagger," intoned Master of the Royal Household Vice Admiral Tom Blackburn, "for services to popular music."

Jagger stepped forward, smiling, as Charles's equerry handed him the sword that belonged to the Queen's father, King George VI, when, as Duke of York, he was colonel of the Scots Guards. Another aide rushed to place the traditional red-and-gold velvet-upholstered investiture stool in position. Pausing to bow before Charles, Mick then stepped forward and, grasping the wooden railing attached to the stool with his right hand, knelt before the prince and bowed his head.

"I dub thee," Charles said as he tapped Mick gently on his left shoulder and then on his right, "Sir Michael Jagger." With that, Mick popped up and Charles handed off the sword to one aide even as a red velvet cushion was being placed before him by another. On the cushion was a medal signifying Mick's new rank that Charles then pinned on Jagger's lapel. After a brief handshake and a few pleasantries, Mick bowed his head slightly and took five large steps backward before turning to leave.

♦

"I went fucking berserk when I heard," said Richards, still fuming. "I thought it was ludicrous to take one of those gongs from the establishment when they did their very best to throw us in jail and kill us at one time. It's not what the Stones is about, is it? I don't want to step onstage with someone wearing a fucking coronet and sporting the old ermine. I told Mick, 'It's a fucking paltry honor.'"

Keith also pointed out that his friend was probably disappointed that Prince Charles had knighted him, and not the Queen. "I guess," Richards said, "that makes him more of a 'cur' than a 'sir.'"

Mick's old flame Marianne Faithfull, who was revived by Jagger when she once tried to kill herself, was more charitable. "Mick's a tremendous snob," she said of the knighthood. "He always wanted that so much. That's why I'm sort of compassionate about it."

Once outside the palace with his proud father and daughters, Mick was besieged with reporters' questions. What was it like, he was asked, to receive such an honor from the Establishment he had railed against for so long? "I don't think the establishment as we knew it exists anymore," he replied, adding that "it's very nice to have honors given to you as long as you don't take it all too seriously. You should wear them lightly and not get carried away with your own self-importance."

Jagger grew visibly irritable when Keith's objections were brought up. "It is a bit like a bawling child who hasn't got an ice cream," Mick shot back. "One gets one, and they all want one. It's nothing new. I think he'd like to get the same honor himself." Besides, he went on, "Keith likes to make a fuss . . . He's not a particularly happy person." (Richards was under no illusions about his ever being offered a knighthood. "They knew I would tell them where to put it," he said, adding about the royals, "I wouldn't let that family near me with a sharp stick, much less a sword.")

Jagger was not about to let anyone spoil the moment—not even Keith. "I suppose people will call me 'Sir Mick,'" he mused, hesitating for a moment. "But 'Sir Michael' has a nice ring to it."

Back at his estate in rural Connecticut, Richards called the Stones' drummer, Charlie Watts. "What *is* all this shit?" Keith asked.

"You know he's always wanted a knighthood," Watts answered, just as surprised that Keith seemed so clueless about what made his soul mate tick.

"No, no," Keith said wistfully, recalling the Mick he'd grown up with—and the man he thought he understood better than anyone. "I didn't know. I didn't know . . ."

I was born in a crossfire hurricane.

—"JUMPIN' JACK FLASH"

◆   ◆   ◆

Mick and I knew each other because we happened to live very close, just a few doors away . . . but then we moved "across the tracks."

—KEITH RICHARDS

◆   ◆   ◆

As far back as I can remember, he said the one thing he wanted most was to be rich.

—CHRIS JAGGER, MICK'S BROTHER

2

◆ ◆ ◆

The Glimmer Twins Grow Up,
Next Door and Worlds Apart

DARTFORD, KENT

*T*hey were born in the same hospital just 145 days apart—Mick, on July 26, 1943; Keith, on December 18—and met when they were seven. By then, Mick (Mike, to family and friends) was a model student, the teacher's pet, and by all accounts the tallest kid in his class. Keith, by contrast, was a self-described runt who spent much of his time fleeing the bullies who pursued him on the way home from school.

Several years later, they formed a friendship that helped reshape popular music. In the meantime, they themselves were being shaped—by the sights, sounds, and smells of Dartford, the London suburb where Jagger and Richards were born and raised.

The "pungent mixture" of "horseshit and coal smoke" was what Keith remembered most about his childhood. For him, postwar Dartford was "somewhere to get out of." Yet both Mick and Keith came to believe there was something about that place and time—the texture of life there—that nurtured talent.

Joe Jagger spotted the first signs within moments of Mick's birth—and so did the nurses on duty that day in the maternity ward of Dartford's Livingstone Hospital. They agreed that of all the infants born to wartime brides that day, Michael Philip Jagger not only had the most distinctive cry but also was the only one that could be heard above the nerve-fraying whine of air-raid sirens.

The "crossfire hurricane" little Mike Jagger was born into was of man's making. While most of the seventy thousand British civilians killed during the German aerial blitz of 1940 and 1941 lived in central London, the Jaggers had the misfortune of residing in what came to be called "the Graveyard"—the narrow industrial corridor between the southeastern coast of Kent and Greater London that took a relentless pounding from Hitler's Luftwaffe.

The newest Jagger was too young to have any conscious memory of the horrors of war—not even the direct hit that incinerated the house next door and the eight people who lived inside. But there is little doubt that the nightmare-inducing sounds of combat—the menacing drone of unmanned V-1 rockets, the staccato bursts of British antiaircraft fire, the earsplitting thunderclap of the exploding German bombs—were deeply embedded in his subconscious. For the rest of his life, the sound of a siren—any siren—would send a chill up Jagger's spine.

Mick's hometown was also known for its fireworks plant, founded by Joseph Wells in 1837, and for its Dickensian mental hospitals; at one point, there were as many as five separate institutions, all operated by Britain's infamously draconian Metropolitan Asylums Board. The fireworks factory was blown to smithereens in 1953, killing four workers and blowing out hundreds of windows throughout Dartford, but the asylums survived well into the twenty-first century. Even after the war ended and the air raids ceased, sirens sounded at least once a week—this time to alert locals that yet another mental patient had wandered off asylum grounds.

Against this surreal backdrop, Eva Scutts Jagger struggled to maintain appearances, as any decent British housewife would. She was outgoing and charming, but also, according to a family friend, "a bit of a snob. She put on airs."

If Mick's mother suffered from a deep-seated inferiority complex, the Scutts family's roots in Australia had everything to do with it. Like many Aussie transplants living in England, Eva was convinced that her nasal accent and open manner marked her as the product of a race of vulgar, ex-convict outcasts.

It was a fear that she'd inherited from her own mother, a London native who moved to Sydney shortly after marrying Eva's boat-builder father. It was a decision that Mick's grandmother, a frustrated singer with a particular fondness for Gilbert and Sullivan, regretted instantly. Nor did it help that Eva, born in 1913, was far more interested in spending time with her father and her brothers on the Sydney docks than in learning the finer points of etiquette and decorum.

Determined to rescue her daughter from a life of drudgery Down Under and desperate to return to a more "civilized" environment, Eva's mother convinced her husband to pack up and move to England—or watch her go alone.

Once the family had settled in Dartford, Eva's mum routinely made the thirty-five-minute train ride into London to attend shows at the Palladium and plays on the West End. At Dartford's Rialto Cinema, mother and daughter hunkered down in their seats and gazed up at Greta Garbo, Gary Cooper, Ronald Coleman, Bette Davis, and other screen favorites of the time.

The Great Depression hit London's working class especially hard, but at age twenty-two, Eva was able to land a job as a hairdresser. Her first week on the job, she made the mistake of tuning into crooner Bing Crosby on the radio. Enraged, her boss berated her in front of a shop full of customers. "That's not music!" the older man bellowed. "You don't call that singing!" Decades later, when Elvis, the Beatles, and her own son would come under fire for pioneering their own brand of music, Eva would describe the incident to anyone who attacked rock and roll as nothing more than noise.

This was 1935—the year that witnessed the birth of swing music and the big band era—and pretty, fun-loving Eva was not about to miss any of it. On weekends, she kicked up her heels— literally—at Dartford's handful of bars and nightclubs. Along the way, she dated some of the town's more notorious rakes— unattached young men who were every bit as determined to have a good time as she was.

When it came to finding a potential mate, however, Eva had an entirely different sort of suitor in mind. Enter Basil Fanshawe "Joe" Jagger, a gangling, somewhat diffident gym teacher at a local high school. By conventional measures, he was precisely the kind of man that Eva's mother wanted for her daughter: college educated, gentlemanly, and well regarded in his chosen profession. Most important, his family represented a climb up several rungs of the social ladder.

"My mum is very working class," Mick said, "and my father is bourgeois . . . so I come from somewhere in between. Neither one thing or the other."

Eva and Joe married on December 7, 1940—exactly one year before the Japanese attack on Pearl Harbor. Both were twenty-seven, and Eva, older than most brides of the era, was eager to quit her job and become a proper suburban English housewife.

Joe, meanwhile, proved himself to be anything but a standard-issue high school PE teacher. A serious student of exercise physiology, Jagger was eventually hired to lecture at St. Mary's College, the highly regarded Catholic teachers college in nearby Strawberry Hill, Twickenham.

On the way to becoming one of the United Kingdom's leading

physical fitness experts, Joe established his credentials as England's preeminent authority on the very American sport of basketball. After writing a book designed to explain the sport to his countrymen, Jagger Senior was rewarded with a seat on the prestigious British Sports Council.

Eva gave birth to her first child on July 26, 1943—the same week that Britons packed theaters to watch Humphrey Bogart and Ingrid Bergman try to resist each other in *Casablanca* and Royal Air Force pilots responded to Hitler's blitz by virtually leveling Hamburg. In a Church of England ceremony attended by the infant's grandparents and a smattering of uncles and aunts, the Jaggers christened their newborn son Michael Philip. He would eventually become the most famous "Mick" in history, but for the first twenty years of his life, he would answer to the markedly more pedestrian, softer "Mike." To his parents, in fact, he would *always* be Mike.

When he was four, Mick, who had been the center of his parents' world, was forced to confront the fact that he was about to be upstaged. His baby brother, Christopher, was born on December 19, 1947, and the following summer, the normally well-behaved Mick reacted to the new family dynamic in dramatic fashion. While the Jaggers were vacationing at the seashore, Eva recalled, Mick suddenly "broke away from me and bolted down the beach, just knocking over all the other children's sand castles as he ran. He was clearly angry."

Mick bridled at the notion of sharing the spotlight with anyone—especially not an adorable sibling. "As far as I was concerned," Jagger said of his brother, "he was nothing more than a punching bag, and I used to beat him up regularly."

Notwithstanding its still-thriving mental hospitals and extensive bomb damage, Dartford emerged from the war in somewhat better shape than several neighboring communities. The bustling town center boasted a new supermarket—soon to be taken over by Safeway, the US-based chain—as well as tea shops, coffee bars, and pubs with names like the Fox and Hounds, the Jolly Miller, and the Dart.

The Jaggers lived at 39 Denver Road, conveniently situated just around the corner from the Dart and a laundromat. Their two-story duplex—the family occupied the right half—was part of a sprawling subdivision built in 1928 to house working-class families.

Mick's second-floor bedroom overlooked the Jaggers' small backyard, where from the age of three he would be schooled by his exercise-obsessed dad on the proper way to perform push-ups and lift weights. Daily calisthenics were only part of the Jaggers' no-nonsense approach to child rearing. Mick and Chris were expected to help out with household chores, take turns saying grace before meals, and adhere to a set of rules strictly enforced by both Eva and Joe. Even the slightest infraction meant a slap across the bottom—or across the face. Understandably, the Jagger boys rarely crossed their parents.

Even before the arrival of his little brother, Mick displayed a keen interest in music—and an even keener interest in showing off. At family gatherings, when the children would be asked to sing a nursery rhyme, Mick insisted on being the center of attention. "I'd be the loudest hollering out the words," he recalled. "Even if I forgot the lyrics, I'd still keep right on going. Boy, I must have been a noisy one . . ."

There was no record player in the house—Joe Jagger wanted his children exercising, not listening to music—but Mick was allowed to listen to popular and classical music on the government-owned BBC radio station and to jazz on commercial Radio Luxembourg, a forerunner of pirate radio and for a time the most powerful station in Europe. The first Jagger moves were not to rock and roll—the musical form did not exist yet—but to Benny Goodman and Glenn Miller. "He jumped around and swiveled his hips," Eva remembered, "and it wasn't really like anything else I'd ever seen. We laughed, of course, because here he was, only four or five, and jumping around with this big grin on his face. It was like the music had flipped this switch inside him."

Not that Mick needed music to start him up. In spite of the grueling physical drills his father put him through each morning, the boy spent the balance of the day climbing trees and clamoring over fences, hurling rocks, and dashing about the neighborhood with his playmates. All of which resulted in the usual scrapes and bruises—and one injury that landed him in the local emergency room. While pursuing another youngster through his backyard, Mick stumbled, reached out to steady himself—and impaled his hand on a spiked fence. "A very gruesome business," Eva said, "but I think he was rather proud of his bloody bandage."

The product of strict discipline and high expectations, Mick enrolled at Maypole Primary School at age five and quickly proved to be a model student. Located directly across from Bexley Hospital, one of Dartford's more infamous mental institutions, Maypole was a brick-and-mortar monstrosity straight out of *Oliver Twist*.

Mick loved it there, and over a two-year period impressed his teachers with his sunny disposition and his eagerness to please. "He was bright, cheerful, always volunteering to help out in the classroom," said Ken Llewellyn, one of Mick's teachers at Maypole. "Almost too good, really . . ."

From Maypole, Mick moved on to Wentworth County Primary, a modern, single-story yellow brick-and-glass structure just two blocks from the Jaggers' house. It was here that he experienced his first fleeting encounter with destiny in the form of a cowboy-obsessed schoolmate named Keith Richards.

◆

Even though the Richardses lived just two blocks from the Jaggers at 33 Chastilian Road, the two families were worlds apart. While Joe's career was taking off and the Jagger finances with it, Bert Richards was barely scraping by as a foreman at the General Electric plant in nearby Hammersmith. Lacking the education and drive of Mick's dad, the elder Richards was, in Keith's words, "the most unambitious man in the world." His mother, Doris, did what she could to augment the family's meager income by demonstrating Hotpoint washing machines to local housewives, but it would not be enough to afford either a telephone or a refrigerator.

"We weren't great friends then," Jagger said of Richards, "but we knew each other. Keith used to dress in a cowboy outfit, with holsters and a hat, and he had these big ears that stuck out. I asked him what he wanted to do when he grew up. He said he wanted to be like Roy Rogers and play guitar."

Jagger was unimpressed by Keith's infatuation with an American cowboy star, but, Mick remembered, "the bit about the guitar did interest me." In fact, ever since Eva bought him a guitar while on holiday in Spain, Mick had been indulging a newfound passion for Latin music. He sat for hours in his room, strumming away while singing soulful ballads that seemed surprisingly authentic, considering that the Spanish-sounding lyrics were pure gibberish.

An only child, Keith was also periodically carted out to sing for his relatives. As early as age two, Doris Richards insisted, her son was able to sing along in perfect pitch whenever Sarah Vaughan, Louis Armstrong, Nat King Cole, or Ella Fitzgerald came on the radio. When he was seven, she gave him a saxophone. While Mick dragged his guitar along wherever he went, Keith—who would have to wait until he was ten to be lent a gut-string classical guitar by his eccentric grandfather Gus Dupree—was weighed down by a sax that was nearly as big as he was.

An early love of music wasn't the only thing Mick and Keith had in common. At Wentworth, both boys were model students—almost "too good," as their teacher had observed. Mick avoided being picked on because of his height—he towered over most of his fellow students—but Keith, who would not shoot up until adolescence, was bullied relentlessly. As a result, Richards kept to himself, retreating to a tent that he pitched in his backyard.

The gap between Mick and Keith would widen in 1954, when both families moved out of the old neighborhood and, in every sense of the word, in decidedly opposite directions. Buoyed by Joe's growing success as one of the country's leading fitness experts, the Jaggers relocated not only to a leafy suburb of Dartford called Wilmington but also to an upper class enclave within that leafy suburb known as the Close. With its circular drive, arched leaded windows, and quarter acre of carefully manicured lawn, the Jaggers' new home even had a name—Newlands—that was carved into a sign that hung from a branch of the apple tree shading their front porch.

Keith was not so lucky. The railway ran straight through the center of Dartford, and now the Richardses literally lived on the other side of the tracks from the Jaggers—on Spielman Road on Temple Hill, later described by its most famous ex-inhabitant as a "fucking soul-destroying housing project."

While Keith, nicknamed "Monkey" because of his protruding ears, was taunted and pummeled by his schoolmates ("I would live in fear all day"), Mick continued to flourish at school. Their final year at Wentworth Primary, all students took the dreaded Eleven Plus exams that determined their academic futures—and the course of their lives. Those who did well were admitted to one of the elite grammar (secondary) schools that ultimately fed into the university system and the possibility of pursuing a lucrative profession. Those who did not do so well were consigned to a trade school and, for all intents and purposes, a working-class life.

Mick aced the tests and was soon being fitted for one of Dartford Grammar's crimson blazers. ("Ooh, the ones in the red uniforms," Keith chided years later.) Founded in 1576, ivy-covered Dartford Grammar, with its Etonian playing fields, arched Gothic windows, and Tudor architecture, was obscured from view by an elegant curved brick wall—a genteel outpost in the working-class wasteland that was postwar Dartford.

Ever the dutiful son and diligent student, Mick earned high marks, assisted his instructors in the classroom, and competed in rugby and cricket. Since the draft was still in effect and he and his fellow students were expected to join the military as officers, Mick signed up with Britain's version of the ROTC: the Combined Cadet Force (CCF). As with everything else he undertook at the time, young Jagger was serious about his soldier's training. One of his teachers, William Wilkinson, remembered that Mick was "a very hard worker all around—an overachiever . . . More than any other student, he went out of his way to be helpful. We were all very impressed."

Mick, however, was not a joiner. He did not belong to any clubs or student organizations, run for any class office, sign up with the choir or the band, or act in any school productions. To please his father, he did become captain of Dartford Grammar's basketball team, although apparently this had less to do with his acumen as a player ("He wasn't really very good," said former teammate Keith Hawkins) than with his ability to lead. "He clearly," Hawkins added, "liked to be in charge."

Across town, Keith's life was on a wholly different trajectory. He took the Eleven Plus exams one year after Mick and only did well enough to qualify for entrance to Dartford Technical High School. Once again, Keith was singled out as the school pansy. It didn't help that he was also one of the stars of the Dartford Technical boys' choir, and actually sang Handel's "Hallelujah" chorus for Queen Elizabeth as a Westminster Abbey choirboy—an early taste of musical success that ended abruptly when his voice cracked in the middle of another royal performance.

Going their distinctly separate ways, Keith and Mick did not speak for the next six years. But Jagger did catch the occasional glimpse of him sprinting home from school, the usual pack of toughs nipping at his heels.

While Keith was preoccupied with simple survival, twelve-year-old Mick sampled his first, intoxicating sip of fame. His father had been hired as a consultant to the BBC television series *Seeing Sport,* and he required the services of a fit young man to demonstrate the finer points of rock climbing and canoeing.

Mick relished the attention. "I was a star already," he later said. "I was thinking, 'Never mind the bloody canoe, how does my hair look?'" Perhaps, but Joe Jagger took the series—and his son's role in it—very seriously. With his father looking on, Mick did hundreds of sit-ups and push-ups, and then ran twenty to thirty laps around the yard each afternoon.

"He wanted more than anything to please his parents, particularly his father," said Mick's schoolmate Dick Taylor. "I think he was afraid of him." On more than one occasion, Taylor recalled, Mick would "only be a few feet out the door before his father shouted, 'Don't go out until you do your weights!'"

It did not take long for Mick to figure out that he could capitalize on his fitness expertise by teaching physical education to the children of soldiers stationed at a nearby US Army base. In the process, he learned the rules of other great American pastimes such as baseball and football. He also learned a lot about American music—specifically, rhythm and blues—from an African American army cook named Jose.

When he was finished putting pupils who were really no

younger than he was through their paces, Mick sat for hours listening to Jose's recordings of such blues legends as Leadbelly, Robert Johnson, Howlin' Wolf, and Muddy Waters. "This was the first time I heard black music," Mick remembered. "In fact, it was my first encounter with American thought."

Soon Mick had amassed a sizable record collection of his own, financed in part by taking on a variety of additional jobs. He hand delivered Christmas cards during the holidays, and when summer rolled around, he donned a white jacket and matching white paper hat to sell ice cream from a pushcart. It was while peddling ice cream in front of Dartford Town Hall, that, after years spent apart, Mick had a fleeting encounter with Keith Richards. "It just clicked in my mind that day," Richards said later. "I bought a choc ice—and then I didn't see him again."

For the first time, Mick was willing to risk running afoul of his autocratic dad by playing the latest hits by Chuck Berry, Fats Domino, and Little Richard—all dismissed by Joe as nothing more than "jungle music."

"Yeah," Mick routinely deadpanned to his father's critique, "that's right—jungle music. That's a very good description."

Mick began to rebel in other ways as well. Another Dartford friend, Clive Robson, recalled that it was Jagger who hatched a scheme to duck out of the school's weekly five-mile cross-country run over Dartford Heath. "Jagger worked out that if you broke off at a certain point," Robson said, "you could hide in the dunes, have an illicit smoke, and rejoin the homeward run half an hour later."

In a portent of things to come, over at Dartford Tech they also had a weekly five-mile cross-country run, and Keith Richards was cutting out midway for a smoke with his buddies as well. He was eventually caught and disciplined for cheating. Mick, by contrast, was never found out.

Not surprisingly, Jagger also soon ran afoul of Dartford Grammar's strict blazers-only dress code. "He would wear those tight pants even then," his housemaster said, "and his hair began to spill over his ears." Mick caused a sensation when, during a coed mixer, he walked in wearing not his regulation crimson blazer but "a bright blue jacket with these shimmering threads. The girls," the housemaster said, "swarmed around him."

Dartford Grammar's crusty headmaster, Ronald Loftus "Lofty" Hudson, was so incensed by boys wearing tight pants that he called a special assembly to address the issue. In the middle of the lecture, fellow student David Herrington said, "in walks Jagger wearing the tightest jeans I'd ever seen." Red with rage, Hudson sent him home on the spot. According to Herrington, Mick "just smiled."

Hormones had much to do with the overnight change in Mick's behavior. "When I was thirteen, all I wanted to do was have sex," he said. "I didn't know much about it. I was repressed. It was never discussed with me." Forced to cope with his first sexual stirrings in an all-male environment, Jagger followed in the footsteps of generations of proper (and equally repressed) English schoolboys before him. "I had my first sexual experiences with boys at school," Mick said. "I think that's true of almost every boy." Apparently this was not true of Keith, in large part because he did not share Mick's English boarding school experience. Instead Richards commuted from his home to working-class Dartford Technical, where the environment was anything but old school.

However commonplace they may have been, these early homoerotic fumblings of Mick's strongly influenced his life and work. They also shaped one of the most complicated and sexually ambiguous personas in pop culture history.

There was nothing ambiguous about his taste in music, however. At fifteen, Mick and his friend and fellow blues aficionado Dick Taylor attended a Buddy Holly concert at the Odeon Theater in nearby Woolwich. "Mick was transfixed," Taylor said, particularly when Holly played his hit "Not Fade Away," which eventually became a staple of the Rolling Stones' repertoire. "You could see the little wheels going round in his head, trying to learn as much as he could."

At the time, Taylor recalled, British rock-and-roll fans were split into two camps. "It was either Elvis or Buddy." Jagger, who for some reason regarded the then twenty-three-year-old Presley as "ancient," was squarely in the Holly camp.

Still, blues was his first love. "We all liked rock, of course," said Dick Taylor, "but what interested me most about Jagger was his interest in the blues. So few people in England knew about it, and here was this guy who knew everything there was about Muddy Waters and Bo Diddley."

Jagger and Taylor soon got together with two like-minded classmates, Bob Beckwith and Allen Etherington, to form Little Boy Blue and the Blue Boys, with Mick as lead singer. Mick's parents thought his first efforts at sounding like he was from the Mississippi Delta were, in Eva's words, "hysterical. We tried hard not to laugh."

Mick's new hairstyle, however, was no laughing matter. Despite the fact that Holly's thick-rimmed glasses, tight black suits, and aw-shucks demeanor made him the nerdy answer to Presley's sneering rebel, Jagger set out to ruffle some feathers at school by adopting a shaggier, more bohemian look.

"I was shocked," said Eva. "Even though it wasn't really long by today's standards, I held up my hands in horror when it started growing over his ears." Eventually she insisted on at least trimming his hair herself. Halfway through the haircut, Mick broke down in tears and fled.

Tight jeans and long hair were only part of Mick's new image as campus rebel. By way of raising Headmaster Hudson's hackles even more than he had already, Mick started questioning the capitalist system in general and the British government's anticommunist Cold War policies in particular. When parliament voted to abolish the draft, Mick led his fellow students in a wholesale exodus from Dartford Grammar's Combined Cadet Force.

He was only slightly more committed to the school's basketball team. "Jagger was an average player," team coach Arthur Page observed. If Mick didn't succeed at something right away, Page added, "then he gave up and moved on to something else."

Before giving up basketball, Mick experienced something on the court that altered his life—and perhaps even the course of musical history. During one especially heated game, Jagger collided with an opposing team member and bit off the tip of his own tongue. With blood spilling down the front of his jersey and before he fully realized what had happened, Mick swallowed the severed tip.

Mick didn't talk for nearly a week. "We all wondered if that was it—if Mick's singing days were over," said Dick Taylor, echoing his fellow Blue Boys' fears. When Mick finally did open his mouth again to sing, his bandmates were stunned. Along with the tip of his tongue went a bit of upper-class polish. Mick now sounded grittier, tougher, more authentically street.

"He sounded so weird—the way he sounds now, actually," Taylor said. "That accident just changed his voice completely. Biting off the tip of his tongue might have been the best thing that ever happened to Mick Jagger."

His newfound sound and evolving rebel image aside, Mick remained something of a closet intellectual. He enjoyed the classics—Blake, Baudelaire, and Rimbaud were his favorite writers—as well as biographies of nineteenth-century political figures such as Benjamin Disraeli, William Gladstone, and Abraham Lincoln.

It was a side he kept hidden. Instead Mick preferred to boast to chums about his success at seducing members of the opposite sex. He finally joined a club—the photography club—for the sole purpose, he claimed, of cornering female visitors in the darkroom. He also bragged about luring girls out onto Dartford Heath for furtive after-school make-out sessions. According to his friend Clive Robson, Mick "had quite a reputation."

None of it was true. Far from being a Lothario, Mick was ignored by the girls at the neighboring schools. "There were some good-looking boys around that we all kind of drooled over," said one girl, but Jagger "certainly wasn't one of them. We all thought he was kind of ugly, really."

Sixteen-year-old Mick soon learned one foolproof way to attract the female attention he craved. Eva had decided to return to work selling Avon cosmetics, and whenever she and Joe were gone, Mick would invite some young woman to come over and try out some items from his mum's sample case.

Sitting side by side at Eva's dressing table, Mick and his date giggled as they applied cosmetics to each other. "He just seemed happy letting me put lipstick and mascara on him," one said of these odd and largely platonic encounters. "It did strike me as very strange at the time, but it was all in fun." She went on to say that, at least for her, dating Mick was more like "being with one of the girls."

Notwithstanding his shaggy mane and decidedly unconventional approach to dating, Mick still harbored dreams of becoming rich—not as a performer but as a businessman. Aiming for admission to the prestigious London School of Economics—which included David Rockefeller, George Soros, and John Fitzgerald Kennedy among its alumni—Jagger threw himself into his studies during his final months at Dartford Grammar. Almost entirely on the strength of his final exams, he managed to graduate twelfth in a class of twenty-five—enough to coax a grudging letter of recommendation from Dartford's implacable headmaster.

"Jagger is a lad of good general character," Mr. Hudson wrote, "though he has been rather slow to mature. The pleasing quality which is now emerging is that of persistence when he makes up his mind to tackle something . . . He should be successful in his subjects, though he is unlikely to do brilliantly in any of them." Years later, Hudson regretted giving even this half-hearted endorsement. "The more famous the Rolling Stones became," teacher William Wilkinson said, "the more Hudson hated him."

Still, Mick's test scores and Hudson's recommendation were enough to get Mick into the London School of Economics on a state scholarship—and offer him his first taste of life outside the suffocating confines of Dartford. "The overwhelming thing about life in the suburbs is the envy, the gossip and pettiness," he said. "I hated it, and I was glad to escape—even if it was for only a few hours a day."

Not that he shared any of these feelings with his parents. At home, he continued to help Eva with household chores and to obey his father's every command. "He still couldn't go anywhere without his father shouting behind him that he needed to do his weights or push-ups," Dick Taylor said. "And he would drop to his knees and do them! Here he was a grown man, and not once did I ever see him hesitate to do exactly what his parents wanted."

One of the things they insisted on was that Mick pay for his own expenses. The summer before he started classes at LSE, Jagger earned $15 a week as an orderly at Bexley Mental Hospital. He later said that Bexley was brimming with "nymphomaniac nurses and nymphomaniac patients" who tried to seduce young orderlies. Mick had less to fear from the patients than he did from the nurses. One, a dark-haired Italian who had just emigrated to England, yanked him into a linen closet where, surrounded by sheets, mops, and bedpans, Mick lost his virginity standing up.

Like college freshmen everywhere, most first-year students at

LSE were instantly swept up in the campus social whirl. Not Mick, who initially seemed to most of his fellow students as standoffish and shy. "He was almost reclusive," said one. "Most of us who commuted to school would make arrangements to stay with friends in the city, but he always declined."

It took more than a month for Mick to begin to show some real independence. He began to cultivate friends with interests in the arts—student actors in particular—and before long was accepting their invitations to stay over in the city and debate the relative acting skills of Sir John Gielgud and Sir Laurence Olivier over the requisite half-dozen pints of ale.

This would be a turning point in his life—a moment in which, unencumbered by his past and in the company of strangers in an exciting new environment, the skinny young man with the oversized lips could reinvent himself. From now on, to anyone outside his immediate family, he was no longer Mike. He was Mick.

Along with Jagger's new name and attitude came a new image, an important part of which was a wildly exaggerated sexual past—and present. "He was a complete fraud," said Jilly, one of the attractive University of London coeds who moved in similar circles. "Whenever I got near him in private, he'd back away . . . I think he was just terribly inexperienced and insecure at the time."

Jagger soon overcame those insecurities, not with one of his new London acquaintances but with the aid of a plump and rather plain Dartford shopgirl named Bridget. Jagger was nineteen—a year or more behind most of his chums in landing a girlfriend, but he would spend the rest of his life more than making up for lost time.

While Jagger was living his new, liberated life as Mick, his long-lost childhood pal Keith Richards was at Sidcup Art College enjoying his first taste of freedom as "Ricky." A habitual truant at Dartford Tech, Richards had been expelled thirty minutes before graduation after failing to attend a graduation day assembly. ("The last nail in the coffin," he recalled.)

It was just as well. In postwar Britain, art schools proliferated as an alternative to college for those with even a modicum of talent in the visual or performing arts. For whatever reason, these schools spawned fewer painters and sculptors of note than they did rock superstars, including John Lennon, David Bowie, Eric Clapton, Jimmy Page, and Pete Townshend.

By the time Keith reached Sidcup Art College, his mother, Doris, had bought him a guitar of his own—a Rosetti acoustic—for £7. Hooked on rock and roll from the moment he first heard Elvis's "Heartbreak Hotel," Keith shied away from learning to read music and taught himself to play by ear ("straight from the heart to the fingers"), listening endlessly to recordings by John Lee Hooker, Muddy Waters, Chuck Berry, and Buddy Holly.

At Sidcup, Keith met another self-taught musician: Mick's Dartford Grammar schoolmate and fellow Blue Boy Dick Taylor. The two hit it off instantly. Although Taylor had started out playing drums, he now discovered that he shared Richards's passion for mimicking legendary bluesmen like Waters and Hooker on acoustic guitar.

Like Mick, Keith had cultivated a bad-boy image at school— and was determined to look the part. "He always wore tight jeans, purple shirt, and blue denim jacket, no matter what the weather," Taylor said. "He never wore anything else, ever."

Surprisingly, Taylor was the superior musician—at least for the moment. Richards eagerly soaked up what he could from his more polished classmate. To fuel their late-night sessions and still be able to attend art classes the next day, they began taking drugs, including diet pills, nasal sprays, and even the British equivalent of Midol. "It seemed relatively harmless at the time," Taylor said, "until you look at what it ultimately led to for Keith."

Keith knew about his friend's group—Little Boy Blue and the Blue Boys—but Taylor never asked him to join it. "Keith was really the school's rocker," he said. "It just never occurred to me that he'd be interested . . . and Keith was too shy to ask."

That changed one fateful morning in December 1961, when Mick and Keith bumped into each other at the Dartford train station on the way to their respective schools.

Keith, his guitar hanging from his shoulder, noticed Jagger was holding several albums under his arm. But it was Mick who approached him. "We recognized each other straight off," Richards said. "'Hi, man,' I say. 'Where are you going?' he says. And under his arms he's got Chuck Berry, Little Walter, and Muddy Waters."

"Chuck Berry!" Richards shouted when he saw that Mick was carrying Berry's newest release, *Rockin' at the Hops*. Keith assumed he was the only person in Dartford—aside from Taylor and a few others—who had ever even heard of Berry.

"You're into Chuck Berry, man? Really?" Richards asked.

It was better than that. Since Berry's albums weren't even released in the UK, Mick wrote directly to Chess Records in Chicago requesting copies. They had just arrived in the mail. "Did we hit it off?" Richards said later. "The guy's got Chuck Berry and Muddy Waters under his arm—the real shit—you're gonna hit it off."

On the train, Richards showed Jagger his guitar and asked him if he played. Mick replied sheepishly that he sang with a local band, just for fun. As the train pulled into the Sidcup station, Richards turned to Jagger and invited him to tea. "And bring your records!" he shouted as the train doors closed behind him. Later that day, Taylor recalled, "Keith came up to me and said, 'I've met your Mick.'" Taylor finally asked Keith if he'd be interested in playing with the Blue Boys. "It seemed logical for us all to get together," Taylor said, "which we did."

Mick Jagger and Keith Richards bonded instantly, and not just over music. "We were born brothers by different parents by accident," Keith said. Yet, despite the fact that they grew up in the same town, there were major differences. A full step up the social ladder from Richards, Jagger was an obedient, industrious son who was perfectly willing to play by the rules if that was what it took to get ahead. Richards was an unapologetic delinquent—"a real lout," Taylor said admiringly—and a loner.

Keith respected Mick from the start. "Keith was attracted to his intelligence, his dramatic flair, his streak of ambition," Taylor observed. But it was Mick's obsession with Keith that formed the bedrock on which the reputation of the world's greatest rock-and-roll band was built.

"Keith is a much freer person than Mick," Taylor said. "The only thing he is obsessed about is his guitar, the music—Mick valued and nurtured that from the very beginning." Or, more to the point: "Keith had the balls to tell everybody to fuck off while he did what he wanted to do. Mick is too calculating, too ambitious, for that."

Phil May, another Sidcup student who went on to form his own group called the Pretty Things, sat in with the Blue Boys occasionally. "They were all very amateurish at this stage of the game," May said, "but Mick was quite unique even then. He could get inside a blues lyric and give it expression. He acted out a lyric instead of just performing it."

By the early spring of 1962, Mick was eager to try out his style before a paying audience. While leafing through the popular British entertainment weekly *New Musical Express,* he spotted a tiny item announcing the March 17 opening of a jazz club in nearby Ealing. The owner, Alex Korner, had played banjo and guitar for Chris Barber's Jazz Band for more than sixteen years and now, at thirty-three, was regarded as the father of England's R & B movement.

"When you walked into that club," Dick Taylor said, "it was like being on Chicago's South Side—or at least the way we all imagined it to be." Musty and dank, the tiny basement club was located across from the train station and beneath a bakery and a jewelry store. Water leaked from the ceiling pipes constantly, making it necessary, Mick remembered, to put "a horrible sheet which was revoltingly dirty" over the stage. Despite these precautions, water dripped onto the amplifiers nearly every night, sending a shower of sparks into the crowd. Wires snaking through puddles on the stage crackled and glowed.

The distinct possibility that they might be electrocuted scarcely mattered to Mick and his pals. For three weeks running, they showed up to hear Korner on guitar, goateed saxophonist Dick Heckstall-Smith, the two-hundred-pound Cyril "Squirrel" Davies on harmonica, and a morose-looking Harrow Art School student named Charlie Watts on drums. "By week three, we said, 'We can do this,'" Taylor recalled. "'We can do *better* than this.'"

Mingling with other R & B aficionados in the audience such as Eric Burdon, Jeff Beck, and Eric Clapton was a short, ruddy-faced towhead who played alto sax with a rock band called the Ramrods. His name was Brian Jones, and like Mick, he was raised in a relatively prosperous London suburb. Unlike Jagger, he was anything but a dutiful son. At age sixteen, he impregnated his fourteen-year-old girlfriend and was summarily kicked out of school.

Leaving home at seventeen, Jones worked a variety of jobs (truck driver, optician's assistant, conductor on a double-decker bus) and moonlighted with a number of traditional jazz bands at clubs around London. When he was nineteen, Jones abandoned his then girlfriend Pat Andrews after she gave birth to their child in 1961. Undeterred, Andrews eventually tracked down Brian and, their son Julian in hand, moved in with him.

Back at the Ealing, where every Saturday night aspiring singers were encouraged to audition for Korner's group Blues Incorporated, Mick knocked back pints of ale as he screwed up his courage to perform in public for the first time.

By the time he climbed onto the stage and fumbled with the microphone, he was, by his own admission, "quite drunk." No matter. Backed by Richards, Korner, and Watts, Mick delivered a rendition of Chuck Berry's "Around and Around" that brought the club's famously churlish audience to its feet.

Korner and the club's other in-house musicians, who viewed Richards's high-octane playing as nothing more than noise, shoved Keith aside to congratulate Mick—the first in a series of slights, both real and imagined, that would define their relationship over the next half century.

Mick was invited back on the spot, to substitute the following week for Blues Incorporated's regular vocalist, six-foot-seven-inch-tall "Long John" Baldry. It was Jagger's first paying gig—just a few shillings and free beer—but it was enough for him to quit his own group that May and sign on with Blues Incorporated as the band's permanent backup singer. Keith, Dick Taylor, and the other Blue Boys understood that this was a golden opportunity for Mick. But they also marveled at the seeming ease with which he left his old friends behind.

In truth, Korner had thought long and hard about hiring Mick. Despite the young singer's clear command of the material and undeniable stage presence, his stage mannerisms may have struck the club's hard-drinking, working-class clientele as a tad fey. At this stage, Mick was far from the over-the-top, gender-bending peacock he became. But he was already prancing about the stage, writhing suggestively, and making sweeping, feminine gestures with his hands. "Frankly, it was wildly embarrassing first time around with it," Korner said. "Imagine just how shocking Mick was then in the early days."

It would have been even more shocking to the blues aficionados who crammed into the Ealing on Saturday nights if they had known just who Mick was impersonating onstage. He was inspired not so much by Chuck Berry or even Little Richard as he was by Marilyn Monroe. What he offered was a wicked parody of Marilyn, consciously mimicking her style—the swivel-hipped walk, the pouty lips, the playful hair toss.

"I'm not sure why," Jagger told Korner, "but I identify with Marilyn." When Monroe died in August 1962—just three months after Mick began singing professionally—he was shattered. "Monroe was a seductress," Korner said, "and that's the way Mick saw himself. He's helped to alter the whole idea of what it is to be male."

Still, Mick felt there was something missing—until a newcomer named P. P. Pond took to the stage one night and started singing blues great Robert Johnson's "Dust My Broom." What grabbed the rapt attention of both Jagger and Richards that night wasn't Pond but the slide guitarist who accompanied him: a blond young man in a perfectly tailored suit whom Pond introduced to the crowd as Elmo Lewis.

Lewis's mastery of the instrument—particularly his fingering technique and his hard-driving style—left Keith shaking his head in wonder. Mick was equally impressed by the way Lewis leaned into the crowd, taunting them, and then abruptly spun around in retreat. Jagger sensed in this Elmo Lewis a latent cruelty that was both sensual and exciting. That night, Mick decided to adopt the young man's exquisitely surly visage.

As soon as the set was over, Mick rushed up to the stage and offered to buy Lewis a drink. The intriguing stranger accepted, but only as long as Jagger called him by his real name: Brian Jones.

Within a matter of weeks, Jones had taken charge and formed a band that included elements of his own group and the Blue Boys. He decided unilaterally that they would be called the Rolling Stones, after the Muddy Waters song "Rollin' Stone." Everyone hated the name, especially Mick. Ironically, Jagger's principal objection was that he considered himself to be an R & B singer, and the word *rollin'* might imply that they were a rock-and-roll band. No one pressed the issue because, for the time being, at least, this was Jones's band.

Still, when *Jazz News* ran a story on July 11 about the band's debut the next evening at London's popular Marquee Club, it was Mick who stepped up as group spokesman. He also went on record with his doubts about being called the Rolling Stones. "I hope they don't think," he told the paper, "that we're a rock-and-roll outfit."

That is precisely what they thought when Mick, wearing his customary bright blue pullover, began prancing around the stage while Keith and Brian (still calling himself Elmo Lewis) lit into their respective guitars. "It was a case of instant dislike," said Dick Taylor, the Stones' bass player. "The sight of us—and particularly Mick—was more than they could handle."

There was a vocal minority in the audience, however, that disagreed with the jazz purists—and they made their feelings known by cheering as loudly as the club regulars booed. While the Marquee's manager, Harold Pendleton, said that he never would have booked Mick in the first place if he'd known how he sang, there was no doubt that this new group sparked a level of excitement the likes of which he'd never seen. Pendleton made it clear to Mick and his bandmates that he personally "loathed" their brand of music, but he nevertheless invited them back to perform Thursday nights.

Even without a solid drummer—they had yet to coax Charlie Watts aboard—the Rolling Stones were drawing larger and larger crowds. Sensing the coming sea change in musical tastes, Pendleton brought in another edgy group, the High Numbers, to play Tuesdays. They later changed their name to The Who.

Notwithstanding his group's success at pulling crowds into the Marquee Club, Mick, still unconvinced that music was a viable career option for him, kept up his studies at the London School of Economics. For a time, he toyed with the notion of becoming either a journalist or a politician, quickly abandoning both fields because they "seemed like too much hard work." Nor was he willing to risk disappointing his parents or, for that matter, give up the government grant that was covering his expenses.

Mick did make one major step toward independence by moving out of his parents' house and joining Brian and Keith in their two-bedroom flat at 102 Edith Grove in Chelsea. Dank and fetid, with a bathtub in the kitchen, a single lightbulb dangling from the ceiling, paint flaking off the walls, and a communal toilet two flights up, the apartment was far from Mick's comfy upper-middle-class existence in Dartford.

Surprisingly, Jagger felt right at home. Soon the floor was carpeted with cigarette butts, moldy, half-eaten sandwiches, and empty beer bottles. Rats skittered across the floor. By way of adding to the ambiance, Mick, Keith, and Brian smeared excrement on the walls and signed it.

For a time, they were joined at the flat by an odd character named Jimmy Phelge. If anything, his personal habits were even more repugnant than those of his roommates. When Mick returned home from school, Phelge would greet him at the front door wearing nothing but his urine-stained, feces-streaked underpants on his head. Unable to kick in his share of the rent, Phelge lasted at Edith Grove for less than a month.

"I thought, 'Do people really live like this?'" said Dick Taylor, who had always known Jagger to be compulsively neat. "This was clearly his way of rebelling against his parents. It was quite amusing to see Mick in this pigsty . . . wallowing in absolute filth." Periodically, the two middle-aged women who lived downstairs (Keith described them as "two old boots") dropped in to tidy up. In turn, Brian, Keith, and Mick alternated having sex with the women. "They seemed," Keith said, "satisfied with the arrangement."

By way of leaving his bourgeois background far behind him, Mick also changed the way he spoke. Overnight, he traded his proper upper-class accent for a cockney twang. Keith, meantime, gradually became more refined in his speech. "We switched accents," Mick quipped later.

That winter of 1962 they were less concerned with their music than they were with matters of sheer survival. Without money to pay for the coin-operated electric heater in their flat, Keith, Brian, and Mick slept together every night in the same double bed, huddling together for warmth.

This curious sleeping arrangement merely underscored the Stones' homoerotic nexus. To his roommates' amazement, Mick, perhaps still inspired by the ghost of the recently deceased Marilyn, took on a decidedly feminine role inside the house. Mick wore pancake makeup and heavy mascara, and painted his toenails red to match his lipstick. He exchanged his pullover for a powder-blue linen house-coat, a lavender hairnet, stockings, and high heels.

"Mick was wavin' his hands everywhere," Keith recalled. "'Oh! Don't!'—a real King's Road queen. Brian and I immediately went enormously butch, sort of laughing at Mick. That terrible switching-around confusion of roles, that still goes on. Mick stayed on that queen kick for about six months."

Jagger was not only exploring the bisexual aspects of his own personality, but the power that such gender bending gave him over the others. By shedding his cloak of masculinity, he was able to make Brian and Keith doubt their own. If he could provoke such a strong reaction from his friends, what, he wondered, would be the effects on an audience?

Mick was, in fact, jealous of Brian for having stolen Keith away from him. Jagger still insisted on keeping up with his studies, and while he was attending classes all day, his roommates remained back at the flat, practicing all day and leaving only long enough to scrounge up enough money to buy cigarettes. When the thermometer plunged during the daylight hours, Brian and Keith huddled in their bed without Mick, telling dirty jokes and cracking each other up making funny faces. "The Nanker"—nose pushed up, eyelids pulled down—was a Jones specialty that never failed to send Richards into convulsive fits of hysterical laughter.

It didn't help that Mick had not fully committed himself to the group the way his roommates had. He was still hedging his bets by remaining in school, and, although he received his school stipend and a generous allowance from his parents, he made no effort to share what he had with his friends. While Mick went out alone to dine at restaurants, Keith and Brian were left to crash neighborhood parties in search of food or break into neighbors' apartments so they could rifle through dresser drawers looking for spare change.

Once he realized that Brian was determined to replace him with his old singer P. P. Pond (alias Paul Jones, soon to join the group Manfred Mann as lead singer), Mick set out to sever the bond between Jones and Richards once and for all. Jagger embarked on what would turn out to be the first in a lifetime of deftly played sex games. He seduced Pat Andrews, the mother of Brian's son Julian. Although Brian was not in love with Pat and had cheated on her openly, being cuckolded by Mick—the "flaming King's Road queen"—was too much for Jones's fragile ego. "I figure the only reason he balled Pat, who was certainly not very attractive," said Ian Stewart, the burly shipping clerk who had already signed on as the group's pianist, "was to get at Brian."

Once he was satisfied that Brian was feeling shaken and vulnerable, Mick moved in for the kill. If he was going to drive a wedge between Keith and Brian, he was going to have to seduce Brian. And he did, according to Anita Pallenberg, the leggy German model who eventually carried on affairs with Brian, Keith, and Mick. It was from Brian that Pallenberg learned the details of his relationship with Mick.

However, Mick's plan backfired. The brief sexual fling with Jones left him feeling emotionally raw—and wondering who seduced whom. "Brian did break up a lot of things by actually going to bed with Mick," Pallenberg said. "And I think Mick always resented him for having fallen for it. In later years, there have always been rumors about Mick being gay, but then it was as if Brian violated Mick's privacy by revealing his weak side."

This strange triangle had tragic consequences for Brian. But its professional, physical, and emotional components also unleashed creative forces that the three men could never have summoned as individuals.

In the meantime, however, Mick cast a gimlet eye in the direction of another up-and-coming group with a name he hated almost as much as the Rolling Stones. When he learned that the Beatles had scored their first hit, "Love Me Do," in November 1962, Jagger rushed into the bathroom and promptly threw up. He doubted that there was enough room for two major pop groups from Britain. The Beatles had beaten the Stones to the punch.

England was, in fact, already giving birth to a cultural renaissance that extended far beyond pop music. Mary Quant was crowned the new queen of a fashion mecca called Carnaby Street, and Edwardian jackets, Cuban-heeled boots, black tights, and vinyl miniskirts became the uniform of the young. Models like Twiggy and Jean Shrimpton soon appeared on the covers of fashion magazines wearing the startling wedge cuts by an innovative hairdresser named Vidal Sassoon, and fashion-conscious young men eschewed the close-cropped hairstyles of the postwar era for the bowl-shaped mod look popularized by those four young trendsetters from Liverpool.

That year the Oscar-winning film *Tom Jones* was released, James Bond was everyone's favorite action hero, and British movie stars such as Peter O'Toole, Albert Finney, Vanessa and Lynn Redgrave, Alan Bates, and Julie Christie were on the verge of becoming household names in the United States. David Frost's satirical TV series *That Was the Week That Was* would become an enormous hit on both sides of the Atlantic, while stage shows like *Beyond the Fringe, Stop the World—I Want to Get Off,* and *Oliver!* played to sellout crowds in the West End and on Broadway.

These were just the opening shots in what came to be known as the British Invasion, and Mick was eager to enlist. But, still far from convinced that he could actually earn a living as a singer, Jagger kept up his college studies as the band went through one shakeup after another. Dick Taylor exited the group to enroll in the Royal College of Art. (Eventually he resumed his music career playing bass for the Pretty Things.) Replacing Taylor was Bill Wyman (real name: Bill Perks), a married storage clerk who had played part-time with bands in and around London. Wyman, who at twenty-six was significantly older than his bandmates and already had a son, was hired for one reason: he brought his own speaker and amplifiers.

For the time being, R & B veteran Carlo Little agreed to sit in as their drummer. "They were pretty pathetic," he said. "They didn't know where their next penny was coming from, and their personal habits were, well, disgusting. Their clothes looked and smelled like they hadn't been washed in months." Little was, however, impressed with the intensity of Mick's ambition. "He wanted stardom much more than the others," Little said. "That was obvious."

It was also obvious that Mick brought something special to the table. He was simply unlike any performer that Little had ever seen. "There was something very weird about him even in those days," said Little, who played with the band at such dives as the Ricky-Tick club in Windsor and Sutton's Red Lion Pub. "It made you uncomfortable to look at him jerking around, but you couldn't help it. He was just damn exciting."

Mick still had his eye on Charlie Watts, however, and by New Year's 1963, the basset-faced, zoot-suit-wearing drummer finally came aboard. On January 14, 1963, the newly reconstituted Rolling Stones—Jagger, Richards, Jones, Wyman, Watts, and Ian "Stu" Stewart on piano—made their debut at Soho's Flamingo Jazz Club. The Flamingo's black patrons resented Mick's obvious attempt to sound like one of them. The whites in the audience, nearly all jazz hard-liners, simply dismissed them as amateurs.

Broke, despondent, and facing another bone-chilling winter without heat back at Edith Grove, Mick, Keith, and Brian began to come unhinged. Instead of cleaning their linens, they merely tossed them out the window after several months and then burned them on the front lawn. When Keith locked himself out of the flat, he smashed open a window with his guitar case and climbed in. The glass was never replaced, leaving rain and sleet to pour inside. Mick took to greeting guests to the apartment in the nude and, without warning, shouting obscenities at neighbors as he passed them in the hallways.

In what was the most obvious sign that the residents of 102 Edith Grove were teetering on the brink of madness, Mick and Keith would return home from posting flyers advertising upcoming club dates around town and pour any remaining glue in the bathtub. As part of this mad science experiment, Mick would toss old socks, cigarette butts, leftover food, newspapers, and beer bottles into the grotesque, burbling blob. "This glue was kind of growing out of the bathroom into the kitchen and everywhere," Taylor said. "It was crazy."

No one was more horrified by their living conditions than Bill Wyman. "They'd sit in bed with hundreds of half-empty bottles with fungus growing out of them," he said. "They lived like rats."

For solace, Mick turned to an aspiring seventeen-year-old singer named Cleo Sylvestre. The daughter of immigrants from Trinidad, Sylvestre was still in school but somehow managed to sneak away each night to catch the Stones wherever they happened to be performing.

"Mick was no heartthrob in those days," recalled Sylvestre, who would go on to a long acting career on British television and on the stage. "None of my friends were jealous." At first she resisted Mick's advances, telling him that she already had a boyfriend. The thought of competing with another person for sexual favors only seemed to fuel his ardor—a trait that characterized his approach to both sexes in the coming decades.

"I was scared to see him, almost," Sylvestre said. "All I wanted was a goodnight kiss, but he wanted sex." Nor was she fooled by his working-class act. "I had a real cockney accent," she said, "so I could tell that his was put on." The young black woman did want to learn whatever she could about American music, however, and it was clear to her from the beginning that Mick was "an incredible performer. He was different, completely original. And when he sang, he sounded totally American."

Over the next eighteen months Mick bombarded Sylvestre with love letters that even then seemed schmaltzy and more than a little juvenile. "I want someone to share everything with, someone to respect, not just someone to sleep with," he wrote in one. "Cleo, what have you done to me?"

A Valentine's Day card Mick sent Sylvestre was the source of inspiration for an early Stones hit. "Let's spend the night together," the card read, "before I fall apart."

Brian, meanwhile, had the group's survival on his mind. The Rolling Stones were now barred from their regular venue—the Marquee Club—because an inebriated Keith had taken a swing at club owner Harold Pendleton.

Salvation for Mick and his bandmates came in the form of Giorgio Gomelsky, a bombastic White Russian impresario who had just opened a blues club at the Station Hotel in the tony London suburb of Richmond. Gomelsky was impressed by the group—and Mick in particular. So much so that, while he waited for an opening in his new club's schedule, he agreed to find bookings for the Stones at other clubs so that they could stop shoplifting to survive.

Bill Wyman watched in amazement as Mick perfected his signature prance at a succession of seedy establishments like Surrey's Eel Pie Island and Ken Colyer's Club. "I thought it took real guts," Wyman said. "I mean, if I were in the audience, I would have thought he was a little queer."

Not Gomelsky, who was such a devout believer in the group from the start that he bought ads in the trades trumpeting the arrival of the "inimitable, incomparable, exhilarating Rolling Stones!"

Soon hundreds of screaming, foot-stomping fans were making the half-hour train ride from central London and cramming into Gomelsky's still-unnamed club every weekend. "They simply went berserk," Gomelsky said, "tearing their shirts off, dancing on the tables." The Stones ended each forty-five-minute set with Bo Diddley's "Doing the Craw-Daddy," and even though Gomelsky had no idea what a crawdaddy was, he thought it sounded like the perfect name for a club.

"Mick was their secret weapon from the beginning," said Phil May, Richards's pal from Sidcup Art College. "He was incredible, electrifying—a complete original. Before Mick, the girls would hug the stage while the guys would hang back at the bar trying to look as disinterested as possible. For the first time, it was mainly guys who fought their way to the front; they literally shoved women and punched other guys to get close to Mick. Jagger was the first performer to appeal to *both* sexes—heterosexual males as well as females and gays. He could arouse both sexes like no one before, or since."

Jagger was not the Stones' only secret weapon. While Mick commanded the spotlight, Brian worked tirelessly behind the scenes to land the Stones a record deal. He enlisted the help of his friend Glyn Johns, a recording engineer at IBC Studio, in cutting a five-song demo. When seven record companies rejected it outright, no one was more devastated than the mercurial Mr. Jones.

There was a bright spot: On April 13, 1963, the *Richmond and Twickenham Times* ran the first newspaper feature ever published about the Rolling Stones. "A musical magnet is drawing the jazz beatniks to Richmond," wrote Barry May, who went on to describe Mick as the "driving force behind the group." Although Jones could just as easily lay claim to the title, he was delighted with the piece and carried it with him everywhere.

Gomelsky went a step further. He hired a crew to film the Rolling Stones for an R & B documentary, and then harangued Peter Jones, editor of the influential music magazine *Record Mirror,* until he agreed to personally cover the event. "I went there very much under pressure," Jones recalled, "but I went. I went because of Giorgio."

Nearly everyone who worked for the affable, backslapping, bear-hugging Russian was openly fond of him. Mick, who offstage often affected a kind of chilly British reserve, found Gomelsky's earthy manner boorish and "irritating." He was, however, perfectly willing to let Gomelsky do all he could for the group—as long as the Stones were not legally obligated to repay him in any way. When

Brian wanted to draw up papers formally designating Giorgio as their manager—Gomelsky had even voluntarily forgone his take of the weekend receipts so that the boys could survive the winter—Mick objected. Not only was the man annoying, Jagger argued, but he was strictly small time, lacking the contacts the group needed to make it in the music industry.

For his part, Gomelsky was not at all concerned. He believed he had an oral agreement with Mick and Brian, and that was good enough for him.

There was no audience at the Crawdaddy when Peter Jones got there—just Mick and the boys up on the stage and Giorgio adjusting camera angles while they performed a Bo Diddley song called "Pretty Thing." Jones remembered that it was "so explosive that even without an audience it just sort of lifted you right out of your seat."

Mick and Brian, well aware that Decca Records owned the *Record Mirror,* cornered the journalist. While Peter Jones listened politely, each repeatedly interrupted the other, making it painfully evident that Mick and Brian were locked in a fierce battle for the title of team leader.

In the piece that ran in the *Record Mirror* that April, Mick made the strange pronouncement that the Stones would play only songs written by Americans. "After all, can you imagine a British-composed R & B number? It just wouldn't make it." Equally odd was the reporter's contention that the Stones' music bore only a "superficial resemblance to rock and roll."

On April 14, 1963, the crowd at the Crawdaddy screamed and stomped its approval as Mick belted out Bo Diddley's "Road Runner." At first Mick didn't notice the four men in matching ankle-length black leather coats being escorted to a table by Giorgio. Although Jagger still felt that Gomelsky would be lacking as a manager because he had no major contacts in the music world, Giorgio did know John, Paul, George, and Ringo, and invited them to the club to see the Rolling Stones.

As he pulled out Lennon's seat for him, Giorgio looked up and winked at Mick, who suddenly turned ashen. Richards could only stare gape mouthed, while Bill Wyman said later that all he could think was "Shit, that's the Beatles!"

As it happened, the Beatles were just as blown away by what they saw that night. Nowhere in the musical cosmos was there anyone like this skinny white Englishman who sounded like a black from the Mississippi Delta and writhed and jerked around the stage like a spastic marionette. It was also clear that, no matter how bizarre his appearance or disjointed his movements, Jagger oozed a kind of sex appeal that excited both men and women.

After their set was over, Mick approached the Fab Four at the bar and asked them to come by Edith Grove for a drink. Like everyone else admitted into this vile sanctum sanctorum, the Beatles promptly proclaimed it to be the most wretched flat they had ever seen. They did, however, deign to stay and drink for another three hours. That night, as they knocked back beer after beer, the nine men who would shape the musical tastes of a generation joked, laughed, swapped stories, and debated the relative merits of bluesmen and rockers both famous and obscure.

John Lennon did not hesitate to let his hosts know that he viewed the music of their adored Jimmy Reed as "crap," but that didn't keep Brian from asking all four Beatles for an autographed photo. After they left, Jones taped the signed eight-by-ten glossy on the filth-streaked living room wall of the Edith Grove flat.

In the coming months, as they plotted to overtake the Beatles as the world's number one group, the photo of John, Paul, George, and Ringo served as more than just an inspiration for Mick and his buddies.

It also doubled as a dartboard.

Mick has always been aware of his place in the universe and what it means. He's always seen himself as a symbol, and if he could push it further, he'd push it further.

—PHIL MAY, MUSICIAN AND FRIEND

◆　◆　◆

Mick has to be the one in control—giving the orders, calling the shots.

—FORMER LOVER CHRISSIE SHRIMPTON

◆　◆　◆

The mouth is almost too large. He is beautiful and ugly, feminine and masculine—a rare phenomenon.

—CECIL BEATON

The fact is that Mick doesn't like women. He never has.

—CHRISSIE SHRIMPTON

◆   ◆   ◆

From when I first met him, I saw Mick was in love with Keith. It is still that way.

—ANITA PALLENBERG

3

• ◆ •

Dirty, Rude, Sullen, Chain-Smoking, Generally Obnoxious—and Brilliant

"*H*e was very giggly, very pretty, very camp," said Chrissie Shrimpton, a seventeen-year-old secretarial student who had been eying Mick ever since he first took to the stage back at Alexis Korner's club in Ealing. She often sat ringside, and although he often locked eyes with her while performing, they'd never actually connected.

Tonight would be different. Betting her girlfriend that she could get Mick to kiss her, Chrissie ran up to the stage between numbers and planted one firmly on his lips. The intensity of the kiss surprised her: Mick's pose was decidedly feminine, and she had half expected him to recoil. Instead she found herself staring breathlessly into his blue eyes and noticing that in one of those eyes was a wedge of brown—one of the many things that "made him different from everybody else."

Although Jagger seemed larger than life on the stage, up close he was anything but: five feet nine inches tall and 130 pounds, with a head that was disproportionately large for his slight frame. He also suffered from a serious case of acne.

None of this mattered to Chrissie, an auburn-haired stunner whose older sister, Jean Shrimpton, was just starting her rise to the top as a fashion model. She recognized the same sex appeal in Mick that a brash young agent named Andrew Oldham saw. "They made the Beatles look like choirboys," said Oldham, the illegitimate son of an American pilot who was killed during the war. "The instant I saw Mick on that stage, I knew what they were all about: sex, pure and simple. Sex—and magic."

Oldham, an unrepentant hustler who at age nineteen was determined to become a "teenage tycoon shit," had worked briefly as a publicist for the Beatles. More important, the tall, blond, ruddy-cheeked Oldham had the ear of Decca Records chairman Sir Edward Lewis. "Sir Edward had a strong gay streak," Peter Jones said, "and Andrew would have been a good catch. He'd listen carefully to whatever Andrew had to say."

Giorgio Gomelsky was called away to his father's funeral that spring of 1963, and Oldham, management contract in hand, seized the moment. Brian Jones handled negotiations for the Stones, and Brian's first suggestion was that Mick, his archrival in the group, be booted out. Oldham's business partner, Eric Easton, agreed. "This Jagger fellow," Easton said, "just can't sing." Oldham's response was swift and unequivocal. "You are both," he told Brian and Easton, "completely insane."

The Stones' pianist, Ian Stewart, was another matter. The brawny, lantern-jawed, crew-cut Stu "didn't have the right look; he just didn't fit," Oldham said. Stewart was out—but not entirely. He agreed to become road manager, and he would still be allowed to take part in recording sessions.

Gomelsky felt completely betrayed. Returning from his father's funeral to discover that the Stones had signed with Andrew Oldham, Giorgio was "angry and deeply hurt," said Peter Jones. "He had done everything for these boys." Jagger, who stood by silently while the band's drummer-of-the-moment Tony Chapman, Stu, and now Gomelsky were discarded, apparently felt no pangs of regret. "It didn't bother Mick," Oldham observed, "one tiny little bit to roll over people on his way to the top. To him, everyone is expendable."

Oldham moved quickly, inviting Decca Records executive Dick Rowe to catch the group's act at the Crawdaddy. Already known as "the man who turned down the Beatles," he did not want to make the same mistake twice. Rowe signed the Stones on May 14, 1963, and within days they were in Olympic Studios in London recording their take on Chuck Berry's "Come On."

Mick hated the song and refused at first to perform it. After a screaming match with Oldham, he relented. None of the Stones, however, would back down when it came to the uniform they were now being required to wear: matching black turtlenecks worn with black pants and Cuban-heeled black boots, or black leather suits with black shirts and ties.

Even as they quarreled with Oldham's obvious attempts to mold them in the Beatles' image, Mick and the boys agreed to wear matching hound's-tooth blazers when they lip-synched "Come On" on the pop music program *Thank Your Lucky Stars*. The June 7, 1963 appearance on Great Britain's commercial ITV network marked the Stones' first time on television, and as soon as it was over, Mick tore off his jacket and tossed it in the trash. His fellow Stones followed suit.

No matter. Even in their comparatively conservative attire, Mick's moves offended adults throughout the United Kingdom as much as it thrilled their children. The father of one of Mick's old friends made his feelings known by aiming his gun at the black-and-white image of Jagger on TV and firing it into the screen.

With Mick as the group's sneering centerpiece, the Rolling

Stones were soon splashed across the cover of nearly every fan magazine in the UK. By July, "Come On" was climbing up the charts, topping off at a respectable, if unspectacular, number twenty-one.

At last, Mick and Keith were able to move out of their grimy flat at Edith Grove and into more commodious digs on Mapesbury Road in West Hampstead. They were joined by Andrew Oldham and Chrissie Shrimpton, who, through Mick, had secured a clerical job at Decca Records.

Brian, still confident that he was generally acknowledged to be the band's leader, left to live with his current girlfriend, Linda Lawrence, at her family's home in Windsor. Oldham, acknowledged by Keith to be both "a fantastic hustler" and "an incredible bullshitter," rushed in to fill the power vacuum created by Brian's abrupt exit.

Oldham's gift to his new roommates that September 1963 was their next hit single—courtesy of the Beatles. Cornering Lennon and McCartney as they were getting out of a cab, Oldham told them that the Stones were desperately looking for a new song to record. As it happened, the songwriting duo had just finished a tune that they thought would be ideal for the Stones' hard-driving sound—and Mick's gritty drawl in particular.

John and Paul piled back into the cab and headed for the Stones' rehearsal studio, where they ran through "I Wanna Be Your Man" with them. Once Brian had added his distinctive slide guitar to the piece and Mick had slithered and jerked his way through the number, it was clear that they had found their second British hit. (The very next day, the Beatles went ahead and recorded their own version for inclusion on their second album. Ringo sang the lead.)

A week later, they returned the favor by opening for the Beatles at London's Royal Albert Hall, whipping the audience into a frenzy even before the Fab Four took the stage. This was never left to chance. Oldham planted himself in every audience and emitted girlish screams until the real girls followed suit. Oldham, who also paid teenage boys to create pandemonium by pushing their way past the girls to the front of the stage, reveled in the "fakery, hype, and hustle" that he said were part and parcel of the music game.

By this time, Jagger and Lennon had already become fast friends—Mick was in awe of John's songwriting talent, and Lennon envied Jagger's raw sound and even rawer physicality onstage. Their personal relationship made it possible for the two groups to work in tandem to create the illusion of fierce competition.

At the press reception following the Albert Hall concert, Mick impressed magazine writer Keith Altham with his fake cockney accent and bad boy persona. "They were not working class the way the Beatles were," said Altham, who later became the Stones' press agent. "They were solidly middle class. Mick was particularly adroit at playing the guttersnipe."

Oldham soon recognized that he had made a grave error in trying to offer up the Stones as a slightly scruffier version of the squeaky-clean, unfailingly polite, mildly androgynous Beatles. The Stones would have to take their image to the opposite extreme, positioning themselves as the anti-Beatles—dirty, rude, sullen, chain-smoking, and generally as obnoxious as humanly possible. Although they didn't require much encouraging, Oldham urged all the band members to spit, chew gum, belch, drink alcohol, swear, and, when possible, blow smoke in interviewers' faces. Oldham also dreamt up the provocative line that fast became the group's mantra: "Would you let your daughter marry a Rolling Stone?" "By the time I was finished," Oldham said, "every parent in England was disgusted by the Rolling Stones."

Mick did more than just play the guttersnipe. On the Stones' first national tour of England in the early fall of 1963—they were fourth on the bill behind Bo Diddley, the Everly Brothers, and Little Richard—Jagger experimented with his sexual persona in a way that was certain to push buttons in buttoned-down Britain. Borrowing some makeup pointers from the irrepressibly ostentatious Little Richard, Mick began wearing heavy mascara and even lipstick when he *wasn't* performing. Now, observed one musician, Jagger was "tarted up like some transvestite . . . Even for us, it was pretty shocking."

Oldham, who like the Stones had a preference for skintight jeans, black turtlenecks, boots, and dark glasses, did not object to Mick's increasingly feminine look. Indeed, Oldham often seemed more flamboyant than some of the acts he managed, so it came as little surprise when he began wearing mascara and pancake makeup around the office.

Even Chrissie Shrimpton, who was in the throes of a stormy and sometimes violent affair with Mick, was aware of the gossip regarding his sexuality. She understood completely. "Mick was very masculine minded. He was very strong and aggressive," she explained. "But physically he was very feminine. Even to me, he seemed outrageously camp."

She was not alone. Although Chrissie clung to the belief that Mick's fey posturing was strictly for effect, she began to wonder after Oldham's then-girlfriend, Sheila Klein, pulled her aside at a concert. "Do Mick and Andrew sleep in the same bed?" Klein wanted to know.

Shaken, Chrissie replied, "Not when I'm there, because I sleep with Mick." Shrimpton soon discovered that Jagger and Oldham had shared the same bed when their girlfriends weren't around. "I did see Mick and Andrew in bed together," Chrissie said. The two men were sleeping in the nude, and Shrimpton said that she "was so naive at the time, I thought they looked very innocent and sweet together. But it's obvious Mick was bisexual even then."

Chrissie wasn't the only person to find Mick and Oldham cuddling up together. Oldham's mother discovered the pair beneath the sheets and was, according to Andrew, "none too pleased." Oldham's mum objected mainly because she did not like Mick. "She preferred Keith," Oldham said, "because she'd seen him be kind to her dogs."

As for the connection between the two men: "We had the same wonder, awe, and conspiracy as to what we were about," Oldham later tried to explain. "We seemed to be getting our way with the world."

Ironically, at the same time Mick was determined that all the Stones appear to be carefree bachelors. While they were building their fan base, it was essential for record buyers and concertgoers to fantasize freely about them—and that meant that none of the Stones could appear to be in a serious relationship.

Taking upon himself the role of enforcer, Mick pressured Charlie Watts and his longtime fiancée, Shirley, to cancel their wedding until future notice. He also ordered Wyman not to refer to his wife and child when speaking to the press. Brian, meantime, was instructed not to talk about his pregnant girlfriend Linda Lawrence, or, for that matter, his brood of out-of-wedlock children and their mothers.

Like the Stones' other women, Chrissie was kept in the shadows while Mick publicly laughed off any suggestion that he had a girlfriend. Privately, he reassured a simmering Shrimpton that once the Stones were a household name on both sides of the Atlantic, he would proclaim their love from the rooftops.

In the meantime, there were to be no public displays of affection. The Stones' girlfriends were not even permitted to go near the recording studio—and they knew that they had Mick to blame for these rules.

"Mick really doesn't respect women," Shrimpton said. "He likes to have sex with them, but he also has a fundamental animosity toward them." Whenever they met Mick, the Stones women snapped a Nazi salute and shouted "Heil Jagger!" Needless to say, Chrissie said, "it made him furious, but that *is* how we all felt."

Chrissie had to content herself with furtive meetings in the shadows. Even the simple act of holding hands became problematic. If someone recognized him, Mick would cast off her hand and step away as if they were strangers. After weeks of such treatment, things came to a head when, while walking down a London street, a group of autograph seekers suddenly materialized. This time, Mick shoved Shrimpton to the curb so that he could mingle with his giggling, awestruck fans. After the last autograph was signed and Mick went to fetch her, Chrissie greeted him with a swift kick to the groin.

As it happened, Mick's no-girlfriends rule only exacerbated what was an already volatile situation. "We were very passionate from the beginning," Chrissie said. "Everything about our relationship was intense." Despite Mick's attempts at keeping its very existence under wraps, their tempestuous romance was characterized by screaming fights outside restaurants and hotels, slamming doors, and smashed crockery. She hit Mick often, and he did not always shrink from hitting her back. "We wore sunglasses to hide our black eyes," she said, "and makeup to hide the bruises."

In January 1964 the Stones toured Britain again, this time sharing the bill with the hugely popular American girl group the Ronettes. Ronnie Bennett, whose plaintive rendition of "Be My Baby" became a pop classic, was engaged to the mercurial songwriter-producer Phil Spector at the time.

None of which mattered to Mick, whom Ronnie described as "sexy, provocative, and gorgeous." Nevertheless, when he started getting close to her, Ronnie turned down Jagger—and, risking the vengeful wrath of the notoriously jealous Spector, began a clandestine affair with Keith. Undaunted, Mick moved on to Ronnie's sister Estelle. Their affair lasted the duration of the tour.

Their heterosexual prowess notwithstanding, all the Stones were now targeted for ridicule wherever they went. After one of their concerts with the Ronettes, the group stopped in at a cafeteria and was instantly showered with insults from American tourists seated at a nearby table. Mick ignored the shouts of "Queer!" and "Homo!" for a time, then leapt to his feet and defiantly confronted the hecklers. Within seconds, both Jagger and Richards lay sprawled on the floor.

On another occasion, Jagger and interior designer Nick Haslam were dining at a King's Road restaurant when an older man seated at the next table leaned over and, shoving his face at Mick, asked loudly, "Are you a man or a woman?"

The restaurant fell silent as Mick stared at the man, expressionless. Without saying a word, Jagger stood up, unzipped his pants, and produced the evidence.

Nothing compared with the chaos generated by the Stones whenever they took the stage in the spring of 1964. Whipped into a writhing frenzy, fans invariably surged toward the stage only to be pushed back by security guards. Fistfights broke out, chairs were tossed, and ambulances waited outside to cart off the dozen or so young women who could be counted on to faint at every Stones concert.

Oldham knew it was not enough. If the Stones were to challenge their friendly archrivals the Beatles for supremacy in the pop music world, they would have to do what Lennon and McCartney were doing. They would have to produce their own material. Oldham was convinced Jagger and Richards had latent talent as songwriters, based on the way they'd tweaked Buddy Holly's "Not Fade Away."

That song became their third single, and far and away their biggest UK hit to date.

Before this, neither Mick nor Keith had given any thought at all to becoming songwriters. The notion of becoming another Lennon and McCartney struck both men as "preposterous," Mick would say later.

Oldham persisted. He locked Jagger and Richards in a room and refused to let them out until they had written a song. They came out with two—both of which Oldham deemed to be "bloody awful." One of these, "Tell Me," was included on their first album, released in the UK by Decca on April 17, 1964. At Oldham's insistence, there were no words on the album cover—just a stark photograph of the group. Overnight, the Rolling Stones' debut album shot to number one. (The US version did include the group's name on the cover along with the line "England's Newest Hitmakers.")

Already exhibiting business savvy, Jagger joined with Oldham to set up a separate company to handle the royalties from any songs written by individual group members. They named the new firm Nanker Phelge Music, Ltd.—*Nanker* for the funny face Brian used to crack everyone up back at Edith Grove, and *Phelge* after their untidy former roommate, Jimmy Phelge.

Oldham wasted no time in persuading Jagger and Richards to write a song for another client, a young woman named Adrienne Poster (later Posta). To promote the release of her first single, "Shang a Doo Lang," Oldham threw a fifteenth birthday party for Posta on April 9, Good Friday.

That night would change Mick's life, although the birthday girl had nothing to do with it. Neither would Chrissie Shrimpton, although by this time, he had asked her to marry him, and she had accepted.

Marianne Faithfull was seventeen and still attending a convent school when she walked into the party with Cambridge art student John Dunbar. They knew no one there but had been asked by two other guests, Paul McCartney and his girlfriend Jane Asher, if they'd like to tag along.

Faithfull was the daughter of a onetime ballet dancer, the Baroness Eva Sacher-Masoch, and British wartime intelligence officer-turned-linguistics professor Glyn Faithfull. Her parents parted ways when Marianne was seven, and the Baroness Sacher-Masoch had struggled to pay for her daughter's convent education while making ends meet in the middle-class suburb of Reading. Given the path of self-destruction that Marianne was about to put herself on, it seems prescient that a maternal ancestor had lent the family name to the term *masochism*.

A childhood bout with tuberculosis had shaped Faithfull's outlook on life and imbued her with a kind of translucent beauty. It also helped that she had a porcelain complexion, saucer-sized cobalt-blue eyes, corn-silk hair, and a kind of aristocratic hauteur that made her stand out even in this high-wattage crowd.

Decked out in a flowing lavender blouse and white pants, Oldham glided across the room and introduced himself. "She had this remarkable quality—ethereal and at the same time, very modern," he said. It didn't matter to Oldham if she could sing. "It was her look that interested me—that virginal, angelic, pure look was gold, as far as I was concerned." Moreover, it would have been impossible to invent a stage name that was better suited to this exquisite creature than the one she already had.

Chrissie also took notice, and watched as Mick loped up to Faithfull, introduced himself—and promptly spilled a glass of Dom Perignon down the front of her blouse. Without apologizing, Jagger wiped off her breasts with his bare hand, and she fled to the kitchen.

Faithfull left that night fuming over the stunt Jagger pulled.

"Marianne was really disgusted by them at first," said Barry Miles, a friend of Faithfull's who later joined the Stones' inner circle. "She told me, 'What horrible, ugly, dirty, pimply people.' She thought they looked greasy and sort of disgusting."

None of which stopped Faithfull from signing a recording contract with Oldham the very next afternoon. "They saw me as a commodity: a hunk of matter to be used and discarded," said Faithfull, who left her first recording session "pissed off" at the offhand manner in which she was treated. She forgave Mick and Keith when the gentle ballad they wrote for her—"As Tears Go By"—became a worldwide hit late that summer.

Gentle was hardly the word used to describe the Stones or their growing reputation for wreaking havoc across England. Crowds went wild wherever they performed, smashing windows, stoning busses, overturning cars. "The fans were like animals," complained one Scottish promoter. "The girls were the worst."

On home turf, the Stones were now overtaking their only real rivals. Their debut album toppled the Beatles from the number one position, and at least one poll rated Mick as the top male singer in England—well ahead of any Beatle.

America was another matter. Having yet to score a hit record there ("Not Fade Away" reached number two in the UK but bombed in the States), Mick worried that it was premature to tour the States. Oldham, however, was confident that hype could make up for any absence of radio airplay.

Mick's doubts evaporated when the band arrived on June 1, 1964, at New York's newly renamed John F. Kennedy International Airport (it had been only six months since JFK's assassination) and was mobbed by hundreds of screaming fans.

It was a very different story three days later when the Stones' appearance on ABC's prime-time variety show, *The Hollywood Pal-*

ace, was sabotaged by that week's host, Dean Martin. Making no secret of his distaste for these shaggy invaders and what they called music, Martin held his nose when he introduced them, rolled his eyes after each song, and at one point pleaded with the audience to stay tuned because he did not want to be left alone with the Rolling Stones.

With the next stop, however, came another surge of confidence. More than five thousand fans turned out for their first American concert in San Bernardino, waving banners, breaking through police barricades, and rushing the stage. "It seemed just like home," Mick said.

The euphoria didn't last. As the Rolling Stones moved on into the US heartland, only a few hundred people would show up in arenas that seated up to fifteen thousand. Their roller-coaster ride continued when they reached New York, where thousands filled Seventh Avenue outside Carnegie Hall awaiting the Stones' arrival. After the concert, which benefited from plants in the audience hired by Oldham to "stir things up," police struggled to hold back the mob so that the Stones could make their escape. The next day, Carnegie Hall issued a blanket rule forbidding rock groups to perform there in the future.

The near riot caused by the Rolling Stones' Carnegie Hall debut buoyed Mick's spirits, but it was too little, too late. As Mick had predicted, without a major hit record on the US charts, the Stones were unable to crack such a huge and diverse market. Their all-important first American tour was an unmitigated flop.

Even before their plane touched down at Heathrow, Oldham was planning a European tour to rebuild their battered self-image. While the group's manager mapped out its next move with all the precision of a seasoned field commander, Mick, Chrissie, and Keith decided to move out of their shared flat and into larger accommodations at 10A Holly Hill in Hampstead. This time they did not ask Andrew to join them.

Chrissie no longer had to worry about the nature of Mick's relationship with his manager, but she did have to contend with the fans who seemed to pop up everywhere. While making love one night, they heard giggling and discovered two young girls hiding in their bedroom closet. When the intruders asked who Chrissie was, Mick replied "Nobody" and sent them on their way. Shrimpton then slapped Mick hard across the face, and the two returned to bed.

For the remainder of the summer, the Stones wreaked havoc throughout the UK and Europe. In Belfast, more than five hundred fans had to be carried away on stretchers. In Blackpool, a Steinway grand piano was pushed off the stage, Watts's drums were smashed to bits, and the red velvet stage curtains were yanked down and shredded. After the Stones' concert at Paris's Olympia Theater, rampaging male fans roamed the streets, attacking patrons at sidewalk cafes and smashing store windows.

According to Oldham, "Mick stirred up some incredibly intense feelings in many males. Sex, rage, rebellion—he brought it all to the surface."

No one, least of all Mick, denied that he was the catalyst for the violence that was taking place. "I get a strange feeling onstage. I feel all this energy coming from an audience," he explained. "They need something from life and are trying to get it from us.

"What I'm doing is a sexual thing," Jagger went on, pointing out that what he did onstage was essentially a coquettish striptease. "What really upsets people is that I'm a man and not a woman." But, he hastened to add, "I don't stand in front of a mirror practicing to be sexy, you know."

That, of course, is precisely what Mick did. Shrimpton watched as Mick pranced and posed for hours in front of their bedroom mirror. She was under orders not to let anyone in on the secret. But Chrissie could keep other secrets, too—like the fact that Charlie had defied Mick's decree against marriage and finally eloped with his longtime girlfriend, Shirley.

When Mick found out that Watts had gone behind his back to damage the group's sexy bad-boy image, he was livid. But this paled in comparison to his simmering resentment toward Brian. "Mick loathed Brian, and you couldn't blame him," Phil May said. Subsisting on a steady diet of amphetamines washed down with Jack Daniel's, Jones routinely failed to show up for concerts and seemed to take sadistic pleasure in physically and emotionally abusing his girlfriends. "Brian was a brilliant musician," May added, "but a complete asshole."

Mick had grown accustomed to cleaning up the wreckage that Brian left behind. When one of Brian's countless lovers announced that she was pregnant with his fifth documented illegitimate child, Mick and Andrew paid her $2,000 to relinquish any claims on Brian's earnings and sent her packing—all without ever letting Brian in on the deal.

By fall, with their debut album and two new singles—"Time Is on My Side" and "It's All Over Now"—destined to become hits in the United States, Mick agreed to take another stab at America, this time to promote their second album, *12 x 5*.

The tour's most important performance would not be at a stadium in front of thousands but inside CBS's four-hundred-seat Studio 50. On October 25, 1964, the Rolling Stones debuted on *The Ed Sullivan Show* singing "Around and Around" and "Time Is on My Side." Having made television history with Elvis and, just eight months earlier, the Beatles, Sullivan was thrilled that he could prove his eye for fresh young talent yet again. Backstage after the Stones' performance, he shook Mick's hand and praised the group for generating more excitement among audience members than any act in the show's history—including Presley and the Fab Four.

The next day, however, CBS was swamped with thousands of phone calls and letters from outraged parents. Reacting to public opinion, Sullivan engaged in some furious backpedaling. "I was shocked when I saw them," he told one reporter. "I promise you they'll never be back on the show . . . It took me seventeen years to build up this show, and I'm not going to have it destroyed in a matter of weeks." (Once the Stones were embraced by mainstream America, Sullivan reversed himself and welcomed them back with open arms—five more times.)

There was no such hesitation among New York's cognoscenti, who fawned over Mick and his fellow rocker reprobates as soon as they disembarked at JFK. At a "Mods and Rockers Ball" given in their honor by photographer–nightclub owner Jerry Schatzberg, Mick met Andy Warhol for the first time. Jagger was in awe of the weird, white-blond painter of Campbell's soup cans, and was already convinced that he would ultimately be seen as one of the giants of twentieth-century art. Warhol, in turn, was beguiled by Jagger's unique blend of raw, unschooled talent and gender-bending glamour. Mick would ultimately regard their personal and professional bond, which lasted until Warhol's death twenty-four years later, to be one of the most important in his life.

The Warhol crowd offered their guests more than just hospitality. Drugs were not widely available in England—not even to wealthy rock stars. For the first time, Mick and his bandmates now found themselves with access to all manner of illegal substances. Wherever the Stones went in the States, outstretched hands offered them pot, cocaine, LSD, amphetamines, and even heroin and morphine. Watts and Wyman, who at twenty-eight was the creaky elder of the group, approached it all with caution. But for Richards, Jones, and Oldham, there would be no turning back.

Mick took the middle road, although he would soon graduate from the occasional joint to harder stuff. He claimed later that he was little more than a symbol of the psychedelic sixties. In truth, drugs became an important part of Mick's life, and would remain so for decades.

Their last gig before heading home was an all-star show at the Santa Monica Civic Auditorium, where they were given top billing above Marvin Gaye, Smokey Robinson and the Miracles, and the Beach Boys. Only James Brown, whose first big pop hits "Papa's Got a Brand New Bag" and "I Got You (I Feel Good)" were just around the corner, objected. "I'm going to make the Rolling Stones wish," the Godfather of Soul vowed, "they never set foot in America."

In the end, Brown was so impressed with Mick's moves that he congratulated him as he walked offstage. Mick, in turn, would incorporate some of Brown's patented moves into his routine—although, incredibly, he discovered he was not quite limber enough to replicate Brown's trademark hip-wrenching splits.

Drugs and James Brown's moves weren't the only things Mick picked up in America. Jagger wrote home to Chrissie every day, but that didn't keep him from taking advantage of the groupies who followed them from town to town. The Stones, Oldham said rather indelicately, returned to England "with lots of clap—the price they paid for their indiscriminate screwing."

By 1965, Mick's reputation as both anarchist and corruptor of youth had gone global—thanks in large part to Oldham, who, among other things, was likening the Stones to the bloodthirsty teddy boy–like thugs in Anthony Burgess's futuristic novel *A Clockwork Orange*.

All of which, of course, made them that much more appealing

to Britain's pedigreed elite. "It was suddenly very chic to be seen chatting with a rock star," recalled Brian Morris, owner of the popular nightclub the Ad Lib. "Especially a Beatle or a Stone. Mick was probably the most sought-after socially, since he was thought to be the most dangerous."

Oddly enough, the American actor Dennis Hopper would be instrumental in helping get Mick's foot in the door with England's aristocracy. Hopper, who shared a taste for cocaine with socially connected London gallery owner Robert Fraser, introduced Jagger to Fraser.

In turn, Fraser took Jagger to meet his old Eton College classmate Christopher Gibbs. A Chelsea antique dealer, Gibbs introduced the Moroccan print drapes, carpeting, pillows, brass lamps, and fixtures that would define the classic ethnic "hippie" look. Mick had craved entree into the rarefied worlds of breeding and refinement since his boyhood in Dartford, and Gibbs was more than willing to play Pygmalion to Mick's Galatea. "I'm here," Mick whispered to trendsetting men's designer Michael Fish at one of Gibbs's elegant dinner parties, "to learn how to be a gentleman."

It wasn't going to be easy. When he wasn't dining with the right people at Gibbs's tastefully decorated flat on London's Cheyne Walk, Mick joined his fellow Stones in playing the irredeemable hooligan. Driving home from a concert late one night in Jagger's black Daimler, they stopped at an East London gas station to use the restroom. The attendant refused to give them the key, a heated argument ensued, and Mick responded by relieving himself against the service station wall. Keith and Bill Wyman followed Mick's lead, and after three months of blaring headlines, the Stones found themselves convicted of "insulting behavior"—an offense for which they were fined £5 apiece. The judge intoned, "You have become guilty of behavior not becoming of a young gentleman." Precisely.

By the time the act occasionally billed as "Mick Jagger and the Rolling Stones" invaded the United States again in April 1965, there was no doubt whom people were coming to see. It wasn't Brian Jones. While Mick never missed a concert date, the group's founder, now seriously addicted to amphetamines, began to pile up absences.

"Brian was complicated, moody, difficult to read," recalled photographer Gered Mankowitz, who shot the Stones' album covers during this period and became a member of their inner circle. "He had a cruel streak." According to Mankowitz, Jones "took pleasure in watching other people's pain." And, apparently, in inflicting it. Brian savagely beat many of the young girls he picked up on the road. Such violent behavior offended even the certifiably misogynistic Mick. After a particularly brutal attack on a sixteen-year-old girl, the tour's roadies, with Jagger's consent, repaid Brian by sending him to the hospital with two fractured ribs.

If Mick ever had doubts about the Stones' ability to score a string of hits in the complicated US market, they vanished in 1965 with such blockbuster singles as "The Last Time," "Play with Fire," "Heart of Stone," and "Get Off of My Cloud."

All would pale in comparison to the 1965 Rolling Stones release that many would consider the greatest rock-and-roll song ever written. The melody for "(I Can't Get No) Satisfaction" came to Keith Richards in a dream on the night of May 9. He woke up in his flat in Carlton Hill, St. John's Wood, grabbed his guitar, and recorded the riff. Then he dropped his guitar pick and fell back to sleep.

The next morning, Richards, who had been ingesting copious amounts of cocaine and amphetamines to stay awake, woke up and remembered nothing. But he noticed that the new tape he had put in his portable Philips cassette player the night before had run to the end. "Then I pushed rewind, and there was 'Satisfaction,'" he recalled. That, and forty minutes of Richards snoring.

Several days later, the Stones were in Clearwater, Florida, working on new material. As was typical of their collaboration at the time, Richards gave Mick the melody and a theme on which to build. "The words to this are 'I can't get no satisfaction,'" Keith recalled. "That was just a working title. It could just as well have been 'Auntie Millie's Caught Her Left Tit in the Mangle.' I thought of it as an album filler. I never thought it was anything like commercial enough to be a single."

Mick sat on the edge of the bed in their hotel room and poured out the frustrations he was feeling on the road. A few days later, they recorded the acoustic version of "Satisfaction" at Chess Studios in Chicago, and, later, one with the classic Gibson foot switch "fuzz tone" effect at RCA Recording Studios in Los Angeles.

Mick and Keith were still perfecting the record—or so they thought—when they were riding through Minnesota and heard it on the radio. Oldham had unilaterally made the decision to release it as their new single, and within ten days, it became their first number one US hit. "At first I was mortified," Richards said. "As far as I was concerned, that was just the dub. If I had my way, 'Satisfaction' would never have been released." Fortunately for all concerned, it was.

"Satisfaction" had been perched at number one for a month by the time someone actually decoded the most provocative line: "Baby, better come back / maybe next week / 'cause you see I'm on / a losin' streak." The obvious reference to menstruation was enough to get the song banned in some parts of the country, while others merely deleted the offending stanza. Either way, Mick was delighted at the widespread outrage—which he had been aiming for all along.

Jagger was less thrilled to hear that Marianne Faithfull—for whom he was now carrying a torch—was pregnant and had married the baby's father, John Dunbar, in May. Mick eased his pain after taping the popular American TV show *Shindig!* by taking two of the show's dancers back to his pink Ambassador Hotel bungalow. Mick told his longtime friend Rodney Bingenheimer that it was "a wild party—mattresses on the floors, bouncing off the walls, an incredible night." One of the women Jagger slept with that night became a top choreographer and recorded a number one song in her own right. The other went on to movie stardom and an Oscar nomination.

Back in England, all four Beatles wound up on the Queen's Birthday Honours List, each being made a Member of the Most Excellent Order of the British Empire (MBE). Yet it was Mick who now moved with ease through the world of titled aristocrats.

It was at the sixteenth birthday party of Lady Victoria Ormsby-Gore, daughter of onetime British ambassador to the United States Sir David Ormsby-Gore, that Jagger made his most important royal contact. When Princess Margaret, wearing one of her customary cleavage-baring gowns, motioned for him to join her table, Mick sprang to his feet—leaving behind an indignant Chrissie.

Shrimpton had reason for concern. Even though Margaret was still years from divorcing Lord Snowdon, she was already famous for her liaisons with younger men. "There was a flirtation going on there, definitely," said Lady Elsa Bowker, whose husband, Sir James Bowker, had served as Britain's ambassador to Austria and Burma. "Princess Margaret was only in her thirties at the time, and quite attractive. And as everybody knows, she was attracted to younger men."

Mick's particular blend of raw sex appeal mixed with an uncanny ability to play the perfect English gentleman—he even traded his cockney accent for a lisping upper-class mumble when in the company of blue bloods—made Jagger an object of desire even among the royals. Princess Margaret and Mick "spoke on the phone constantly," said one courtier, "and she invited him to social events. Like many other women, she found him sexy and exciting. If you saw them laughing together, dancing, the way she'd put her hand on his knee and giggle at his stories like a schoolgirl, you'd have thought there was something going on."

Princess Margaret's sister, the Queen, was not amused. "The Queen could tolerate the Beatles because they were clean cut and sort of sweet—at least, that was their reputation at the time," said Harold Brooks-Baker, publisher of *Burke's Peerage*. The Stones were an entirely different matter. "Princess Margaret caused more than her share of scandal. The last thing the Queen wanted was her sister running off with Mick Jagger!"

Chrissie felt the same way and let Mick know it. After another violent encounter—this time Shrimpton used a diamond engagement ring Mick had given her (one of five) to slash his face, leaving a scar that would be visible for years—the couple agreed to wed once the Stones returned for a fourth US tour in the fall of 1965.

Before they left for America, there were some business issues to settle. On Mick's twenty-second birthday, the Stones met with rotund New York accountant-turned-show-business-manager Allen Klein and listened to him lay out his plans for taking the Rolling Stones to the next level. This included squeezing every penny that was due them from record companies and promoters.

Klein certainly looked like someone who would deliver on his promise. According to Stephanie Bluestone, who handled the Stones' financial accounts, Klein always carried a gun and swaggered around the office swigging Scotch out of a bottle. "Allen Klein," Bluestone said, "was a dreadful, dreadful man. He was greasy and fat and vulgar." He was also surrounded by "dangerous people, people operating just this side of the law."

The deal Klein arrived at with the Stones, arranged by a drug-addled Andrew Oldham, would cost Oldham the group he had been so instrumental in making an international phenomenon. "Klein was obviously out to grab the Stones away from me," he said. "I was just too fucked up to notice."

Perhaps. But Oldham was a paragon of sanity compared to Brian, whose behavior grew more erratic with every passing day. Convinced that Mick and Oldham were plotting against him and thoroughly intimidated by the ease with which Jagger and Richards churned out hit after hit, Jones sank deeper into addiction and paranoia. "Having to come into the studio and learn a song Mick and I had written would bring him down," Richards said of Brian. "It was like an open wound."

When he was around, Jones was difficult, insulting, obnoxious. Mick and Keith returned the favor by teasing him constantly—about his stubby legs, his pageboy bangs, the dark, drooping bags under his eyes. "You had to be strong to be a Stone," Bill Wyman said. "The fainthearted or ultrasensitive would not have stood the jibes that poured from Mick and Keith." Added Oldham: "The Rolling Stones and I may have been childishly cruel to Brian on occasion, but he asked for it."

For the most part, Brian was simply AWOL. "We got to rely on him *not* being there," Keith said of Jones's absences from recording sessions and on tour. "And if he turned up, it was a miracle."

Jones did turn up when the Stones played Munich in September 1965, just before leaving for the United States. It was there that a leggy, blonde, eighteen-year-old aspiring Swiss-German model named Anita Pallenberg offered Mick hashish ("Oh no, we can't smoke before we go onstage," he replied) but wound up moving in with Brian instead. Pallenberg would play a key role in the Stones saga for the next fifteen years, and before making her exit, she would descend into a world of insanity, drugs, occultism, and death. "Anita was an exotic, ambitious, sexy, decadent, *dangerous* woman," Gered Mankowitz said. "In a word, she was trouble."

Her impact was felt instantly. The next day in Berlin, Mick, aware that this was the very amphitheater where Hitler had addressed cheering Nazi throngs, suddenly began goose-stepping in the middle of "Satisfaction." More than one hundred people were injured during the riots that followed. (Later, Pallenberg persuaded Jones to be photographed in a Nazi uniform with his foot on the neck of a doll—an image that was understandably denounced in the press as glaringly anti-Semitic.)

That fall, the Stones juggernaut rolled on. With their not-so-subtle drug paean "Get Off of My Cloud" topping the charts, the Stones once again invaded the United States and received their customary reception from fans. "It was terrifying," Mankowitz recalled. "Fans pounded on the windows, rocked the car back and forth. Then they climbed up onto the roof, and it started to collapse. We had to hold it up with our hands."

The most memorable night on that particular tour was November 9, 1965—the night of the great blackout that plunged all of New York City (and most of the Northeast) into darkness. Mankowitz and Watts walked into their suite at Manhattan's City Squire Hotel to find Brian and Bob Dylan surrounded by naked girls, drinking, jamming, and, of course, smoking dope—all by candlelight.

To be sure, Mick took advantage of everything the groupies had to offer. But by the time the tour ended, he was frustrated, exhausted, lonely, and desperately missing Chrissie. He sobbed when he spoke to her on the phone, and each day took time to sit down to write her a love letter. (Shrimpton would ultimately amass more than six hundred such letters.)

When it came time to check out of the City Squire, Jagger vented his frustrations by leading his fellow Stones in the now traditional rock star room trashing. They smashed lamps and TV sets, overturned tables and chairs, threw towels and bedding out the window, and, according to Mankowitz, engaged in Mick's favorite farewell ritual: peeing in the sinks.

Until now, Mick had resisted LSD; at a party thrown in LA by *One Flew Over the Cuckoo's Nest* author Ken Kesey, Keith and Brian both dropped acid, but Mick declined. "He was afraid of losing control," Chrissie said, "and that's the most important thing to him, more important than love or even money: control."

However much he may have missed Chrissie when he was on the road, in no time at all they were back at each other's throats—a situation aggravated by drug use. They were now smoking pot on a more or less constant basis, and it soon became clear to Shrimpton that Mick had relented and was experimenting with LSD. "He just acted very strange and talked gibberish," she recalled. "I had absolutely no idea what he was talking about, but since I was smoking grass, I thought that maybe it was me."

The Stones' February 1966 release "19th Nervous Breakdown" spoke volumes about the ongoing tensions between Mick and Chrissie. She was delighted when he told her that his next hit, "Lady Jane," was about her and not about Henry VIII's doomed wife Jane Seymour. In fact, Mick took it from D. H. Lawrence's *Lady Chatterley's Lover*; "Lady Jane" is the protagonist's name for Lady Chatterley's vagina.

Chrissie threw tantrums and seethed, but Mick was able to turn his rage into hit songs. Of the many overtly misogynist tunes that made up their next album, *Aftermath*, none resonated more than "Under My Thumb," with its cringe-inducing line about the "squirming dog who's just had her day." Even "Mother's Little Helper," which ostensibly (and rather hypocritically) took aim at prescription drug abuse, had a line that Chrissie took personally: "What a drag it is getting old." At twenty, she was already worried that Mick would trade her in for a younger model.

Age actually had nothing to do with it. First Jagger had to go through his own nervous breakdown, sent home for bed rest after he was overtaken by physical and emotional fatigue in the middle of yet another European concert tour in June 1966.

More hell-bent than ever on climbing up Britain's steep and spiraling social ladder, Mick needed a mate who was already a rung or two above him—someone like Marianne Faithfull. "Jagger loved her," said Mankowitz, who had a ringside seat for their romance. "What man wouldn't? She was this dangerous combination of convent girl, English rose, and pop star all in a very sexy body. Marianne looked at Mick, and he just fell apart."

Faithfull, for all her breeding, was more businesslike in her approach. "My first move was to get a Rolling Stone as a boyfriend," she confessed. "I slept with three, and then I decided the lead singer was the best." Faithfull's decision to leave her husband, John Dunbar, was reached with equal, clear-headed ease. "I went with the one who had the most money," she said with a shrug. "And that was Mick."

Mick, who had already crept up the *Billboard* charts singing the Stones' uncharacteristically restrained version of "As Tears Go By," was hardly her first choice. First she slept with Brian while they were both on an LSD trip. The Stone who fascinated her most, however, was Richards. She hoped theirs would be a lasting relationship, but after they slept together, Keith told her that Mick was hopelessly smitten with her.

"There was Keith in the sheets," Faithfull said, "explaining to me that nobody had to know about this night because Mick was in love with me . . . I just thought, 'Oh, dear, well it's a shame.'"

Even after she had decided on her Stone, Faithfull was anything but. While the Stones were in New York that September of 1966 promoting their new hit single "Have You Seen Your Mother, Baby, Standing in the Shadow?"—at Mick's insistence, all five posed for the record sleeve in full drag—Faithfull carried on with Jimi Hendrix. (Just two years earlier, when he was an unknown guitarist going by the name of Jimmy James, Hendrix auditioned for Mick and was turned down. Hendrix got his revenge not only by sleeping with Faithfull but also by stealing Keith's girlfriend Linda Keith.)

Of course, Mick was scarcely a model of fidelity. While he still hid his affair with Marianne from the dangerously jealous Chrissie, Jagger also carried on for months with Ikette P. P. Arnold, one of Ike and Tina Turner's backup singers. More important, it was while touring England with Ike and Tina ("God, who's that boy with the big lips?" Tina Turner asked when she first saw Jagger standing in the wings) that Mick picked up several moves to add to his repertoire. "Mick wanted to *be* Tina Turner," Allen Klein said. "He told me that when he's performing, that's the image he has of himself."

On December 18, 1966, Chrissie was packing for their planned Christmas trip to the Bahamas when Mick informed her coldly that he had canceled their plane tickets and was going off to spend the rest of the day with Marianne. "It was incredibly shocking and very cruel," said Shrimpton, who was "amazed" that Jagger still insisted that his relationship with Faithfull was strictly business. "Mick can be sweet and caring," Chrissie said, "but he is also manipulative and possessive . . . he is a master of verbal abuse. He has a vicious, vicious mouth."

That night, Mick came home to find that Shrimpton had tried to kill herself with an overdose of barbiturates, and very nearly succeeded. (In an eerie twist of fate, on that same day, Mick's playboy friend Tara Browne, heir to the Guinness brewery fortune, ran a light and was killed—a tragedy that would inspire the Beatles classic "A Day in the Life.")

On Christmas Eve, Mick threw Chrissie out of the apartment they shared. "Mick," she recalled wistfully of their breakup, "completely broke me in the end. But until he did, I was always stronger than him."

Just weeks later, Mick was mugging his way through another appearance on the *The Ed Sullivan Show,* rolling his eyes skyward every time he sang the Sullivan-mandated line "Let's spend some *time* together" instead of "Let's spend the night together."

Mick gloried in his outlaw role. But on February 5, 1967, when the UK paper *News of the World* ran a purported interview with Jagger in which he freely discussed his use of hashish and speed, he was outraged. The interviewer, it turned out, thought that he'd talked to Mick, when he'd really talked to Brian. No matter that Mick *was* regularly ingesting hashish, speed, and, for that matter, LSD. Jagger announced on television the next day that he intended to sue *News of the World,* then the most-read newspaper on the planet, for libel.

Not long after, Mick was cautioned that the unmarked van parked outside his flat in Harley House, on London's Marylebone Road, was there to spy on him—and that his phone line was being tapped. More than forty-four years before a phone hacking scandal would nearly topple a media empire, shake a Conservative Party government to its foundations, and bring an end to the 168-year-old tabloid, *News of the World* was already engaged in widespread eavesdropping and wiretapping activities—all while engaged in a kind of unholy alliance with the authorities.

Beyond being able to use the press to promote his own agenda, Jagger was no fan of Fleet Street. But the idea that a major publication would actually engage in illegal phone tapping seemed, he would later tell his attorney, "crazy." Waving off the warnings, he headed off to spend a weekend at Redlands, Keith's baronial, moat-ringed estate in the English countryside. Jagger and Marianne would be joined by, among others, an upper-class hanger-on named Nicky Kramer, art gallery owner Robert Fraser, the ever-present Christopher Gibbs, and George Harrison and his then wife, Pattie. The guest of honor was not a Stone or a Beatle but a young Californian who would later be identified in court as "Dr. X": David Schneiderman. "Acid King David," as his friends called him, brought along a monogrammed valise crammed with every illegal substance imaginable. Topping the list of hallucinogens was DMT (dimethyltryptamine), a powerful psychedelic that Mick and Keith were both eager to try for the first time.

That Saturday, an "anonymous informant" (Keith's Belgian chauffeur Patrick) tipped off *News of the World* to a sex-and-drugs bacchanal at Redlands that was to last the entire weekend. It was not until eight o'clock Sunday evening—at which time, everyone at the party was, in Richards's words, "tripping on acid and in a completely freaked-out state"—that Keith was informed someone was banging at the front door. Peering outside the window, Richards saw "this whole lot of dwarves outside, and they're all wearing the same clothes!" The "dwarves" were nineteen police officers armed with a search warrant.

Once they stepped inside, police beheld a surreal tableau. Marianne, clad only in a tawny fur rug, reclined on a sofa while Mick, whose head was between her legs, nibbled on a strategically placed Mars bar. Several Mars bars were always on hand, Richards explained later, using a rather unfortunate choice of words, "because on acid, you get a sugar lack, and suddenly you're munching away."

After scouring the premises, the police somehow missed a vial of heroin someone had simply jammed under the cushions of a drawing room couch. As for Acid King David's portable pharmacy, when police opened the briefcase and saw that it was loaded with foil-wrapped packets, Schneiderman claimed it was film. "Please, please officers, shut it! You'll ruin my photographs!" They obliged, and Schneiderman not only made a hasty departure but disappeared. (Decades later it was revealed that Schneiderman, who had agreed to set up the bust to avoid being prosecuted on separate drug charges, fled to Los Angeles where he lived under the alias "David Jove" until his death in 2004.)

What the police did manage to find during the 1967 Redlands raid was heroin stashed in the lining of Robert Fraser's coat, and, in the breast pocket of Mick's favorite green velvet jacket, four amphetamine tablets. Jagger told Detective-Constable John Challen that the "pep pills" had been prescribed by his physician. They actually belonged to Faithfull, and—although she later offered to confess this to the police—Mick nobly insisted on taking the blame.

The next day, Keith's regular drug dealer, "Spanish Tony" Sanchez, had an explanation for why the raid was going unreported in the press. The police, he said, were waiting for a bribe. Told that the whole matter would go away for $12,000, Sanchez was dispatched with the cash.

After a month passed with no charges being filed, Mick finally felt comfortable enough to head off to Morocco on vacation. In Marrakech, he and Marianne (who, for some reason, Mick had taken to calling "Marian") met up with Gibbs, Fraser, and the legendary photographer and costume designer Cecil Beaton.

From the start, Beaton, then sixty-three years old, was smitten with Mick. "We sat next to each other," Beaton wrote in his diary, "as he drank a Vodka Collins and smoked with pointed finger held high. His skin is chicken-breast white and of a fine quality. He has an inborn elegance."

As for Jagger's sex appeal, Beaton described it as "unique. He is sexy, yet completely sexless. He could nearly be a eunuch. As a model, he is a natural." One part of Mick's anatomy held a special fascination for Beaton. At one point during Jagger's Moroccan sojourn, Sir Cecil instructed Mick to pull down his pants so he could photograph Jagger's derriere. Beaton then committed a "portrait" of the rock star's backside to canvas. The painting was eventually auctioned off at Sotheby's for the then respectable sum of $4,000.

On March 18, 1967, Mick awoke to headlines that, despite the $12,000 bribe arranged by Spanish Tony Sanchez, he and Keith were to face drug charges after all. The trial would not begin for another two months, during which time they were committed to a nine-country European tour. Since Mick and Keith were now on Interpol's watch list, every time they arrived at a new destination, they were forced to undergo a degrading full-body search.

Undaunted, Mick and the Stones kicked off the tour by invading Poland. When more than three thousand fans pushed past police barricades and stormed the arena where they were performing in Warsaw, tanks rolled into the center of the city to subdue them with tear gas and water cannons. Similarly violent scenes would be repeated in Milan, Italy, and Zurich, Switzerland, where Mick was actually assaulted onstage by a crazed fan and beaten to the floor before police could pull off his attacker.

Once back in London, Jagger continued apace with the other half of his curious double life—as the coquettish darling of cafe society. Among Mick's new admirers was beat poet Allen Ginsberg, who brought along his friend Tom Driberg when he dropped in on Jagger in April 1967. Both men were openly gay, and when sixty-one-year-old Driberg, who also happened to be a controversial member of parliament, put his hand on Mick's thigh and made a crude remark about Jagger's "basket," Ginsberg was taken aback.

"I also had eyes for Jagger myself," Ginsberg said, "but I was very circumspect about Jagger's body. Yet here was Driberg coming on crude." Apparently Mick was anything but offended. He reportedly told his friend Barry Miles on several occasions that he had spent a night in bed with Driberg and Ginsberg.

Whether or not the relationship with Driberg was, in fact, intimate, the two men forged a personal bond that would endure for more than a decade. "Many of Mick's closest friends," said Spanish Tony Sanchez, "are men who he knows long to go to bed with him. The feminine side of his complex personality seems to delight in their flattery and admiration."

As he faced serious drug charges, Mick now had a powerful ally who could—and would—stand up in the House of Commons and speak passionately in his defense. Driberg was in awe of Mick's mesmeric hold over the young and would spend years trying to convince him to run for office as a Labour Party candidate.

Although it was widely known that Driberg had been a member of Britain's Communist Party for twenty years before switching to Labour, it was revealed only after his death that Driberg was, in fact, a spy. Shortly after entering parliament in 1942, Driberg became a double agent, recruited by Britain's MI5 security service *and* by Russia's infamous KGB to report on the private lives of his fellow lawmakers. After Driberg was elevated to the peerage by Queen Elizabeth in 1974, those inside the tight-knit intelligence community dubbed Mick's close friend and mentor "Lord of the Spies."

Even had he known that his friend Tom Driberg would go down in British history as a traitor, it was doubtful that Mick would have turned his back on him. After all, as he joined Keith and their friend Robert Fraser in pleading not guilty to drug charges that May, Jagger knew full well that he would need all the influential friends he could get. Within hours of the arraignment in the Redlands case, reporters just happened to be on hand when police barged into Brian Jones's Chelsea flat and arrested him for possession of hashish, amphetamines, and cocaine. Judging by the next morning's headlines, one thing was patently obvious: British authorities intended to make examples of those arrogant corrupters of England's (and for that matter the world's) youth—the Rolling Stones.

In Mick Jagger's mind, only one thing came first:
Mick Jagger.

—KEITH ALTHAM, LONGTIME PUBLICIST AND FRIEND

◆   ◆   ◆

You know what is the greatest tragedy to me?
That c— is a great entertainer.

—BILL GRAHAM, LEGENDARY ROCK PROMOTER

4

◆ ◆ ◆

Angels and Demons

JUNE 29, 1967

𝓜ick's knees buckled, the color drained from his face, and, for a moment, he felt as if he were about to collapse. Keith had just been sentenced to a year in prison, and now the bewigged Judge Leslie Block was telling Jagger that he was to spend three months behind bars. "I just went dead when I was sentenced," recalled Mick, who could hear the crowd of eight hundred supporters outside the West Sussex courthouse in Chichester chanting "Shame!" and "Let them go!" The experience, Jagger added, "was just like a James Cagney film. Then everything went black."

Moments later, Marianne and Mick were together in his holding cell, holding each other as they wept. It was not the only time the case had driven Mick to tears. Convicted after just two days, he was handcuffed and sent to Lewes Prison to await sentencing. At that time, Jagger cried as he was fingerprinted, photographed, and handed a prison uniform.

Now that he faced the prospect of sharing a cell with another convicted felon in London's forbidding nineteenth-century Brixton Prison for ninety days, Mick was devastated—and terrified. Tears streaming down his face, a haggard, trembling Jagger told visitors that he doubted he could survive the experience.

Mick and Keith, who had been dispatched with Fraser to the equally medieval Wormwood Scrubs Prison, could take solace in the fact that their conviction and sentencing had ignited worldwide protest. Demonstrators gathered outside British embassies in scores of countries to call for the immediate release of Mick and Keith. Disc jockeys everywhere vowed to play Stones' recordings around the clock until the rockers were set free. And in a show of solidarity, The Who recorded a double-sided single of appropriately titled Stones songs—"The Last Time" and "Under My Thumb"—that became a hit in Britain that July.

In the House of Commons, Mick's friend and political mentor Tom Driberg stood to express "revulsion" at the way Jagger and Richards were being punished "as if they were murderers." The day after Driberg's impassioned plea, Mick and Keith were released on £7,000 bail (about $15,000 at the time) to await the outcome of their appeal.

The drive to "Free Mick and Keith" raged on in the court of public opinion. Most newspapers ran editorials denouncing the Stones' harsh punishment as "another case of British hypocrisy" (the London *Evening News*) or "monstrously out of proportion" (the *Sunday Express*). But the coup de grace was delivered by William Rees-Mogg, editor of the musty *Times* of London. The title of Rees-Mogg's editorial condemning the sentences, borrowed from the eighteenth-century English poet Alexander Pope, would become one of the most famous in the history of British journalism: "Who Breaks a Butterfly on a Wheel?"

On July 31, England's lord chief justice, Lord Parker, reversed Keith's conviction for lack of evidence and then—creating a momentary surge of panic—upheld Mick's. Within seconds, however, Lord Parker tossed out Jagger's prison sentence and replaced it with a year on probation.

Mick responded by gobbling down several Valium tablets and heading off in a Rolls-Royce limousine to his first televised press conference. After fielding reporters' questions for fifteen minutes ("I've been pushed into the limelight . . . I don't try to impose my views on people like some pop stars do"), Mick grabbed Marianne and climbed aboard a helicopter that then carried them to a Georgian estate in Essex. As TV cameras continued to roll, Mick sat down with a panel of political leaders, clerics, and publishing executives to discuss such weighty matters as drug policy, social rebellion, and the future of Britain's youth.

"I didn't set myself up as a leader in society," he said, opting for the measured speech of a gentleman over his usual faux cockney patois. "It's society that's pushed one into that position."

Overnight, a scandalous drug trial had transformed Mick into one of the world's most sought-after experts on important issues of the day. Comporting himself before the TV cameras with intelligence and a degree of maturity beyond his twenty-four years, Jagger seemed every inch the model citizen. Privately, he relished his victory over the Establishment that had tried and failed so miserably to destroy him—the very same entrenched institutions that now sent their gray-haired minions to court him.

It wasn't long before Mick reverted to form, however—and for sound business reasons. The Stones' power did not reside in reasoned debate or tempered public discourse. It resided in unfettered expression, youthful rebellion, and anarchy. Within days of his release from prison, Mick was calling for all three.

"The time is right now—revolution is valid," Jagger told reporters, who dutifully appeared at his hastily called press conferences to record his every offhand comment and rumination on the socio-political scene. "Anarchy is the only slight glimmer of hope," he declared. The financially savvy and already outrageously wealthy rock star also stated on the record: "There should be no such thing as private property."

Even as he called for his fans to man the barricades, Mick was furnishing his newly acquired Queen Anne–style mansion at 48 Cheyne Walk with costly antiques, Flemish tapestries, and Persian rugs hand selected by the excruciatingly tasteful Christopher Gibbs. Jagger shared his chic new residence on the banks of the Thames with Marianne, her toddler son, Nicholas—and a freshly minted Bentley.

Just a few steps away was Gibbs's stately brick-and-stone manor, once the home of the American painter James McNeill Whistler. It was here, in dimly lit rooms decorated in the Moroccan style and redolent of incense, that Gibbs played host to the most famous names in the worlds of music, art, fashion, cinema, business, and politics.

When Allen Ginsberg passed through London on his way back from Italy that summer, Gibbs threw a party and invited Princess Margaret as well as several of her titled cousins, five cabinet members, a smattering of Oxford and Cambridge intellectuals, and his uber-wealthy neighbors Paul Getty II and Getty's comely wife, Talitha. (Talitha Getty, who, as usual, wore a transparent dress with no underwear, would succumb a few years later to a heroin overdose.)

None shone brighter than Mick and Marianne—she braless in a tight purple blouse and miniskirt, he wearing a mulberry tunic with flouncy Victorian sleeves. It was while they were chatting with the Queen's only sibling that a butler began passing around a silver tray heaped with brownies made from a recipe in the *Alice B. Toklas Cookbook*. In this particular case, however, the cook decided to double the amount of hashish normally called for in the recipe. According to one of the guests that evening, Mick's friend John Michel, what the guests were ingesting was "very toxic, very dangerous.

"People began freaking out," Michel continued. "All these ladies and lords, curators of the British Museum, various members of parliament, were rushed away in their chauffeur-driven cars to have their stomachs pumped." Not to mention Princess Margaret. Shortly before midnight, the Queen was awakened at Buckingham Palace and told that her sister had been rushed to the hospital suffering from "severe food poisoning."

Even with their significantly greater tolerance for drugs, Jagger and Faithfull bolted outside and began sprinting up and down Cheyne Walk—"very high but very happy," he told John Michel. Fortunately for all concerned, the British press never got wind of the incident. If they had, Michel said, "the impact of the scandal on the government and on the royal family would have been enormous."

Mick's notoriety notwithstanding, the Beatles dominated the musical landscape in the summer of 1967 with their landmark *Sgt. Pepper's Lonely Hearts Club Band* album. The Stones even played a small part in the success of the Beatles' mostly live recording of "All You Need Is Love," adding their voices to those of others in the studio audience. The Beatles returned the favor on the Stones' similarly titled single "We Love You," but when it failed to match the success of "All You Need Is Love," Jagger refocused his attention on what had made *Sgt. Pepper* the Beatles' greatest musical achievement to date.

The Beatles had taken a decidedly psychedelic turn, to be sure. But the Stones had to do more than just offer a variation on *Sgt.*

Pepper's trippy peace, love, and LSD theme. Their concept album would take an abrupt turn toward the sinister and the macabre. Borrowing a line from language found on all British passports—"Her Britannic Majesty's Principal Secretary of State for Foreign and Commonwealth Affairs Requests . . ."—Mick came up with *Their Satanic Majesties Request.*

The album, recorded at Olympic Studios in London, effectively marked the end of Andrew Oldham's highly profitable and exceedingly close relationship with the Stones. Having frittered away his fortune on drugs, his creative drive waning, Oldham was diagnosed as suffering from clinical depression. After spending the weekend recovering from electroshock therapy sessions, he would show up at the studio ready to contribute his ideas as he had always done.

Mick made it painfully clear that he no longer wanted Oldham around. "When it came to the look, the image of the Stones," photographer Gered Mankowitz said, "they had always deferred to Andrew's genius." No longer. "By not consulting Andrew on this, Mick was basically telling him he was finished. I remember the look on Andrew's face so clearly."

Mankowitz was "astounded" at how "callous" Mick could be—and how patently ungrateful he could be to people who had been instrumental in his rise to the top. "If someone opens a door for you, and *everything* you want is on the other side of that door," he said, "then you can't dismiss him as a doorman."

Jagger insisted that the Stones no longer needed an outside manager. Allen Klein would control day-to-day finances, but the Stones themselves—well, really, Mick—would be making the big creative and business decisions. Nevertheless, Oldham would wind up having to sue Klein to get his payoff. Eventually Andrew agreed to walk away from the Stones for $1 million in cash—roughly the equivalent of $9 million today, but a relative pittance in light of the fact that the group would end up grossing billions.

If Jagger had no problem turning his back on Oldham as he had on Giorgio Gomelsky and so many others, he was equally unmoved by the plight of Brian Jones. Within days of Oldham's departure, Brian was sentenced to six months in dreaded Wormwood Scrubs Prison. Jones had long suffered from respiratory problems, and the verdict triggered a severe asthma attack.

Not that Jones seemed particularly worthy of anyone's sympathy. Sprung on bail after one day pending an appeal, Brian picked up two teenage girls, took them back to his apartment for an LSD-laced threesome, then beat them so viciously that they ran bleeding and naked into the street.

Jones's prison sentence would later be replaced with three years' probation, but only after a psychiatrist told the court that Jones suffered from "Oedipal fixations" as well as "suicidal tendencies," and that his imprisonment would result in a "complete break with reality, a psychotic breakdown."

Jagger's own grip on reality seemed tenuous at best. Shuttered from the outside world in their dimly lit Cheyne Walk townhouse, he and Marianne smoked hashish, dropped acid, made love, and— they would both admit later—played dress-up.

For years, Keith and Brian had traded clothes with Pallenberg and their other girlfriends, and now the waifish Mick was wriggling into Marianne's frocks while she pulled on his bell-bottoms and ruffled shirts. When he was in the mood, Jagger might go all the way, decking himself out in Faithfull's jewelry and one of her feather boas, then squeezing into high heels to offer a leg-pumping rendition of "River Deep—Mountain High" worthy of his idol Tina Turner.

Playful cross-dressing was not uncommon among the British upper classes and gave little indication of whether the participants were either gay or straight. For their part, Jagger and Faithfull were game for pretty much anything.

"I did have girlfriends, and I did have affairs with them," Marianne recalled. "Mick knew about my girlfriends." Indeed, if he happened to come home to find Faithfull in bed with a woman, more often than not he jumped in with them.

To Marianne, Mick's willingness to accept her lesbian adventures made sense. Jagger would have felt jealous, she said, if he were competing with another man for her affections. "His attitude was that he'd much prefer me to have a girlfriend than a boyfriend," she explained. "Same as I preferred him to be in bed with a man rather than a woman."

Marianne added that her countrymen have always taken a more relaxed view of homosexuality, which she went on to suggest is really "at the heart of narcissism. It's just the desire, a very strong desire, to have people be in love with you. Whether it's a man or a woman isn't really important."

One of the men Jagger was allegedly found in bed with was a young Eric Clapton, who had just recorded "Sunshine of Your Love" as guitarist for the virtuosic power trio Cream. Clapton and Jagger actually traced their friendship back to the Ealing Jazz Club, when Mick was still with the Blue Boys and before Eric had started his first major group, the Yardbirds.

"Eric and Mick were caught in bed together, it's true," John Dunbar said. "It was a very narcissistic scene, very ambivalent sexually. Bisexuality and androgyny were not only accepted, they were encouraged."

Not everyone in the Stones' inner circle was aware of an intimate relationship between Jagger and Clapton, although virtually all knew of their close personal friendship. Marianne's ex-husband, however, certainly appeared to be in a position to know who was sleeping with whom. Throughout this period, Dunbar not only remained close to Faithfull and Jagger, he occupied a unique position at the epicenter of Swinging London as co-owner of London's trendy Indica Gallery. It was at the Indica that Dunbar introduced his friend John Lennon to an unknown avant-garde artist named Yoko Ono in November 1966.

English-born journalist Victor Bockris, an acquaintance of Mick's who covered the music scene in London during this period, knew that many of Jagger's peers were up to the same "shenanigans." Their behavior, he said, was "extremely hedonistic, dope induced." Clapton, who later battled heroin addiction for years, was, Bockris said, "very much a part of that. Nothing was sacred; the idea was to break every taboo. This was a time period where there was no sense of finger-pointing if you were bisexual. It wasn't perceived as something to be ashamed of. Everyone was experimenting, including heterosexual rock stars." Added Dunbar: "Bisexuality and androgyny were not only accepted but encouraged."

Although he would strike a very different pose in the future, the Eric Clapton of 1967 was also, Gered Mankowitz remembered, "a pretty daringly androgynous creature." Sporting a wardrobe of frilly psychedelic tops, flowing caftans, and platform heels, Clapton also was one of the first male rockers to perm his straight hair into an Afro and wear nail polish—something that even Mick rarely did.

It seemed logical to those who knew both men at the time that they would gravitate toward each other. Based on his work with the Yardbirds, John Mayall's Bluesbreakers, and Cream, Clapton was already being hailed in some circles as rock's greatest guitarist. Certainly that was the overwhelming sentiment in the UK, where the slogan "Clapton is God" was scrawled on walls from London to Edinburgh. "They were both being worshiped," Dunbar said, "and they were isolated by sycophants." Inevitably, "rock stars of their magnitude begin to believe their own press. They become deluded, as fooled by it as the public is."

There may have been another, more deep-seated psychological reason that Mick found intimate relationships with men to be especially satisfying. "I think it has a lot to do with Mick's attitude that all women are groupies," Dunbar said. "It's a more equal mating with other men because they're your peers."

More than anything else, Mick wanted his peers to be peers of the realm. The "aristos," said Dunbar, "would never really accept him as an equal. He was and remains a curiosity for them."

What was missing, Jagger managed to convince himself, was the one thing that every true English gentleman had: a country house. Keith Richards had Redlands, Bill Wyman had Gedding Hall in Suffolk—so it was only natural that Mick set out in search of a stately English home befitting his station.

He settled on Stargroves, a palatial Elizabethan manor in the Berkshire town of Newbury. Decades later, the area would be overrun with paparazzi and tourists hoping for a glimpse of another Berkshire resident, Kate Middleton.

It had been eleven months since their last big album, *Between the Buttons,* which marked their breakaway from their blues roots and the foray into psychedelia. Now Jagger hoped that *Their Satanic Majesties Request* would duplicate the mammoth success of *Sgt. Pepper.*

It seemed only logical that it would. After all, the Beatles and the Stones were closer personally, creatively, and commercially than they had ever been. They secretly contributed to each other's projects, and even started timing the release of their singles—at the time, artists as hot as the Beatles and Stones were expected to crank them out at the rate of one every eight or nine weeks—so that the two groups would not be in direct competition as they had in the past. It was a scheme designed to ensure that the Stones would never deprive the Beatles of a number one record, and vice-versa.

From then on, Lennon and Jagger would check in with each other every five or six weeks to let the other know the status of their group's next recording. A typical exchange:

"I don't like ours the way it is. We're going back into the studio. You?"

"We're all set to go with one."

"Your turn, then. You go."

"It was," Allen Klein said, "an incredibly shrewd strategy." Even more important, while the rest of the world saw them as bitter rivals, Mick viewed the Beatles—John and Paul in particular—as the Stones' musical brethren. At one point, Jagger wanted to make this partnership official. A few months earlier the Beatles' longtime manager and mentor, Brian Epstein, died from an accidental overdose of sleeping pills, stunning the entertainment world. Now, with Oldham also out of the picture, Mick proposed that the Beatles and the Rolling Stones share a studio and management office in London. John and Paul signed on with the plan immediately, but after a studio was picked out, the less-than-ecumenical Klein scuttled the merger.

As he eagerly awaited the release of the new album, Mick pondered new ways in which to scandalize fans' parents and provoke the Establishment. It quickly became clear that, when it came to offending upstanding, clean-living citizens, satanism would be awfully hard to top. All the elements certainly seemed to be there: violence, anarchy, heresy, spectacle, sex. It simply took Mick's breath away. Jagger would no longer settle for being a run-of-the-mill antihero. He would be the Antichrist.

Mick stopped reading his favorite Beat Generation writers—Burroughs, Jack Kerouac, Ginsberg—and began devouring such occult bibles as *The Book of the Damned, Manuscripts of Witch-*

craft, and *The Master and Margarita,* a Russian novel in which Lucifer drops in on Moscow to assay his handiwork after the Bolshevik Revolution. That book would inspire a later Stones hit, "Sympathy for the Devil."

As his guide in matters of the occult, Mick had Kenneth Anger, a former child actor who now claimed to be a *magus*: a kind of satanic Merlin. Along with Tom Driberg, Anger had been a disciple of the "Great Beast" Aleister Crowley, Britain's infamous father of modern-century witchcraft.

Anger was fond of casting spells and leveling curses, and soon found a willing acolyte in the highly impressionable (and perpetually unstable) Anita Pallenberg. While riding in Keith's Bentley on the road between Fez and Marrakech, Pallenberg encountered the aftermath of a violent car crash. She instructed the chauffeur to pull over, ran up to one of the accident victims lying on the side of the road, and dipped her silk scarf in his blood. Anger had told Pallenberg that a dying person's blood possessed magical powers, so from then on she used the scarf to put curses on her enemies. Eventually she would use it to cast a spell on Mick.

Anger's powers of persuasion were difficult to overstate. Hoping to spread his dark message through film, he leaned on his Hollywood experience to make several underground films, including the cult classics *Fireworks* (1947) and *Scorpio Rising* (1963). None would be darker or more disturbing than the film he hoped would be his masterpiece—*Lucifer Rising.*

Life would later imitate art. In the title role of the devil, Anger wound up casting an unknown rocker named Bobby Beausoleil. After the two quarreled on the set, Beausoleil, who had already grown close to Charles Manson's merry band of homicidal misfits, ran off and committed a brutal murder. He then used his victim's blood to scrawl satanic messages on the wall.

In the end, with Beausoleil on death row, Anger would ask Mick if he cared to step into the role of Lucifer. Jagger actually gave the idea serious consideration before declining politely. He promised, however, that he would write the music and record the score for Anger's film—a promise Mick failed to keep.

On December 12, 1967—coincidentally the very same day that Brian and Mick appeared in court to hear Jones's prison sentence thrown out on appeal—*Their Satanic Majesties Request* arrived in record stores with a resounding thud. Critics slammed the Stones for failing miserably in their attempt to imitate *Sgt. Pepper's,* and even though *Their Satanic Majesties Request* somehow made it to number two on the US charts, most of the one million copies shipped went unsold. Despite this, and the fact that it produced one memorable hit single—"She's a Rainbow" (the Stones' too-obvious answer to "Lucy in the Sky with Diamonds")—Mick later conceded that the album was "rubbish."

For Mick and the Stones, 1968 loomed as a make-or-break year. Already written off by many after *Their Satanic Majesties Request,* they had to face the fact that they had not topped the British charts since "Paint It, Black" two years earlier. "We *had* to have a number one hit," Bill Wyman said.

They were certainly not at a loss for sources of inspiration. In the postwar era, it would be difficult to find a twelve-month period more fraught with sociopolitical upheaval than 1968. In the States, already torn apart by the Vietnam War, life was simply one mind-spinning headline after another: President Lyndon Johnson's decision not to seek reelection, the assassinations of Martin Luther King and Robert F. Kennedy, bloody confrontations between protesters and police outside the Democratic Convention in Chicago, and race riots in Washington, DC, Kansas City, Chicago, and Baltimore.

Nothing dominated the news more consistently than Vietnam. In major cities around the world, antiwar demonstrators clashed violently with police. When antiwar marchers stormed the US embassy in London that spring, Mick was not about to forgo an opportunity to showcase himself as spokesman for the world's discontented youth. Without the slightest trace of self-consciousness, Jagger drove to the embassy in a chauffeur-driven limousine and locked arms with the dissidents. At one point, he actually led the protest against the United States—stopping periodically to sign autographs and pose for photographs before speeding away in his Bentley.

The immediate result was Mick's "Street Fighting Man," which that summer and fall would become the anthem for placard-waving, rock-throwing demonstrators from Berkeley to Paris. Seizing the moment, Tom Driberg again pressed Mick to run for parliament.

For the first time, Jagger seemed as if he might be interested. "If a man with anarchist feelings did go into politics," he asked Driberg, "where would he fit?" While the future Lord Bradwell tried to convince Mick that the "old order is breaking up" and that "the Labour Party is somewhere a young man should be when it happens," Mick listened intently.

It became clear that Mick was thinking of more extreme social change. "The Trotskyites may be right," Driberg told his friend. "Revolution may be starting at this moment." Driberg, who believed that Jagger could attract countless young voters and provide his party with a much-needed shot in the arm, later admitted he was caught up in the moment. "One begins to share that revolutionary hope," Driberg recalled, "when one is in the company of someone like Mick."

It was left to Bill Wyman to jump-start the Stones' stalled career. When Mick and Keith walked into the studio and heard Brian and Charlie Watts building on a piano riff started by Wyman, they stopped in their tracks. Keith remembered things somewhat differently, claiming that inspiration struck him in much the same way as it had for "Satisfaction," and that he promptly recorded the opening riff on his ever-present cassette player. "'Flash,'" Keith explained, "is basically 'Satisfaction' in reverse." There was no dispute regarding the inspiration for the lyrics. While staying with Keith at Redlands, Mick awoke one rainy morning to the sound of the estate's gardener, Jack Dyer, clomping outside his window in heavy boots. When Jagger asked Keith who it was, Richards replied, "Oh, that's Jack. That's Jumping Jack." After picking up his guitar and trying to build a melody around the phrase "jumping Jack," Mick took one look at Keith and blurted, "Flash!"

Jagger took less than an hour to write the lyrics. Casting Mick as one part Nimble Jack and four parts spawn of Satan, "Jumpin' Jack Flash" went straight to number one in England and to number three in America.

That summer, amid repeated pleas from Allen Klein that they sack Brian Jones once and for all, Mick and Keith made a last-ditch effort to bring Brian back into the fold. It wasn't going to be easy. Once again charged with drug possession, Jones, still convinced that Mick was trying to maneuver him out of the group he'd created, was behaving more irrationally than ever. Out of necessity, the other Stones no longer even bothered to include him in recording sessions. Instead, when he was sober enough to play, they had him lay down his tracks on the dulcimer or the sitar alone in a separate studio.

As Jones nervously awaited his next trial, Jagger and Richards invited him to join them at Redlands for the weekend. But instead of mending fences, Brian and Mick quarreled bitterly. After accusing Mick of trying to replace him with Eric Clapton, Brian shrieked that he was going to kill himself and then jumped into Redlands' moat, vanishing beneath the still, black surface. Mick went in to rescue him, only to discover that Jones was crouching in four feet of water.

"I hope you do go to jail," Mick screamed, "and for a bloody long time too!"

If Brian did go to jail, it meant that the Stones would have to cancel their planned tour to promote the new album, *Beggars Banquet*—unless they decided at long last that his services were no longer required. Not yet quite prepared to pull that trigger, Mick hoped that Brian would be able to avoid prison as he had done in the past. Of course, that meant staying out of trouble—and out of the papers.

It was decided that Brian should spend the remainder of the summer at Redlands with his new girlfriend, a stunning blonde model named Suki Poitier. (Poitier had survived the crash that killed Guinness heir Tara Browne, but years later, she would die in a separate auto accident.)

Within a week, however, Mick was back—this time responding to Marianne Faithfull's premonition that Jones's life was in peril. He was a double Pisces, the water sign. It was all there in the *I Ching*: death by drowning. No sooner had Jagger arrived than the two men began fighting again. This time Brian tried to plunge a kitchen knife into Mick's chest—Jagger bounded out of reach—and when he failed, again declared his wish to die and dove back into the moat. Jagger went in to save him again—three more times. The last time, Mick carried Brian, limp, sobbing, and clearly very drunk, back to his room.

Brian's paranoid psychosis aside, Mick was in no position to criticize anyone for his consumption of illegal drugs. Sensitive to the fact that the authorities were ready to pounce at any time, Mick and Keith decided to open a club of their own—a place where they could, at least to some extent, operate in an environment that they controlled.

Vesuvio marked its grand opening in July 1968 with a twenty-fifth birthday bash for Mick attended by John and Yoko, Paul McCartney, and the crème de la crème of British society. Co-owned by Richards's pal and longtime drug supplier Spanish Tony Sanchez, Vesuvio offered methedrine-spiked punch and joints laid out at every place setting. Mick and Marianne went off to a private room to share the birthday boy's main present that night: a pipe off of which they took hits of pure Thai opium.

More of a surprise that summer was news that Faithfull was expecting a baby. Now subsisting largely on a steady diet of drugs and alcohol, Marianne took plenty of pills—but not always her birth control pills.

No matter. Mick was thrilled with the news. The world was still years from the use of ultrasound to determine a baby's sex, but the expectant parents quickly became convinced that Marianne was expecting a girl. They went so far as to pick out a name: Carena.

As it happened, Faithfull was still married to John Dunbar. Even though Dunbar agreed to give her a divorce, Faithfull's sense of self was far too precarious for her to risk becoming Mrs. Mick Jagger. She had no intention of marrying Mick simply to make their baby legitimate, and he agreed. "Marriage?" he joked. "It's all right, for those that wash." On a more serious note, he added that he would marry a woman he loved "if she really did need it . . . But I'm not with that kind of woman."

As dumbstruck as he was by her deceptively chaste beauty and regal bearing, Mick was equally in awe of Marianne's proven talent as an actress. She already had parts in several West End productions and two small film roles under her belt, and now she was telling Mick that it was time for him to make the jump to acting.

There was certainly no shortage of opportunities. He had already turned down dozens of movie scripts because, Dunbar observed, he was "wary of taking risks . . . The whole idea scared him. That's where Marianne came in. She kept propping up his ego and gave him the confidence to at least give acting a try."

Unfortunately, Mick's congenitally suspicious nature meant that he would not accept one of the scripts sent to him by someone he didn't personally know—no matter how big the name. Instead, when his American friend Donald Cammell, an heir to the Cammell shipping fortune and a sometime painter living in Paris, offered him the starring role in a film called *Performance,* Mick jumped at the chance.

It helped that the movie, about a sadistic cockney mobster who begins to doubt his own sexuality after a curious encounter with a has-been rock star, was written expressly for Mick. With Jagger on board and noted cinematographer Nicolas Roeg agreeing to back him up as codirector, Cammell had no trouble selling the project to Warner Bros.

Marlon Brando originally toyed with the idea of playing the thug opposite Mick, but when he finally turned it down, the Harrow-educated English actor James Fox was hired for the part. Fox and Jagger knew each other well. They "had a sort of romance," said their mutual pal Cammell, "but they were both such closet queens."

While Fox eagerly immersed himself in his role as a hoodlum, Mick was asked to take the role of the reclusive, bisexual Turner as far as he could. That meant flouncing about in body stockings, frilly blouses, and flowing caftans. Beyond having Joan Crawford red lipstick and eye shadow smeared on his face for every scene, Mick was told to simply "be you."

Marianne disagreed. She told Mick to imagine he was "poor, freaked-out, deluded, androgynous, druggie Brian" with a dash of Keith's "beautiful lawlessness." When Mick makes his first appearance on-screen dressed in a black leotard and belt with huge silver buckle, Fox delivers a telling line. "You'll look funny," the gangster says to the rock star, "when you're fifty."

Faithfull's own shot at a role in the film evaporated when doctors cautioned her that there might be complications in her pregnancy. The part—that of Mick's nymphomaniacal secretary—went to Keith's girlfriend Anita Pallenberg, who also happened to be expecting a baby. She had an abortion, and was before the cameras bright and early the next morning.

Keith did not stand in the way of Anita doing the film—even after he read a scene in the script that called for Mick, Anita, and a boyish eighteen-year-old actress named Michele "Mouche" Breton to engage in a steamy threesome. All that changed, however, when it became clear that the sex Anita and Mick were having on camera was very real—a fact that Pallenberg did not attempt to conceal. She did, however, hide the fact that she was also sleeping with Cammell, a former lover. Richards detested Cammell—"a Svengali, utterly predatory, a manipulator of women," Keith later wrote. "The most destructive little turd I've ever met."

Consumed with jealousy, Keith parked outside the set every day and sat in his blue Bentley, fuming. With good reason. His suspicion that Cammell was really out to film "third-rate porn" had merit. The uncut version of *Performance* was eventually entered at a pornographic film festival in Amsterdam—and won first prize.

Pallenberg used the ticklish situation during filming to taunt Keith, claiming that bedding Mick had been her goal all along; that she had slept with Keith *and* Brian just to get to Jagger. If she sought to drive a wedge between the two men, her plan was working. For the first—but certainly not the last—time, the partnership of Jagger and Richards was in peril.

"High drama" is the way that Sandy Lieberson, the Stones' agent at the time, described the mood during filming. Everyone in the cast, Lieberson said, was "extremely volatile. They made sure there were lots of eruptions, arguments, tantrums. Mick in particular is very high strung, very mercurial. I got the impression everything had to be very *large,* or he just didn't feel alive."

Featuring enough profanity, drugs, and violence to earn it an X rating, *Performance* was definitely out to shock moviegoers. It certainly shocked studio executives, who for some reason had believed all along that they had signed up for a musical romp along the lines of the Beatles' box office hits *A Hard Day's Night* and *Help!* At an early screening, one woman who had seen one graphic sex scene too many vomited on a studio boss's shoe before she could make it to the exit.

After two years of legal wrangling, the film was finally released in 1970 to lukewarm reviews. Most critics, however, were fascinated by Mick's performance—particularly, as Roger Greenspun of the *New York Times* put it, Jagger's "sadism, masochism, decorative decadence, and languid omnisexuality."

Still, Roeg said the film "almost destroyed" him. And Fox, shaken by the real-life melodrama on the set—particularly by what he called Mick's "mind games"—quit acting altogether and spent the next twenty years spreading the gospel as a member of a Christian sect called the Navigators. Cammell would make three more minor movies before committing suicide by shooting himself in the head—an act he dutifully recorded on videotape while his wife was in the next room.

As for the Stones, Jagger's betrayal with Pallenberg "probably put a bigger gap between me and Mick than anything else," Keith said. "And probably forever." Of course, it turned out that in the years prior to her pregnancy, Keith was also cheating with Marianne. Making a hurried exit out the window one night when Mick returned to Cheyne Walk, Richards left his socks behind. "I'm still looking for your socks" was an inside joke that Marianne would share with Keith for the next forty years.

Faithfull was halfway through her seventh month when, on November 22, 1968, she suffered a miscarriage. Incredibly, Yoko

Ono, also seven months pregnant, miscarried John Lennon's baby on the same day. Marianne was told that in her case, they could pinpoint the cause: her years of drug abuse.

Marianne was overcome with guilt, but Mick bounced back quickly—too quickly. Soon he was immersed in plans for the release of the new album, which was to ship the same week as the Beatles' self-titled double album, better known as the White Album. It was the first time in years that the two groups had gone head-to-head with new LPs, and in the wake of the *Their Satanic Majesties Request* debacle, Mick was terrified.

He needn't have been. This time the Stones proved more than a match for their rivals musically, as *Beggars Banquet*—containing the gritty tracks "Sympathy for the Devil," "Stray Cat Blues," and "Street Fighting Man"—was hailed as their best album to date. In "Street Fighting Man," wrote *Rolling Stone* magazine's Jon Landau, the Stones "were the first band to say, 'Up against the wall, motherfucker!'" The *New York Times* simply called Mick "demonic . . . also wildly exciting."

Mick was determined to maintain the momentum. While the Beatles' highly anticipated hour-long TV film *Magical Mystery Tour* had flopped miserably when it aired on the BBC the year before, Jagger was determined to see the Stones triumph where the Fab Four failed in prime time.

With Mick cracking the whip as ringmaster, *The Rolling Stones Rock and Roll Circus* was filmed over a three-day period and featured clowns, fire-eaters, animal acts, and trapeze artists—not to mention guest performances by John Lennon, Eric Clapton, and The Who.

Lennon called the experience "exhilarating," and, following retake after retake, even Jagger seemed satisfied. But when he screened the finished product, Mick was surprised by how tired and old he looked—especially in comparison to The Who's boyish-looking lead singer, Roger Daltrey. *The Rolling Stones Rock and Roll Circus* was shelved, and would not be seen for twenty-eight years.

For the time being, at least, Mick and Keith were able to put their differences aside. Along with Marianne and Anita, in December they took a cruise from Lisbon, Portugal, to Rio de Janeiro, Brazil, that yielded two hit songs: "Honky Tonk Women" and "You Can't Always Get What You Want."

The songwriting duo also returned home with a new nickname. While Keith and Mick knocked back whiskeys at the ship's bar, an older woman who couldn't quite place their faces kept asking who they were. "Come on now, who are you?" she pleaded. "Won't you give us a glimmer?" From that day forward, Mick and Keith called themselves the Glimmer Twins.

Not quite ready to abandon dreams of big-screen stardom, Jagger signed up to play the title role in *Ned Kelly,* Tony Richardson's film biography of the celebrated nineteenth-century Australian bandit. Although Mick scarcely seemed the macho type, it looked as if he might wind up behind bars for real. The day it was announced that he was to appear in the film, police officers stormed through his front door and searched the house. He was eventually convicted of possessing a quarter ounce of marijuana and fined $500.

As the summer of 1969 approached, it became glaringly evident that Brian was in no shape to tour with the band. Mick told Allen Klein that he felt now was the perfect time for Jones and the Stones to make a clean break. For £100,000 (then roughly $200,000) plus the record royalties to all the Stones' songs written up to now, Brian would be asked to leave—permanently. "Mick was very forceful about this," Ian Stewart said. "He said it was imperative we get rid of Brian and replace him with someone who could perform."

Shortly before midnight on June 1, Mick invited a twenty-one-year-old guitarist named Mick Taylor to sit in for Jones on "Honky Tonk Women." Satisfied that Taylor, who had played with John Mayall's Bluesbreakers, possessed what the band was looking for in a new member, Jagger set out the following week for Brian's new country estate in Sussex with Keith and Charlie Watts in tow. Mick's mission: to tell the man who had founded the Rolling Stones that he was fired.

Brian had, in fact, found some measure of peace at bucolic Cotchford Farm, the onetime home of *Winnie-the-Pooh* creator A. A. Milne. Instead of flying into a rage when Mick told him "It's over," Brian simply nodded in agreement. "We shall remain friends," Jones stated in his press release announcing the breakup. "I love those fellows." As Mick and the others sped away, Brian gave no indication that he was devastated. That night, he locked himself in his room and sobbed for hours.

With the pesky business of sacking Brian finally out of the way, Mick turned his attention to the group's business affairs. "He obviously loved the money end of things," Stephanie Bluestone said. "He would walk into the boardroom, and all of these very proper-looking men in dark suits jump to their feet."

Jagger reckoned that the Stones had grossed more than $17 million to date. Yet balance sheets showed that the group was actually in the red. Convinced that Klein was dipping into the till, Mick brought aboard portly merchant banker Prince Rupert Loewenstein—known within Christopher Gibbs's ritzy circle as "the German Dumpling"—as the group's financial advisor. Loewenstein, a descendant of thirteenth-century German king Rudolph I of Habsburg, and a partner in the prestigious London firm of Leopold Joseph, had impressed Mick at the outset by claiming that he had no idea who Jagger was and had never heard of the Rolling Stones.

With Loewenstein's help, Jagger would learn that the American incarnation of their company Nanker Phelge—Nanker Phelge USA—was not just a Stones subsidiary but also an entirely separate entity wholly owned by Klein. Moreover, Klein owned the master tapes and copyrights on all the Stones' work—an arrangement that would continue until the group ended its relationship with Decca Records in 1970.

The Stones, with Mick and Prince Rupert taking the lead, would eventually free themselves from Klein's grasp once and for all. But it would take seven lawsuits spread out over seventeen years. For now, Mick assigned Loewenstein the task of untangling his personal finances. Incredibly, Mick—like the rest of the Stones—was deep in debt.

Such matters were of little concern to Brian, who was nothing short of euphoric in the wake of his unceremonious sacking. Within days of being kicked out of the Rolling Stones, Jones was approached by Jeff Beck, John Lennon, and Jimi Hendrix—among others—with offers of work. "It was as if this dark cloud that had been hanging over Brian's head had just vanished," Stewart said. "He didn't have to worry about Mick plotting against him anymore. He was suddenly full of energy and ideas and optimism."

Jagger was in the mood to try something new as well. Eric Clapton and Steve Winwood—fresh out of the bands Cream and Traffic, respectively—had formed a new "supergroup" called Blind Faith with Cream's Ginger Baker on drums, and when they threw an unprecedented free concert in London's Hyde Park, an astounding 150,000 people had shown up. Mick and Marianne, who like most of the other concertgoers were floating along on a cloud of LSD, jug wine, and pot, agreed on the spot that a Stones free concert might possibly attract twice the crowd. Three days later, Allen Klein announced the concert date: July 5.

Brian read about the planned free concert and joked with his new Swedish girlfriend, Anna Wholin, that he would be the only person Mick would charge to see it. "It didn't bother him," Wholin said. "He was looking forward to starting his own band. It was a time of new beginnings for him."

It had been a particularly dry and pollen-filled summer, and on July 2, Brian was relying more frequently than usual on his "puffer"—the CO2-propelled inhaler that kept his airways clear whenever he sensed the onset of an asthma attack. For most of that day, Cotchford Farm was crawling with workmen who had been hired to do some major repairs on the 150-year-old main house. Brian suggested that once their workday was over, they invite their girlfriends over for a dip in the pool.

Around ten o'clock at night, after watching their favorite TV program—*Rowan & Martin's Laugh-In*—Jones and Wholin decided to join the laborers partying by the pool. Already high from consuming a half bottle of whiskey, several amphetamine pills, and the tranquilizer Mandrax, Brian pulled on a pair of multicolored trunks, jumped into the pool, and began splashing the workers' girlfriends.

Wholin quickly grew tired of Brian's antics and went back to the house to change. The workmen, meanwhile, had also had enough of Jones's juvenile behavior. They began engaging in horseplay of their own—pushing his head underwater, then letting him up just long enough to catch his breath before shoving him beneath the surface again.

Two of Brian's friends, Richard Cadbury and Nicholas Fitzgerald, arrived at eleven o'clock and witnessed the scene. The two men fled when one of the workers lunged at them threatening, "You'll be next!"

By the time Wholin returned, the workmen and their girlfriends had fled, and Brian was at the bottom of the pool, arms outstretched. Wholin was shocked that Jones's live-in construction foreman, Frank Thorogood, and his girlfriend, who happened to be a nurse, were "just *standing there*" looking down at him. The nurse applied CPR while Wholin gave Brian mouth-to-mouth until he suddenly gripped her hand "and then he just stopped moving."

The autopsy chalked up Brian's demise at age twenty-seven to drowning and "severe liver dysfunction." But the coroner's inquest conveyed the mysterious goings-on at Cotchford Farm with language straight out of the nineteenth century. Brian's was a "death by misadventure." (Twenty-five years later, Frank Thorogood made a deathbed confession that he had drowned Jones. Keith was not at all surprised. Brian, Richards said, "pissed off the builders, whining son of a bitch.")

The Stones were in the studio mixing their cover of Stevie Wonder's "I Don't Know Why" (which would pop up on their *Metamorphosis* album years later), when the phone rang at two o'clock on the morning of July 3. Mick was sitting at the control board, ashen faced and near tears, when Keith Altham walked into the room a few moments later.

Once Mick told him that Brian was dead, Altham assumed that the band was going to pack up for the night. "No!" Mick shot back, motioning to the others to get back to work. "It goes on."

The worldwide clamor over Brian's untimely death would certainly not hurt the Stones' new double-sided single "Honky Tonk Women" and "You Can't Always Get What You Want." In another freakish coincidence, the record had been scheduled for release on that same day.

Nor did Mick see any reason to cancel the planned Hyde Park concert, which was to be televised live in England. By billing the event as a memorial to Brian, they could proceed without appearing callous. In truth, Mick *had* to do the concert on July 5—he was due to start filming *Ned Kelly* in Australia just four days later.

By two thirty that day, the throng at Hyde Park had swelled to over three hundred thousand—a blur of flowers, feathers, beads, and tie-dyed T-shirts stretching to the horizon. Leather-jacketed, swastika-wearing Hell's Angels, Britain's anemic answer to California's odious motorcycle gang, were assigned the task of guarding the stage.

A gasp went up from the crowd when Mick, wearing a white "party dress" by the outré designer Michael Fish over tight white pants, suddenly appeared onstage and began blowing kisses to the audience. He was made up in rouge, lipstick, and heavy mascara, and a wooden crucifix dangled from his neck.

Mick then asked for silence and began reading stanzas from Percy B. Shelley's elegy *Adonais*: "Peace, peace! He is not dead, he doth not sleep / He hath awakened from the dream of life." He continued reading for a few minutes, and when he was done, cardboard boxes were opened to release a quarter million white butterflies over the crowd. Not long after, a clanging cowbell announced the beginning of "Honky Tonk Women"—a sound new to the crowd but one that soon become instantly recognizable.

The rest of the concert would have little to do with poetry, as Mick pumped, slithered, jerked, and preened his way through a sweat-soaked hour of Stones hits. Apparently not at all concerned that he was being watched by a potential TV audience of millions, Jagger dropped to his knees and maneuvered his mouth around the handheld microphone in a manner that, to put it gently, was highly suggestive.

Jagger's onstage gymnastics were not enough to offset the band's poor performance. Critics and fans alike voiced their disappointment; TV viewers tuned out. The Hyde Park concert, trumpeted as the musical event of the century, was an unmitigated flop.

Seated on the stage with the rest of the Stones' wives and official girlfriends, Marianne Faithfull was too high to care. More than anyone else in the Stones' inner circle, she seemed most traumatized by Brian's death.

Faithfull was also upset that none of the Stones seemed to care. At one point, she heard Mick sniffling in the bathroom and assumed that the reality of his friend's death had finally caught up with him. Instead he was simply fighting off a transient case of hay fever.

After the concert, Mick told Marianne that he would join her back at 48 Cheyne Walk after he'd tied up some loose ends. Then he ran off to spend the night with his new girlfriend, Marsha Hunt. The African American daughter of a Philadelphia psychiatrist, Hunt had starred in the West End production of *Hair,* but it was only after a wardrobe malfunction exposed her breasts during a live performance on British television that she caught Mick's eye.

Jagger wanted her to be the face of "Honky Tonk Women" on the record sleeve and in ads, but she declined. At first Hunt also resisted his sexual overtures, although he was able to quickly wear her down with stories about Marianne's drug use and the tearful confession that, despite all the adulation, he was really "lonely." At the Hyde Park concert, Hunt was impossible to miss in her VIP seat on a scaffold thirty feet above the stage. She was dressed entirely in fringed white buckskin, but Hunt's most striking feature was her towering Afro—a hairdo that prompted Mick to start calling her "Miss Fuzzy."

Mick said farewell to Hunt in a driving rain the next morning and then headed off to Australia with Marianne—but not before letting Hunt know that he was working on a song about her. He wanted to call it "Brown Sugar."

Since Jagger had to be on the *Ned Kelly* set the day of Brian's funeral in London, he felt he had a built-in excuse for not paying his last respects. Only Bill Wyman and Charlie Watts, out of the scores of people affiliated with the Stones organization, bothered to attend Brian's memorial service.

As soon as Mick and Marianne arrived at their hotel in Sydney, they headed for bed, exhausted by the twenty-four-hour flight. Marianne, still shaken by Brian's untimely death, had a much harder time getting to sleep. While Jagger slept soundly, she followed her nightly ritual of downing a cup of hot chocolate with two sodium amytal sleeping tablets.

Only this time, Marianne did not stop at two pills. Instead she took one hundred and fifty before slipping into bed next to Mick. Soon she found herself in a dreamlike tug-of-war between life and death, alternately floating through space with Brian and being pulled back to life by her son and her mother.

An hour later, Mick awoke with a start and realized that the pillbox on Faithfull's vanity table was empty. He grabbed Marianne, slapped her, and shook her violently. Nothing—she remained unresponsive. Frantic, he called for an ambulance and rode with her to the hospital. Even after she had her stomach pumped, there were grave concerns that, since she was also going through severe heroin withdrawal, she might not withstand the strain. She might never regain consciousness.

Mick stayed at Marianne's side until she was in the clear, something for which—along with his fast thinking in summoning an ambulance—Faithfull would be forever grateful. Marianne spent the next two months recuperating at a hospital outside Sydney. It meant that she had lost the small role in *Ned Kelly* that Mick had promised, but it was just as well. As tensions over the script mounted and Mick became increasingly annoyed with the demands being made by his director, it became clear that Jagger had been woefully miscast as Australia's tough-as-nails answer to Robin Hood.

Since the movie's protagonist was actually born and raised in Ireland, Mick was told that he had to play the part with an Irish accent—a dialect that, for some reason, the normally gifted mimic found all but impossible to pull off.

Then there were the fight scenes for which, despite his athleticism onstage, he seemed woefully ill equipped. To add insult to injury—literally—Mick was the only person to be harmed physically during filming. He nearly had his right hand blown off when a prop gun misfired.

Mick and Marianne returned to London in September to find that they had new neighbors: Keith and Anita had moved into a house at 3 Cheyne Walk just five days before Pallenberg gave birth to their son. They named him Marlon, after Richards's favorite actor.

Keith's move to Cheyne Walk was strategic. The Glimmer Twins wanted to be close together so that they could work on new material and rehearse for their upcoming eighteen-city US tour—the Stones' first in three years. Leaving nothing to chance, they signed up blues legend B. B. King and the sizzling Ike and Tina Turner Review as their opening acts.

Mick and Keith arrived in LA on October 13 and moved into the Laurel Canyon estate occupied by their friend Stephen Stills of Crosby, Stills, Nash, and Young. For the next week, Mick wrote flowery love letters to Marsha Hunt and Marianne while entertaining an endless stream of nameless teenage groupies and veteran camp followers with names such as Suzy Creamcheese, Sable Starr, Sweet Connie, and Suzie Suck.

In the sixties and seventies, when two young women known as Chicago's famous "Plaster Casters" immortalized the private parts of such rock gods as Jagger, Hendrix, Jim Morrison, and all the members (literally) of Led Zeppelin, few groupies managed to reach the exalted status of Pamela Des Barres. Mick paid scant attention to the perky fan from Reseda, California, when she first met him during the Stones' 1966 US tour. But Jagger was obsessed with sleeping with the wives of his friends. Now that Des Barres—then Pamela Miller—was officially the girlfriend of Led Zeppelin's Jimmy Page, Mick would stop at nothing to lure her away from him.

For weeks Mick devoted himself to winning over Miss Pamela, but to no avail. When more conventional techniques failed to work, he was not above getting on his knees and begging.

Not that he was ever starved for female companionship. LA music insider Rodney Bingenheimer remembered going to a party in LA with Jagger and then stopping at the House of Pies on North Vermont Avenue at one in the morning "to pick up girls. All these teenyboppers would come up to Mick and say, 'You look like Mick Jagger!' and he'd say, 'Yes, everybody says that.' Then he'd take a couple home with him."

The tables turned abruptly when, the morning after their first concert in Dallas, it was reported that Marianne had left Jagger for Italian postmodernist painter Mario Schifano, one of Pallenberg's many former lovers. Humiliated, hurt, and concerned about how this might tarnish his image as rock's reigning satyr, Mick called Faithfull in Rome and pleaded through tears for her to come back to him.

Eventually she would. In the meantime, Miss Pamela saw an opportunity to move up in the rock world and finally relented. Jagger seduced her in a booth at the Whisky a Go Go on the Sunset Strip. "Those lips!!! Please!!" Des Barres said. "We made love for hours."

Mick was having less success with American audiences, in part because the band's playing was "ragged" (Jagger's words) but also because the image he had so carefully cultivated now seemed to eclipse the flesh-and-blood man onstage. In city after city, critics voiced their disappointment, and the hysteria that once greeted the Stones' every performance failed to materialize.

All that changed by the time they hit New York on Thanksgiving Day 1969. Jimi Hendrix, Janis Joplin, Mick's old pal Andy Warhol, and the iconic conductor-composer Leonard Bernstein were on hand to witness Jagger work up the crowd to what amounted to a mass grand mal seizure. According to Warhol, Bernstein was, in fact, "excited by Jagger's sexual charisma. Lenny has a crush on Mick." Bernstein was also not shy about letting Jagger know how he felt. Mick was in awe of the great man and admitted to being flattered by the attention, but he would not take Bernstein up on his offer.

By turns a beglittered, sloe-eyed fawn and a strutting cock of the walk, Mick used what Kenneth Anger called "a kind of bisexual charm" to arouse American audiences. Along the way, the Stones obliterated attendance records across the country and racked up ticket receipts in excess of $2 million—up until that time, the largest take in history.

Not everyone, however, was thrilled with the Stones' stratospheric ticket prices—the highest demanded by any rock group to date. After being pilloried by the press for shaking down audiences, Mick held a press conference to announce that the Stones would pay back their American fans with a free concert.

Mick, able to face the press only after one of the reporters present offered him a Valium, insisted that the idea of giving a free concert in America had been percolating for some time. "It was when we fucking got to Los Angeles, the first stop," he snapped. "We decided right then to do it after the tour was over. We wanted to do Los Angeles, because the weather's better. But there's no place to do it there, and we were assured we could do it much more easily in San Francisco."

And why not? San Francisco's Haight-Ashbury district was the birthplace of "flower power" and, by extension, the counterculture itself. Glorious Golden Gate Park seemed a perfect venue for the Stones' first-ever free concert in the States.

The city, citing rampant drug use at previous rock concerts in the park, disagreed. The Stones then relocated the planned concert to Sears Point Raceway, thirty-five miles north of San Francisco. They had already finished building a stage and had started putting up light towers when the raceway's owners demanded an up-front payment of $125,000. Incensed, Mick moved on—but not before telling Sears Point's representatives where they could now put the lighting towers.

Enter car-racing promoter Dick Carter, offering to make his eighty-acre Altamont Raceway available to the Stones completely free of charge. Technically within the city limits of Livermore, some forty-five miles east of San Francisco, Altamont was nothing more than some weathered bleachers and a clapboard announcer's booth overlooking a dusty ellipse. Hidden from civilization, the raceway itself was accessible only by a single dirt road.

Shortly after two in the morning on December 6, 1969, a helicopter landed in the center of the raceway, and out jumped Mick, wearing a red velvet cloak and a floppy matching red beret. With Keith trailing behind him, Mick, at times shivering in the bone-chilling California night air, moved among the thousands already camped out at the site—like a general visiting his troops on the eve of battle.

For the time being, at least, it appeared as if the same mellow peace-and-love vibe that had enveloped Woodstock less than four months earlier might also prevail at Altamont. With the entire area illuminated by diesel-powered floodlights that had been trucked in from San Francisco, fans tossed Frisbees and played touch football.

Most, however, just tried to stay warm, huddling together in sleeping bags and fortifying themselves with swigs from shared bottles of jug wine. Bonfires, fueled by pieces of wood ripped from the fences of neighboring farms, dotted the hillsides. Those who did not have the foresight to bring their own bedrolls crawled into the rusted hulks of abandoned stock cars and prayed for daybreak.

Satisfied that the stage was set for the greatest live event of all time, Mick and Keith climbed aboard their chopper and were whisked back to their Huntington Hotel suite high atop San Francisco's Nob Hill. This predawn visit and the events that would unfold over the coming twenty-four hours were being dutifully recorded for posterity by filmmakers Albert and David Maysles (who later made a documentary of a very different sort, *Grey Gardens*). Mick wanted to pay back Warner Bros., which was refusing to release his sexually explicit film *Performance,* by producing a movie that would upstage its much-ballyhooed Woodstock documentary. *Gimme Shelter* would, as it turned out, do just that.

From the outset, there were those who warned that the concert was headed for disaster. Astrologers consulted their charts and predicted doom, but more significantly, so did seasoned promoters who believed that too little thought had been given to the safety of concertgoers. Rock promoter Bill Graham, operator of the Fillmore West auditorium in San Francisco and the Fillmore East in New York City, made no secret of whom he would blame if things went wrong; later, Graham called Mick a "selfish prick" who was determined to be at the center of a spectacle, no matter what the human cost.

As cars began backing up on Highway 50, local disc jockeys cautioned listeners that they would not be able to drive within miles of the site. Undaunted, young people simply abandoned their cars by the side of the road and made the rest of the way on foot.

By midday, the crowd had grown to 350,000—a ready and willing market for the drug dealers hawking everything from pot, speed, and LSD, to cocaine, hallucinogenic mushrooms, and heroin. There would be hundreds of bad trips and overdoses, with on-site emergency medical personnel doing what they could to stabilize patients before ambulances took them to tiny, understaffed Livermore Hospital nearby.

Meanwhile, only a dozen portable toilets were provided to accommodate a crowd larger than the entire population of Oakland. As might have been expected, fights broke out among the thousands of people who stood in line for hours waiting to use the facilities.

The scene merely got more surreal as the day progressed. Hare Krishnas, their heads shaved and wearing saffron-colored robes, drifted through the crowd waving incense and chanting—at times stepping over couples making love in the dirt. While all this was going on, a stoned teenage boy ambled off alone and jumped into a concrete aqueduct carrying water from the north to the San Joaquin Valley. His body was fished from the culvert more than a mile downstream.

The situation was ripe for chaos even before the Hell's Angels made their grand entrance. The fearsome motorcycle gang came highly recommended by the Grateful Dead, and Jagger was satisfied with the job that their paler English brethren had done patrolling the perimeter of the stage at Hyde Park. The penny-pinching Jagger also thought the price was right: the Angels would provide security in return for ringside seats and all the cold beer they could consume.

For Mick, the Angels also served to bolster the satanic image that he had worked so tirelessly to promote. Covered in tattoos and leather, snarling from beneath Nazi helmets and pirate bandanas, the Angels were a fearsome lot—perfect candidates for the role of Lucifer's murderous minions.

They did not disappoint. Arriving midday, they gunned the engines of their Harleys and steered directly into the crowd, sending people scurrying and bodies flying in all directions. Their first mission was to clear a path to the stage for a yellow school bus that carried the Angels' drugs, booze, and a cache of weapons—guns, knives, chains, lead-tipped pool cues—that they would put to use throughout the day.

The group Santana was first up among the Stones' many stellar opening acts. The fans, responding to Santana's driving Latin beat, pushed forward toward the stage—and were met with a phalanx of knife-wielding, chain-twirling Angels. Gang members kicked at the spectators with steel-tipped boots and beat them senseless with brass knuckles and lead pipes.

"Jesus," Mick said as he gazed down from the Stones' helicopter at the assembled throng. "Have you ever seen so many people in one place in your whole life?" After landing, his euphoria was quickly extinguished when someone jumped out of the crowd screaming, "I hate you! I hate you!" and slugged him in the face. Jagger, in shock, was rushed off to the Stones' trailer while his Angels beat Mick's attacker savagely.

Onstage, the Jefferson Airplane was having problems of its own. While Grace Slick belted out their hit "Somebody to Love," singer Marty Balin tried to help a young African American who was being battered by the Angels—only to have a biker smash a pool cue over his skull, splintering the cue and rendering Balin unconscious.

Not even the soothing harmonies of Crosby, Stills, Nash, and Young could bring a stop to the violence. Instead the peace-and-love crowd was drawn even more strongly to CSNY, prompting the bikers to beat them back with renewed ferocity. Within thirty minutes, the group cut short its performance and boarded the first chopper out. "It's like Vietnam down there," Graham Nash said. "I was scared out of my fucking mind."

It was well past nightfall when Mick donned his trademark Lucifer costume—a black-and-red Harlequin outfit created by British designer (and royal family favorite) Ossie Clark—and launched into "Jumpin' Jack Flash." Halfway through, Mick stopped—not because of the fans but because so many Hell's Angels now crowded the stage that Satan himself could barely move.

A few unfortunate civilians did attempt to get closer to Jagger, and paid a terrible price. One teenager shed his clothes and managed to pull himself onto the stage before a biker kicked the boy squarely in the face, breaking his jaw. During "Sympathy for the Devil," a female fan—also naked—was roughed up and hurled headfirst back into the audience. "Something very funny always happens," Mick said, "when we start that number."

In truth, now that he had unleashed his leather-clad demons, Mick had no idea how to control them. A German shepherd prowled the stage while he tried to execute his signature moves, and Hell's Angels had no compunction about whispering into Jagger's ear even as he was singing.

Not even those closest to Jagger were exempt from mistreatment at the hands of the Stones' storm troopers. When a Hell's Angel spat on her earlier in the day, groupie Pamela Des Barres grabbed the next helicopter out. "As things turned out," she recalled, "it was obviously the smart thing to do."

The Stones had launched into "Under My Thumb" when a tall, eighteen-year-old black man named Meredith Hunter came running through the crowd, pursued by a biker who simply did not like the fact that Hunter's girlfriend was white. Cornered as he reached the stage, Hunter—hard to miss in a green suit and large hat—pulled out a gun in a desperate act of self-defense.

Even in the midst of this chaos, Mick managed to spot a gun barrel glinting under the powerful stage lights. "Fuck, man," Mick called out to Mick Taylor, "there's a cat out there pointing a gun at us!"

Jagger could not hear Meredith Hunter's girlfriend pleading with him not to fire his weapon, nor could he make out the carnage that ensued just a few yards away. Hunter was still waving the gun in the air when one Hell's Angel plunged a knife in his back. As he stumbled forward, another biker stabbed Hunter in the face. Incredibly, Hunter tried to flee his attackers, but they chased him through the crowd, stabbing him repeatedly until he finally crumpled to the ground.

As the Angels stood over him, Hunter lifted himself up by one arm. "I wasn't going to shoot you," he told them. His attackers were not convinced. "Why did you have a gun?" one demanded before grabbing a heavy metal garbage can and bringing it crashing down on Hunter's head. Then gang members took turns stomping the young man, leaving the coup de grace—a swift kick to the face—to be administered by the Hell's Angel who had first singled out Hunter for annihilation. The biker, clearly satisfied with himself, then stood on his head for several minutes before calmly returning to catch the rest of "Under My Thumb."

Spectators who rushed to Hunter's aid after the attack found gaping wounds in his back, side, and right temple. Once he could see the stretcher bearing Hunter being lifted over the heads of the crowd, Mick stopped singing and called for an ambulance.

"This could be the most beautiful evening," Mick told the crowd. "I beg you to get it together. Hell's Angels, everybody—let's relax, get into a groove . . ."

But the mayhem continued. A topless woman who tried to climb onstage was stomped, beaten, and tossed back into the audience in the middle of Mick's chillingly appropriate song about Boston Strangler Albert DeSalvo, "Midnight Rambler."

"Hey hey hey hey hey hey!" Mick hollered. "Hey, fellows, hey, fellows, one of you can control her, man." Unaware that Meredith Hunter's lifeless body lay in the raceway announcer's booth, Mick sang the fitting refrain of "Gimme Shelter" ("Rape, murder, it's just a shot away"), then scooped up roses that were tossed onstage during "Satisfaction" and "Honky Tonk Women." The Stones wrapped up the show with "Street Fighting Man." Given the day's carnage, Jagger could not have picked a more suitable closing number.

Before the Stones exited the stage, Mick leaned forward and blew kisses into the crowd. "We're gonna kiss you good-bye, and we leave you to kiss each other good-bye," he said, as if this were just another show. "You have been so groovy. Good night."

Groovy was hardly the word that came to mind as the Stones sprinted to a waiting chopper and made their getaway. "Shit, that was close," Mick said. "But it's going to make one fucking terrific film."

Mick also knew the controversy surrounding what happened that day would assure that their new album, timed for release that very day, would rocket straight up the charts. After today, the album's title would take on a new resonance, echoing all that Jagger and the Stones now wished to stand for: *Let It Bleed*.

Like refugees fleeing a war zone—which in a sense they were—the 350,000 people who remained in the darkness gathered up their belongings and began the long and perilous journey back to civilization. Not everyone would make it. Two people sleeping by a campfire were crushed to death and two others critically injured when a fan, eager to beat the rush, ran over them with his car.

In the end, the free concert that was meant to be the Stones' thank-you to America could be described best as a disaster of epic proportions: four dead, dozens seriously hurt and requiring hospitalization, hundreds of minor injuries, and an estimated two thousand overdoses ranging from minor freakouts to near fatalities.

Back at his San Francisco hotel suite, Mick was getting stoned with Keith and their rocker pal Gram Parsons, formerly of the Byrds and then with the Flying Burrito Brothers. (Parsons would die four years later of a drug overdose at age twenty-six.) Jagger, still in his harlequin getup, was no longer euphoric.

"I blame myself, it's my fault," he said repeatedly to Des Barres, who joined the party not long after the Stones arrived back from the concert. "Maybe I should just give it all up, rock and roll. I don't deserve it, you know . . . All that fucking shit that happened out there—I'm responsible . . ."

Mick would get no argument from Bill Graham. "What right did you have to leave the way you did," Graham asked in the press, "thanking everybody for a wonderful time and the Angels for helping out? What right does this god have to descend on this country this way?"

For now, Mick sought to ease his mind by proposing a threesome with Des Barres and The Mamas and the Papas singer Michelle Phillips, who had just dropped by to say hello. Phillips, who would go on to star in the *Knots Landing* television series in the 1980s and 1990s, did that and more. Miss Pamela, however, was in no mood; she returned to her hotel room alone, unable to shake the memory of what had transpired only hours earlier in that godforsaken spot called Altamont.

It was several months before the Maysles brothers screened a rough cut of *Gimme Shelter* for the Stones. "Wow," Mick said as he watched Meredith Hunter being murdered. "It's so horrible." So horrible, in fact, that even though Hell's Angel Alan Passaro could not deny he was the first to plunge a knife into Hunter, so many of his fellow Angels were captured on film stabbing the young man that it was difficult to determine who struck the fatal blow. Incredibly, a jury found Passaro not guilty.

The Altamont concert would spawn several lawsuits and earn Mick the undying enmity of the Hell's Angels. "This Mick Jagger put it all on the Angels," fumed Angels leader Sonny Barger, who later did time in a federal prison for conspiring to blow up a rival gang's headquarters. "He used us for dupes, man." Elements within the Angels organization demanded revenge, but it was years before Mick realized how frighteningly close they came to getting it.

Altamont came to be regarded by many as a cultural benchmark—the dark side of Woodstock, and, in the words of singer-songwriter Don McLean, "the day the music died." For the Stones, it would leave a bitter and lasting legacy, but one that, for the moment at least, served Jagger's purposes. Mick had spent years carefully honing his reputation as a dangerous, menacing, even sinister figure. The starkly disturbing image of Jagger, wearing Satan's silks and whipping hundreds of thousands of people into a homicidal frenzy, only solidified his standing as a kind of pop Antichrist.

Altamont cast a shadow over the Stones—and Mick in particular—that would last for decades. It also inspired Don McLean to capture the moment with two more lines in his classic 1971 song "American Pie": *No angel born in hell / Could break that Satan's spell.*

Mick basically has contempt for women.
They only exist as reflections of him.

—MARIANNE FAITHFULL

   ◆   ◆   ◆

Mick looked into Bianca's face and saw—Mick. It was as close as he could get to making love with himself.

—DONALD CAMMELL, FRIEND

   ◆   ◆   ◆

You can only have so much vanity.

—MICK

5

♦ ♦ ♦

Under His Thumb

For Mick, the sixties ended with a bang. Several. With Marianne off in the arms of her Italian lover, Jagger kept company with a dizzying array of women. Marsha Hunt stayed with him at Cheyne Walk for a few days but beat a hasty retreat after Keith and Anita—both strung out on heroin—kept dropping in unannounced.

Once Marsha left, Mick made a point of sleeping with a different girl—or girls—every night. Many were Americans, for whom he had a special fondness. "Women Mick had slept with would come up to us in restaurants," Christopher Gibbs said, "and he'd have absolutely no idea who they were."

Once Marianne was back in London to spend the holidays with her son Nicholas, however, Mick had to win her back. He confronted her and her new boyfriend, Mario Schifano, whom she declared to be Mick's sexual superior, on Christmas Eve. Marianne left it to the two men to fight for her honor, and when she woke up the next morning, Mick was in bed with her, and Schifano was packing his bags for Rome.

Mick didn't love Marianne anymore, and they both knew it. Winning her back, she said, had only to do with "overcoming his public humiliation and preserving his machismo." Faithfull felt that Mick treated her the way he would "a butterfly or an insect on a pin . . . He had me on a pin, and he was watching me flail."

Marianne had no idea that Mick was putting the finishing touches on his plan to get even by asking Marsha Hunt to have his child. "Miss Fuzzy" agreed and seven weeks later broke the news that she was due to give birth to their baby in November. Jagger was jubilant. "Just don't tell anyone," he asked Hunt. "Let's keep it out of the press for now."

Mick, meanwhile, was not about to let Marianne go. After another screaming match in which she again threatened to leave him, Mick sat her down and sang the song he had just written about her, "Wild Horses": *Graceless lady, you know who I am / You know I can't let you slide through my hand.*

Moved beyond words, Marianne threw her arms around Mick and sobbed. "Ohhh, such a beautiful song!" she told him. "You wrote that for me? I love you!"

Not that she harbored any illusions about Mick. She knew that he was seeing Hunt at her flat in St. John's Wood, and that several times a week he was driving up to Stargroves for trysts with any number of young women. He had even held on to the Stones' old apartment at Edith Grove for the occasional romp. It was there, recalled Pamela Des Barres, that Mick "threw me on the mattress and turned me into a cheating trollop—it was fantastic." Des Barres resumed her affair with Mick even as she was dating another friend of his. When someone suddenly knocked on the door, Jagger beat a hasty retreat. "One-two-three," Miss Pamela said, "Mick came and went."

Marianne also faced competition for Jagger's attention from

some unexpected quarters. Over the years, Mick and Mick Taylor had grown close. One morning Marianne and the ubiquitous drug dealer Spanish Tony Sanchez walked into 48 Cheyne Walk and discovered the two Micks "dozing in bed together, like little boys."

Faithfull finally left Jagger, moved in with her mother, and began an affair with Lord Rossmore, an Irish peer sixteen years her senior. Unwilling to let anyone else pull the plug on a relationship, Mick again launched an all-out campaign to win her back. "The only way I could see out of it," she remembered, "was for him or me to die."

Either that, or gain fifty pounds. "Mick is very conceited about his body," Marianne said, "and the women he is seen with." Once she had become a proper matron, Faithfull knew that she had won. "And that was the end of that," she said. "He never came back." Among other things, she blamed her "soul-destroying" five-year affair with Mick with rendering her incapable of having an orgasm. He claimed, in turn, "Marianne nearly killed *me*."

So, it seems, did *Ned Kelly*. The film, released before *Performance* and therefore the first time Mick had seen himself on the big screen, was a critical and commercial debacle. "Jagger is too fey," one critic wrote of Mick's turn as the brawny Australian folk hero, "too vulnerable, and too vague to menace anybody."

Jagger wisely chose not to attend the movie's London premiere, preferring instead to amuse himself by rotating among the members of his floating harem. Among them: Janice Kenner, a stunning blonde from LA, ostensibly hired to be his housekeeper, cook, and "personal assistant"; New Yorker Patti D'Arbanville, a nineteen-year-old model and actress; another leggy Californian, Catherine James; and Brian's ex-girlfriend Suki Poitier.

Even for these women, there were limits when it came to sharing Mick. When one girl came upon Catherine James in bed with Mick at Stargroves, he merely suggested a ménage à trois. James, furious, stormed out. After hastily making love to the interloper, Jagger spent the rest of the evening trying to talk James out of catching the next flight home. He succeeded, but it wasn't long before James decided she "definitely wasn't the right girlfriend for Mick. Eventually I would have killed him in his sleep. I've a jealous nature."

Sometimes it was Mick who was being courted. For nearly a year, Atlantic Records founder Ahmet Ertegun tirelessly pursued Jagger in hopes of landing the Rolling Stones for his label. Mick could not have asked for a more urbane suitor. Son of the Turkish Republic's first ambassador to the United States, the bald, bespectacled, goateed Ertegun cofounded Atlantic in 1947 and promptly signed such legendary R & B acts as Ruth Brown, the Coasters, the Drifters, and Ray Charles. Before and after selling Atlantic to Warner Records in 1967, Ertegun expanded his roster of talent to include the diverse likes of Aretha Franklin; Led Zeppelin; Blind Faith; Crosby, Stills, Nash, and Young; Yes; Ben E. King; Iron Butterfly; Percy Sledge; Cream; the Rascals; Buffalo Springfield; and Bette Midler. Atlantic Records's sterling R & B catalogue notwithstanding, it was Ertegun's innate sense of class that most impressed the eternally upwardly mobile Mick. With his stylish wife, Mica, who with Chesebrough-Pond heiresss Chessy Rayner cofounded the interior design firm of MAC II (for Mica and Chessy), Ahmet was already an established fixture on the Manhattan social scene by the time he began wooing Jagger.

With Keith and Anita strung out on drugs, it fell to Mick to finally wrest the Stones from the grip of Allen Klein. "Jagger *had* to take control," Victor Bockris said. "If Mick didn't make the hard decisions, who would?"

Jagger, backed by Prince Rupert, ordered the Stones' lawyers to file a $29 million lawsuit against Klein, essentially accusing him of siphoning money from the group and into his own pocket. Klein controlled the Stones' copyrights, publishing rights, and master tapes for all works produced up to 1970. Even after his death in 2009, his estate would continue to control those rights.

In the meantime, Prince Rupert convinced Jagger to just swallow hard and accept a $2 million settlement to free the Stones from Klein. That left a confrontation with Decca, which, under the terms of its original contract, was demanding one final album.

Jagger bristled at the way that Decca tried to censor the Stones' songs and album covers, and he was personally offended by the imperious manner of Decca's prim chairman, Sir Edward Lewis. As a sort of good-bye gift, Jagger showed up at Lewis's office with a delightful new number called "Cocksucker Blues." Jagger only had to croon the first two lines—"Where do I get my cock sucked? Where do I get my ass fucked?"—for Sir Edward to grudgingly bid the Stones farewell.

That summer of 1970, the Stones hit the road again: this time a fourteen-city tour of Europe that stretched over six weeks. At every stop along the way, Mick dutifully wrote Marsha, now five months pregnant, about the young women who were keeping him company on the road. "He kept me laughing," Marsha said, "about whose girlfriend he'd had."

As far as the tour itself, there was speculation that the Stones might be wary of inciting violence in the wake of Altamont—that their hell-raising days could be over. That was hardly the case. In city after city—from Stockholm and Hamburg to West Berlin and Rome—the Stones proved they could still inspire chaos as fans took to the streets, overturning cars, setting fires, and smashing store windows. By now law enforcement authorities across the Continent had come to regard the Stones more as a small invading army than as a mere rock group, such was the mayhem they inevitably triggered.

Satisfied that he had not lost his Mephistophelian touch, Mick was especially pleased when the Stones' arrival in Paris sparked the worst street violence since the student riots of May 1968. Yet it was what transpired after the Stones' concert at the Olympia Theater that would alter the course of his life.

"Mick, this is Bianca," Donald Cammell said to his old friend, turning to the svelte, sultry, vaguely dangerous-looking young woman at his side. For the first time, Cammell noticed a striking physical resemblance between them. "You two are going to have a great romance," Cammell went on. "You were made for each other."

There was a haughtiness about Nicaraguan-born Blanca (she traded the *l* for an *i* when she was sixteen) Perez Morena de Macias— a vaguely disdainful air of superiority to equal his own. Bianca was fluent in several languages, but what she said was not nearly so interesting to Mick as the way she said it, in a throaty, flirtatious Eartha Kitt purr.

They spent the night together at Cammell's Paris apartment. Although Bianca said the whole experience that night was like "a bolt of lightning," she also insisted that she "wasn't attracted to Mick for physical reasons. I found him shy, vulnerable, human—the opposite of everything I had ever imagined."

Mick didn't know quite what to make of Bianca, and he said as much to Marsha over the phone the next morning. Still, he informed Hunt that he was taking his latest conquest with him to Italy—"just for a giggle."

Jagger wasn't the only man who found Bianca hard to pin down. For starters, she claimed that she was twenty-one when she met Mick in 1970. In truth, she was twenty-five. At various times, she claimed that her father was either a wealthy commodities broker, a coffee baron, or a career diplomat.

Her uncle was, in fact, Nicaragua's ambassador to Cuba. But when her parents divorced, Bianca's mother was left destitute. To make ends meet, Senora Perez Morena de Macias went to work running a diner in Managua a la Joan Crawford's title character in the 1945 film classic *Mildred Pierce*. Like Pierce's daughter Veda, Bianca was indulged by her doting mother and, as a result, grew up with an inflated sense of self. "I never washed a dish, boiled an egg, or cleaned," she admitted. She also shared Marianne Faithfull's convent school background and the "terrible sexual repression" it bred.

Determined to become Nicaragua's first female ambassador, Bianca studied for two years at Paris's Institut d'Études Politiques— a period during which she said she studied hard and "remained a virgin until eighteen and a half."

It was around this time that she ran out of money and began working odd jobs just to afford her dollar-a-day room in one of Paris's grimier working-class districts. Through a cousin who was cultural affairs attaché at the Nicaraguan embassy, Bianca was able to land a clerical job on the ambassador's staff—and, more important, entree to Paris's endless round of glittering embassy parties.

It was in London, however, that twenty-year-old Bianca met her "almost first lover": actor Michael Caine. Within days, they were living together at his flat in Mayfair. Their fiery relationship—the couple battled it out in restaurants, at parties, in hotel lobbies, on the street—quickly became the talk of cafe society. According to Bianca, Caine "was unkind, superficial, and kept me like I was his geisha." Caine was more charitable, comparing the passionate Bianca to a "panther cub that is potentially dangerous but still needs help."

Bianca's stormy romance with Caine ended after a year, and

she moved back to Paris. Within six months, she was caught up in an affair with Eddie Barclay, a married (ultimately nine times) and very powerful French record executive twenty-four years her senior. They had broken up just days before that first fateful encounter with Mick.

"That day I grew up a little bit," said Bianca, who believed that in Caine and Barclay she was looking for the "protection and affection a father can provide." She was more satisfied with what she found in Mick, whom she curiously described as "more of an older brother."

An older brother who was also, like the other men in her life, very rich. "Bianca," observed her friend Donald Cammell, "is the sort who was always basically saying to herself, 'Well, who's going to be paying the rent five years from now?'"

Others went even further in trying to account for the gaps in Bianca's history—not to mention the fact that through it all, she'd somehow managed to afford a wardrobe by Yves Saint Laurent and Givenchy. They floated the wholly unsubstantiated rumor that Bianca was a "Madame Claude girl," one of the refined, well-educated, gorgeous young companions who moved in the highest circles during the 1960s. Favored by presidents, prime ministers, dictators, diplomats, captains of industry, movie stars, and even a few rock stars, Madame Claude girls often wound up marrying into the upper echelons of society. "You can leaf through the society pages," said social chronicler Cleveland Amory, "and have no trouble at all finding Madame Claude girls who are now respected Park Avenue matrons."

For now, reporters were clamoring to know more about the exotic creature who had replaced Marianne Faithfull in Mick's life. When the press cornered them in London, Jagger refused to even give them her name. "Sorry, I can't tell you who she is," he said.

"That's our business." When it came to the paparazzi, Mick was more protective of his mystery woman than he had ever been of Marianne. At one point, when a photographer shoved a camera in Bianca's face, Jagger chased down the man and punched him squarely in the face. Convicted of assault, Mick was fined $1,400.

Now ensconced with Mick at Stargroves, Bianca began cleaning house. One by one, she ordered the other women in Mick's life to stay away from her man. When Miss Pamela called, she was surprised when a husky-voiced woman answered the phone. "You are never, ever, under any circumstances to call Mick, ever again," Bianca said. "Get the picture?"

Anita Pallenberg was another matter. Now that Marianne was gone, Pallenberg had advanced to the number one position among the Stones' women. This was not just because she was Keith's long-time girlfriend; Pallenberg's previous relationships with Brian and Mick gave her a special standing within the group. Bill Wyman's Swedish girlfriend Astrid Lundstrom, Mick Taylor's fiancée, Rose, and Shirley Watts all kept their distance from Pallenberg.

Unfortunately for Bianca, Pallenberg took an instant dislike to her. Convinced that the bony Nicaraguan had, in fact, once been a man, Pallenberg offered Keith's dealer, Spanish Tony Sanchez, $50,000 if he could prove that she had undergone gender reassignment.

Once she abandoned that absurd notion, Pallenberg turned to the black arts. She placed a number of voodoo curses on Bianca, stabbing pins into dolls and, in one instance, walking around a bewildered Bianca three times with a handwritten curse stuffed in her shoe—one of several voodoo tricks for getting rid of people.

Before long, Bianca learned that Pallenberg was not her only remaining adversary. On November 3, 1970, Mick told a shocked Bianca that Marsha Hunt had given birth to his child that day. Hunt had wisely passed on Mick's name for the little girl—Midnight Dream—and settled instead on Karis.

Although Bianca was now determined to be the mother of Mick's next child, it quickly became clear that he was not exactly the paternal type. Over the next two weeks, he saw his infant daughter just twice—and only then stopping by for a few brief minutes between appointments.

Hunt was upset with Mick's apparent indifference to their baby and let him know it. Jagger would have none of it. "I never loved you," he shouted at her, "and you're mad to think I ever did!"

Hunt broke down, but that seemed to make Mick only that much angrier. "She's my child," he said, pointing to the fact that she was no match for him when it came to hiring lawyers and wielding influence. "I could take her away from you anytime I felt like it."

"Try it," Hunt said, "and I'll blow your brains out."

That Christmas, with the Stones riding high on the success of their critically acclaimed live album *'Get Yer Ya-Ya's Out!,'* *Newsweek* put Mick on its cover, declaring, "Of all the charismatic figures produced by rock—Paul McCartney, Bob Dylan, John Lennon, Jimi Hendrix, Janis Joplin, Eric Clapton—Mick Jagger is undoubtedly the most startling in his sustained flamboyance, his demonic power to affect even people who instinctively recoil from him, his uncompromising refusal to ingratiate."

Even with Marianne out of the picture, Mick was still snorting cocaine at 48 Cheyne Walk—often in the company of his friends Paul and Talitha Getty. According to Spanish Tony Sanchez, they would frequently be joined by Keith and Anita, and he would sometimes have to "calm them down" with heroin.

Incredibly, Mick seemed more than up to the task of managing the Stones' complex finances. "Mick held meetings constantly," said Trevor Churchill, who later headed up Rolling Stones Records in

Europe. While the others would remain seated, Jagger would pace up and down the room, fidgeting and peppering the business types with questions.

"Mick was very much in control," Churchill said. "He was incredibly well versed on the business side. He used to come up with extraordinary things to keep you on your toes." It was not unusual for Jagger to call Churchill or another member of his financial team and ask for the latest album sales figures in Italy or Sweden. Moreover, Mick also personally handled all of the group's banking relationships. "He has a very, very shrewd business mind," Churchill added. "It's impossible to overstate how clever he is in this regard."

There was only one person who had veto power over Mick. "Before he put anything into effect," said their longtime business associate Sandy Lieberson, "Mick ran it by Keith. If Keith said no, then Mick was fucked."

The Stones announced on March 4, 1971, that they would be relocating to France—but not before completing a nine-city "Farewell to Britain" tour. Despite Mick's insistence that the Stones were leaving the UK "for the climate," by jumping ship in fiscal 1971–72 they stood to save millions in taxes retroactive to 1969.

Before they finally made the move to France, the Stones kicked up their heels at several going-away parties held in their honor. At one held where the Stones got their start, the Marquee Club, Keith showed up drunk and wound up taking a swing at the club's manager with his red Gibson guitar.

Mick managed to top Keith at a later farewell bash, this one a decidedly more posh affair at Skindles Hotel in Maidenhead, on the Buckinghamshire bank of the Thames. When the manager asked his rowdy party to leave at four in the morning, Jagger went berserk. Despite efforts by Eric Clapton and John Lennon to restrain the guest of honor, Mick grabbed a chair and tossed it through a plate glass window. "At least you'll be able to pay for it," Lennon cracked, "now that you're leaving the bloody country."

Insisting to the end that the Stones were not turning their backs on their beloved England, Mick and his fellow band members finally went into tax exile in the south of France at the end of March. Wyman settled into a house in the hills of Grasse, Watts bought a farm in the medieval town of Vaucluse, and Keith and Anita leased Nellcôte, a glistening villa overlooking the Mediterranean harbor town of Villefranche.

Mick and Bianca, meanwhile, bided their time at the exclusive Hotel Byblos in Saint-Tropez while they hunted for a house to equal if not surpass Keith's new residence. They found just the right property: a stucco-walled, tile-roofed estate just a half hour down the coast in Biot.

Safely ensconced in their new tax haven, the Stones announced their new $5 million, six-album deal with Ertegun's Atlantic Records. Under the terms of the four-year contract, Atlantic would distribute records made on the Rolling Stones Records label.

Part of the hefty cash advance from Atlantic was earmarked for signing new acts—one of the main reasons that Marshall Chess, son of Chess Records founder Leonard Chess, agreed to head up the new Rolling Stones label. But Mick's natural reticence made that impossible. "Contrary to his public image, he is not a risk taker," Churchill said of Mick. Moreover, the Stones "were just not willing to share the money or the spotlight." When he had the opportunity to sign unknown acts such as Genesis and Queen, both of which would at one point outsell the Rolling Stones, Jagger "just brushed them off," Churchill said. "It was very frustrating to see Mick pass up so many incredible opportunities to make millions."

Exactly one week after inking their deal with Ertegun, the Stones released *Sticky Fingers,* their first album on the new label. It was not enough that the record itself be good; with classic cuts such as "Brown Sugar" and "Wild Horses," that was a fait accompli. Jagger also wanted *Sticky Fingers* to be visually stunning, and to ensure that, he turned to his old friend Andy Warhol.

"Mick borrowed some from Marlon Brando and some from Marilyn Monroe," observed Warhol biographer and Jagger acquaintance Victor Bockris, "but a lot from Andy." In some ways, Bockris added, the envelope-pushing pop art pioneer was "the Mick Jagger of the art world."

Jagger's instructions to Warhol were succinct: "We're out for a little shock value, Andy—as always." Warhol did not disappoint. The result—a bulging, jeans-clad crotch with an actual fly that could be unzipped to reveal the Stones' John Pasche–designed lapping-tongue logo on the obverse side of the cover—fused art and fashion with rock. Mick's Michelin-sized lips—"child-bearing lips," comic Joan Rivers called them—and the tongue they surrounded would soon become as recognizable as the corporate symbols for McDonald's and Coke.

Contrary to popular belief, the denim-encased bulge on the cover did not belong to Jagger. For this purpose, Warhol auditioned a number of male models and then wound up doing what Mick himself often did onstage to obtain the desired effect: Warhol stuffed a rolled-up sock down the front of the model's pants.

With the provocative and hugely successful *Sticky Fingers* album heralding an exciting new era for the Stones, Mick decided it was time for change in his personal life as well. When Bianca told him that she was four months pregnant, he reacted in much the same way as he had when Marsha Hunt informed Mick that she was pregnant. He was ecstatic, overjoyed. In Bianca's case, however, he had come to believe that he was actually in love with the woman carrying his child.

Mick asked Bianca to marry him, and, to his surprise, she refused initially. "I have always had my own identity," she said. "I don't want to live my life totally in Mick's shadow." Jagger hounded her for weeks before she finally said yes.

Eva Jagger burst out in loud sobs when Mick phoned her with the news. Beyond telling members of the immediate family, details of the May 12 nuptials were—for the time being, at least—to remain top secret. Even as he was taking private catechism lessons—necessary if they were to wed at the Roman Catholic Chapel Saint-Anne high above the Côte d'Azur—Mick lied to reporters. "We're definitely *not* getting married," he told them. His assistant Shirley Arnold, meanwhile, was secretly rounding up guests.

The list of invitees quickly grew to seventy-five—all of whom were to be bussed to London's Gatwick Airport and flown to Nice, France, on a chartered jet. Within twenty-four hours, Ringo Starr, film director Roger Vadim, Paul and Linda McCartney (with whom Mick had had a one-night stand before she met her Beatle), The Who drummer Keith Moon, actress Nathalie Delon, Eric Clapton, and the Queen's cousin Lord Lichfield were among the celebrities winging their way to what was already being billed as rock's wedding of the decade. Incredibly, Keith was the only Stone invited, along with Anita. The day before the wedding, Mick called up Bill Wyman, Charlie Watts, and Mick Taylor to inform them that they were welcome at the reception afterward, however. "We were, to put it mildly, shocked," Wyman said later. "Shocked—and hurt."

There were, as it turned out, plenty of hitches on the way to getting hitched. The wedding was to be a two-parter: a brief civil ceremony conducted by the mayor of Saint-Tropez at town hall, followed by the religious ceremony at the Chapel Saint-Anne.

But two hours before the first ceremony was to get underway, Mick and Bianca were already arguing about money. The issue was forced on them by French law, which requires newlyweds to sign a document stating whether or not their property would remain separate or be held jointly.

Not surprisingly, Mick had no interest in giving Bianca a joint claim on his fortune—and certainly not now that he stood to reap an additional $1 million in 1971 based on his new tax exile status. Bianca stood her ground. Rather than be pressured into signing this prenup, she told Mick that she wanted to call the whole thing off.

"Are you trying to make a fool of me in front of all these people?" Jagger screamed, all well within earshot of the wedding party. Trembling, Bianca surrendered, signing over her claim to Mick's millions with Jagger's longtime driver, Alan Dunn, acting as witness.

Next it was Mick's turn to threaten to call off the wedding. When he was told that more than a hundred paparazzi had crammed into town hall, Mick protested, "I am not a fish in a goldfish bowl, and I am not the king of France!" Jagger sent word to the mayor that he would not set foot in town hall unless they were told to clear out.

But Mayor Marius Estezan refused to clear the hall ("Any citizen has a right to be here"), and issued an ultimatum of his own: if the bride and groom weren't there in ten minutes, *he* was calling it quits. Even after the couple showed up holding hands, at times Mick looked as if he might be a runaway groom. At one point, when they were being jostled by the press inside town hall, Mick grabbed Bianca's hand and started to bolt. "I'm not going on," he said. "I'm not doing it like this." The Stones' press agent, Les Perrin, thought otherwise. He spun them back around and gently shoved Mick and Bianca in the mayor's direction.

In a calculated effort to divert attention from her expanding midsection, the very pregnant bride wore a large hat trimmed with rosebuds and a white Yves Saint Laurent suit with a plunging neckline that offered everyone—the mayor and the officiating priest included—the occasional glimpse of nipple.

If the groom's open-collared floral print shirt and off-white summer suit seemed uncharacteristically staid, Keith more than made up for it. Mick's Glimmer Twin wore black leggings and a combat jacket with no shirt underneath. Richards complained loudly when, despite the mayor's insistence that the hall was a public place and that everyone was welcome, gendarmes tried to bar him and Anita from witnessing their friend's wedding. "I've had four fights," he bellowed, "just to get here!"

Then came the mad dash up the hill to the Chapel Saint-Anne, with the press and curious onlookers in hot pursuit. The newlyweds reached the chapel with the mob nipping at their heels, only to find the door bolted shut. It swung open at the last minute, and Mick, livid, pushed his way to the front of the chapel. Then he turned to watch Bianca march down the aisle on the arm of Lord Lichfield—a reminder that, while the Queen would never permit her sister Princess Margaret to attend an event such as this, Jagger's ties to the aristocracy remained strong. Mick flinched only slightly at the music Bianca had selected for the occasion: an organ rendition of the schmaltzy theme from the hit movie *Love Story*.

At one point during the ceremony, Father Lucien Baud spoke directly to Mick. He wished the groom happiness, then glanced at the mob of photographers gathered outside. "But when you are a personality like Mick Jagger," Father Baud added wistfully, "it is too much to hope for privacy for your marriage."

If there was any doubt that Mick had met his match in Bianca, it was dispelled when she showed up at the reception at the Café des Arts in a transparent silk blouse and a sequined turban. She fiddled periodically with the light-catching diamond bracelet on her left wrist—a wedding gift from Mick.

Jagger had picked a reggae group called the Rudies to liven up the festivities. When they struck up the Stones' "It's All Over Now"—an odd choice, considering—Mick grabbed Bianca's hand and led her onto the floor for their first dance together as man and wife. Much to the amusement of the assembled two hundred guests and assorted gate-crashers, "It's All Over Now" would be the evening's most frequently played song.

All hopes for a spontaneous Stones performance were dashed by Keith, who passed out well before midnight. That left it to Mick to provide the entertainment high point of the night. Although thoroughly wasted, Mick joined American R & B singers Doris Troy and former Ikette P. P. Arnold for an electrifying twenty-five-minute soul medley.

Sitting with Roger Vadim and Paul McCartney, the new Mrs. Jagger watched with interest as Mick and Arnold bumped, ground, and sweated their way through one R & B staple after another— all the while blissfully ignorant of the fact that Mick and P. P. had once been lovers. As the night wore on, however, she began to feel ignored—and she let him know it in no uncertain terms. "Mick isn't interested in anyone telling him what to do," Wyman said. "He went right back to his friends and enjoying the party." Bianca, fuming, returned to their suite at the Hotel Byblos.

The newlyweds embarked the next day on a ten-day honeymoon cruise around the islands of Sardinia and Corsica aboard the 120-ton yacht *Romeang*. Would any of their famous friends be accompanying them, an enterprising reporter asked. "You must be joking," Jagger answered.

As soon as they returned, Mick hunkered down with his fellow Stones that summer to produce their new album—actually, a double album that would be released to coincide with their next invasion of the United States in 1972. It had to be a megahit on the scale of *Sticky Fingers*.

Since Keith's stately manor, Nellcôte, was far and away the largest of the Stones' residences in the south of France, Mick agreed that it made sense to record the new album there. In the basement, there was ample space for recording facilities, as well as for the Stones' mushrooming technical and support staff.

What Nellcôte did not have was air conditioning—or, for that matter, reliable electricity. As the temperature soared to 120 degrees that summer, Mick stripped off his clothes just so that he could get through the ordeal of recording "Tumbling Dice" and "Rocks Off." The humidity was so bad, Mick recalled, that he "couldn't stand it. As soon as I opened my mouth to sing, my voice was gone."

Further complicating matters was the power, which periodically dimmed or went out completely. "I'd be right in the middle of a song and everything would be going great and then boom, the lights would go out," Jagger recalled. "We'd have to do the whole fucking thing again." It was, he said, "a bloody nightmare."

Keith and Anita scarcely noticed. Both mired deep in addiction, they were content to surround themselves with a sleazy group of drug dealers, fellow junkies, hangers-on, flunkies, and drifters. If anything, they took pride in their scandalous reputation. When it came time to christen his speedboat, Keith considered *Marlon* but wound up painting *Mandrax*—his favorite prescription quaalude—on the hull.

Believing that this probably was not an ideal environment for a woman who was seven months pregnant, Bianca opted to spend the summer in the Jaggers' suite at Paris's historic L'Hotel. It was at L'Hotel, nestled just off the Seine River on the Rue des Beaux Arts, that Oscar Wilde died—but not before promising, "Either this wallpaper goes, or I do."

It was just as well. True to form, her nemesis Anita Pallenberg was stirring up trouble at Nellcôte by openly pursuing sound-men, tradespeople, pushers—even fellow heroin user Eric Clapton. Soon rumors began flying about Anita and Mick. To allay Bianca's fears that Jagger and Pallenberg were doing a reprise of their torrid love scenes in *Performance,* he agreed to spend time with Bianca in Paris at least three times a week. Mick's absences from the studio meant that the other Stones would have to record without him, leaving the group's lead singer to record his tracks separately.

Bianca gave birth to a six-pound baby girl at Belvedere Nursing Home in Paris on October 21, 1971. It would take her parents two more days to agree on a name: Jade Sheena Jezebel. Why Jade? "Because she is very precious," Mick replied, "and quite, quite perfect."

Two weeks later in London, Eva and Joe Jagger—who still called their son Mike—were cooing over the new grandchild. In Bianca's absence, Mick also invited Marsha to stop by at the Cheyne Walk house so that he could photograph her with Karis and Jade. It was painfully evident to Marsha that Jade, not Karis, was the apple of her father's eye.

A month would pass before Mick spoke with Hunt again, and only then because she had reluctantly asked Mick to help cover Karis's food and clothing expenses. Prior to that, Hunt, who claimed she was broke, received money from Jagger only once: just $500 to help cover some of their child's living expenses. At that time, he did not look her in the eye as he grudgingly wrote out the check. "I guess he couldn't," Hunt observed later.

Although he ignored Karis, Mick lavished attention on Jade. Janie Villiers, Jade's nanny, said that Jagger "enjoyed fatherhood. It made an incongruous scene: Mick Jagger in a silk shirt, white satin trousers, and green eye shadow he wore in the evenings, bringing all his flamboyance and charisma to the nursery."

Bianca, on the other hand, complained of the "tremendous strain" of being a mom: "Nobody knows what a strain it is to keep a house, look after Jade, and be dressed properly all the time." According to Villiers, Bianca spent less time with Jade than Mick did, and when she did pick up the baby, she hoisted her up with "an awkward kind of fireman's lift. Once," Villiers claimed, "she actually dropped Jade down the stairs."

By the following spring, the Stones still had not nailed down the details of their all-important US tour. But they had settled on a title for the album: *Exile on Main St*. Now that he had been a tax exile for nearly a year, Mick admitted to being homesick. He was even telling friends that he might take his old friend Tom Driberg's advice and return to England to run for parliament as a member of the Labour Party. "But," Jagger added slyly, "I haven't got the right wife."

Leaving Bianca behind at their house in the south of France, Mick headed to New York for a series of meetings with Ahmet Ertegun. It was there that he had a chance encounter with James Taylor, the lanky, mustachioed American singer who was fresh off the success of his *Sweet Baby James* album. By the time he was discovered by Mick's old pal Peter Asher, formerly half of the popular duo Peter and Gordon and now a top producer, Taylor had already undergone treatment for suicidal psychosis. Now, like Keith, Anita, Clapton, and so many others who drifted in and out of Mick's life, Taylor was desperately addicted to heroin.

Taylor was eager for Mick to meet his new girlfriend, another rising star in the pop music firmament named Carly Simon. Jagger was certainly familiar with her music—thoughtfully crafted, unusually literate hits such as "That's the Way I've Always Heard It

Should Be" and "Anticipation"—but he was even more interested in her background. Simon's father had founded the publishing house Simon & Schuster, and during Carly's childhood it was not all that unusual for Albert Einstein, Salvador Dali, or John Steinbeck to show up at the dinner table.

Like Taylor, Simon suffered from childhood insecurities that would propel her into the realm of music. When analysis failed to correct Carly's childhood stutter, Andrea Simon suggested that her musically gifted little girl simply sing whatever it was she wanted to say. It worked. Once her true voice emerged beautifully and clearly through song, Carly became confident enough to overcome her stutter.

Mick also couldn't help being drawn to Simon physically. After all, she was very much his type. Tall and bony, with an oversized mouth and untamed hair, she looked like an American version of Bianca. Or, more accurately, she also looked like Mick.

Taylor had just ended a long relationship with folk singer Joni Mitchell when he met Simon at a Carnegie Hall concert in late 1971, and she was still seeing notorious Hollywood Lothario War-ren Beatty. But now Taylor and Simon definitely seemed smitten with each other, and, of course, that meant Mick had to have her.

It did not take long for rumors of Mick's affair with Carly Simon to float across the Atlantic. At their villa in Biot, Bianca reacted appropriately. She opened the door to Mick's enormous walk-in closet, pulled out his favorite shirts, and ripped them to shreds—with her teeth. She made no effort to conceal how she felt about Carly. "There's a certain American female singer," she told several people, "I'd like to tear to pieces."

Bianca wasn't feeling so charitable toward Mick, either. She locked him out of their villa in Biot and, once he'd managed to convince a servant to let him in, threw him out again. Jagger later swore that, while in a "jealous frenzy," she had once threatened him with a gun.

Years later, Bianca told Andy Warhol that of all Mick's lovers, Simon concerned her most. According to Andy, this was because "Carly Simon is intelligent and has the look Mick likes—she looks like Mick and Bianca."

Several months after her affair with Mick, Carly married Taylor and spent the next nine years trying to wean him off heroin. Taylor was not at all bothered by his wife's dalliance with Mick; the three remained close friends. So close that when she went into the studio to record her hit "You're So Vain," Mick gamely sang backup. (Despite speculation that Beatty was the subject of the song, those familiar with the affair—and with Mick's fondness for wearing a particular silk scarf he described as apricot—knew otherwise: "your scarf it was apricot . . . the wife of a close friend, wife of a close friend.")

The apricot scarf would figure in another scene that year, when Mick informed Bianca that she would not be allowed to tag along on the US tour. Mick was standing on the sidewalk surrounded by twenty suitcases and waiting for the limo to take him to the airport when Bianca came out and yelled, "If I can't go, then my silk scarf's not going either! You can just unpack every suitcase until you find it."

Jade's nanny, Janie Villiers, was stunned by what happened next. Mick, who referred to Bianca simply as "B," stamped his foot and began to weep. "B, I was going to wear it for my act," he bawled. "You can't expect me to find it now!" But she did. For the next forty-five minutes, Mick, who never stopped crying, tore through his luggage until he finally located the apricot-colored scarf—in the very last suitcase. "There," he said, tossing the scarf at Bianca. "I hope you're satisfied! Now I'll miss my plane." (After all the histrionics, Bianca did join Mick toward the end of the US tour.)

Mick got his revenge not long after, when he and Marianne Faithfull got together for a one-night stand. Jagger told her about the brief vacation that he and Bianca had taken to Southeast Asia earlier in the year, and how he had trolled through some of Bangkok's famous sex establishments while she shopped. "And I haven't," Mick complained to Marianne, "had a good fuck since."

As Bianca well knew, there would be plenty of women willing to oblige Mick as the Stones—carried on a tsunami of sustained airplay and record sales (more than a million copies of *Exile on Main St.* sold even before they arrived)—once again swept across North America like a Mongol horde. "Mick needed to prove to himself that he was still on top," Ertegun said. "He needn't have worried. Nobody could match him."

Still, as he approached his twenty-ninth birthday, Mick had to face the fact that many of his contemporaries were either dead (Hendrix, Joplin, Jim Morrison, Brian) or, like the Beatles and other groups that led the first wave of the British invasion, already beginning to be seen as quaint relics of a bygone era. Newcomers like the Jackson 5 and David Cassidy now vied for every dollar spent by teenage record buyers, while acts like Alice Cooper, the Grateful Dead, The Who, and Led Zeppelin competed for the allegiance of diehard rock fans. At the same time, Elton John, Lou Reed, and David Bowie cashed in on the glam-rock trend that Mick had pioneered.

Jagger was still breaking new ground. In his effort to recapture the youth market by creating as much pandemonium as possible at the edge of the stage, Mick unilaterally banned VIPs from the first twenty rows of every concert and filled those seats with screaming teenage fans. Jagger fed off their energy. "I can feel 'em down there," he said. "I need each and every one of 'em."

From the moment he hit the stage in a sequined white jumpsuit slashed to the groin, it was clear that Mick was leaving nothing to chance. Decades before Keith would set tongues wagging about the size of Mick's genitalia, Jagger begged the question by continuing to stuff a rolled-up sock down the front of his outfit.

Between nips of Jack Daniel's and a furtive snort or two of coke, Mick, drenched in glistening sweat, snarled and twitched his way through songs like "Midnight Rambler," "Under My Thumb," "Brown Sugar," and "Tumbling Dice." In *Life* magazine's cover story "The Stones Blast Through the Land," Thomas Thompson wrote, "Above all there is Jagger. He is possessed, as few performers are—Callas, El Cordobés, Nureyev come to mind—with a stunning, electric-shock stage capacity." He went on to describe Mick as a "marionette abandoned by the string-puller" and a "cheerleader at an orgy."

For the Stones, perhaps nothing was more gratifying than seeing the mayhem they were still capable of generating. In Vancouver, British Columbia, more than thirty people were rushed to the hospital after an overflow crowd of two thousand clashed with Mounties. More than three thousand fans with counterfeit tickets rioted outside Montreal's Forum. Fans in San Diego set fire to police barricades, touching off a street battle that resulted in fifteen injuries and sixty people being thrown in jail. That was nothing compared to Tucson, Arizona, where police lobbed tear gas grenades into an angry mob. Before it was all over, police had rounded up more than three hundred people.

The scene was repeated in the nation's capital. There police arrested sixty-five rampaging fans. In Rhode Island, only two people were arrested—but they were Mick and Keith, for assaulting a photographer.

Later aboard the "Lapping Tongue," the Stones' private DC-7 with the iconic John Pasche–designed logo on the fuselage, Mick hauled off and slapped an attractive young woman before throwing her off the plane. As it turned out, the young woman was a process server who had just handed Mick a summons from Altamont landowners claiming that their property had been damaged to the tune of $375,000—a not-insubstantial sum at the time. (Jagger often felt free to do as he wished once he was aboard an aircraft. On an earlier flight to LA, a flight attendant made the mistake of telling Mick he was in the wrong seat. "You talk like that to me," Jagger allegedly told stewardess Pauline Laugh as he grabbed her by the arm and spun her around, "and I'll kick you up your ass." He later added that he would have also liked to "have given her a good slap in the face, because she deserved it.")

Such bravado masked a palpable fear on Jagger's part that he would die violently—more specifically, that he would be assassinated in the middle of a performance. For that reason, at least two bodyguards accompanied him on tour. As a last line of defense, Mick also packed his own heat—a .38-caliber pistol that he kept in his jacket pocket when he was not onstage.

Although he now added to his list of phobias and nervous tics a newfound fear of flying—the slightest turbulence could trigger a panic attack—Mick had no interest in slowing down. Far from it; for the Stones, life on the road was more outlandish—and disturbingly surreal—than ever.

Filmmaker Robert Frank captured much of the insanity for a tour documentary tentatively titled *Cocksucker Blues,* which, for reasons that would quickly become apparent, never was released. In one scene, Mick and Keith, both obviously stoned, babble nonsensical answers and roll joints during an interview. In another, Keith is openly shooting up heroin. Among other charming vignettes: Bianca photographing her husband smoking pot in the back of their limousine as it barrels down a country road in the Deep South; Mick walking around the pool of the Stones' LA headquarters, his hands down the front of his swim trunks; another man whose face is concealed masturbating inside his satin pants; naked groupies shooting up themselves and one another; Jagger snorting cocaine through a rolled-up $100 bill just before a performance; and Mick playing the tom-toms aboard the Lapping Tongue while roadies strip three young groupies and start chasing them around the cabin.

In one typically grotesque tableau, Mick sits up in bed holding a mirror to his face and stares into it like the wicked queen in *Snow White*. All around him, groupies and tour members are having sex, snorting coke, or shoving poppers—amyl nitrate—under one another's noses.

Even as battle-hardened a rock journalist as *Rolling Stone*'s Robert Greenfield was stunned by what he witnessed: "Five bottles of Demerol and a bottle of 500 Quaaludes and they're all gone; a quart-sized jar of coke just for an energizer; four Quaaludes to get to sleep, but if you start to speed on them drop a Placidyl . . . $500 of coke laid out in a four-foot line on a mirror . . . one guy keeps his stash in a rubber—calls it *real* prophylactic medicine, ha-ha."

Another witness to the Stones' drug-fueled antics was Truman Capote, on assignment to do a piece for *Rolling Stone* that never ran. "It was a case of dueling bitches from the start," a friend of Truman's commented. "Mick disliked Tru for being 'on' all the time . . . No one laughed because he wasn't funny." Capote, in turn, declared Mick to be a "scared little boy, very much off his turf." As for Jagger's unisex appeal: "Believe me," laughed the author known in cafe society circles as the "Tiny Terror," Jagger "is about as sexy as a pissing toad."

Millions of women would have taken issue with Capote, and one happened to show up at a star-studded LA party in the Stones' honor. "Miss Pamela!" Mick shouted across the room to his on-again, off-again lover. "The girl of my dreams!" Miss Pamela had just discovered that her new beau, an unknown young actor named Don Johnson, was cheating on her with actress Tippi Hedren's fourteen-year-old daughter, Melanie Griffith. She also informed Mick that Johnson was the most well-endowed lover she'd ever had—"which, of course, Mick saw as a challenge to his manhood." And Jagger was, she added wryly, "always up for a challenge."

Since Bianca joined him just twice during the tour ("I just have to be on my own," he explained), Mick freely sampled dishes from the sexual smorgasbord served up to him on the road. This included several buxom Playmates he met while staying at Hugh Hefner's Playboy Mansion in Chicago. Even Hef was impressed with Jagger's prowess. "Mick," he said, "obviously doesn't need any tips from me."

The Stones' second show at New York's Madison Square Garden on July 26, 1972 marked the end of the tour—and Mick's twenty-ninth birthday. After plans to dump five hundred live chickens on the heads of audience members were abandoned, the Stones settled for throwing pies at one another while twenty thousand people sang "Happy Birthday."

The postshow party that Ahmet Ertegun threw at the St. Regis Hotel was a fittingly Fellini-esque finale to the tour. Andy Warhol snapped Polaroids while Warhol Factory actress Pat Ast and transvestite Candy Darling kibitzed with playwright Tennessee Williams. Bob Dylan, in dark glasses and a white fedora, chatted with TV talk show host Dick Cavett before asking to have his picture taken alongside actress Zsa Zsa Gabor. Woody Allen slunk in a corner for most of the evening, and writer George Plimpton gossiped with Capote and Jackie Onassis's sister, Princess Lee Radziwill. Also moving through the crowd, champagne flutes in hand, were many familiar faces on New York's social scene, including jewelry magnate

Gianni Bulgari, supermarket heir Huntington Hartford, socialites C. Z. Guest and Slim Keith, designer Oscar de la Renta, publishing mogul Sy Newhouse, and critic Rex Reed.

At two in the morning, Mick joined in on a jam with Stevie Wonder and his blues idol Muddy Waters. When the whole affair wrapped up shortly before dawn, Dylan described it as "encompassing—the beginning of cosmic consciousness." Syndicated columnist Harriet Van Horne had a different take. She thought that Nero, Caligula, the Marquis de Sade, and the Manson family "would have been perfectly at home at such a Bacchanal as Jagger's birthday party."

Rudolf Nureyev was another name that Van Horne might have added to the list. Although Nureyev could not make it to Jagger's birthday party, the two men were close and did spend several days together that summer.

It had been a decade since his defection from the Soviet Union, and Nureyev was still at the peak of his powers, dazzling audiences around the world with his gravity-defying leaps and his sheer animal presence. Away from the ballet, the flamboyantly exotic figure with the pouting lips and high Tartar cheekbones strutted through life much like Mick—seducing men as well as women, including his famous partner Dame Margot Fonteyn, Leonard Bernstein, the actor Anthony Perkins, and the designers Giorgio Sant' Angelo and Halston.

Mick was drawn to people who resembled him, and, in many ways, Nureyev did. "Me and Nureyev have flaming rows about whether it takes more talent and discipline to be a ballet dancer or a pop singer," Mick said of their friendly rivalry. "He used to put me down a lot, but I think I've converted him. I told him I would have wanted to dance myself, but I never had the opportunity."

Just how intimate the relationship between Jagger and Nureyev had become was apparent that summer, when broadcast journalist Geraldo Rivera invited both men to a party at his Lower East Side apartment. While Rudolf and Mick smoked pot and danced together in his living room, Rivera excused himself and ducked into the kitchen to mix drinks.

"Suddenly," Rivera recalled, "someone snuggled up behind me. I felt an arm around my waist, and I made a kind of half pivot to see who it was. It was Nureyev, and he was moving in time to the music, pressing himself against me from behind. He was being playfully suggestive, overtly sexual, and before I had a chance to even think how to respond, Jagger approached me from the front and started doing the same thing. They were kidding, and giddy, but there was also something seriously competitive going on between them."

As Mick stroked Geraldo's chest, Nureyev ran his fingers through Rivera's hair. "He's a virgin, you know," Nureyev said to Mick.

"Oh, well," Jagger replied with a wink, "we can break him in."

At that moment, Geraldo, who would remain convinced that this was a serious effort by Nureyev and Jagger to seduce him, "squirmed out from between this odd sandwich and laughed the whole thing off." He added, however, "If I were ever going to have a homosexual experience, it would have been that night, with Rudolf Nureyev and Mick Jagger."

Later Bianca shrugged when Geraldo told her the story. "Mick doesn't think much of women," she said matter-of-factly.

In September Mick returned to London and announced he was home for good; the Jaggers were fed up with life in the south of France. So were Keith and Anita, but their reasons for wanting to flee were even more pressing: after years of taunting French officials, Richards and Pallenberg learnt warrants had been issued for their arrest on narcotics charges.

Few things in life were as personally satisfying to Mick as toying with the press. Toward that end, he announced that he was going to retire in four years at the age of thirty-three. "I couldn't bear to end up as an Elvis Presley and sing in Las Vegas with all those housewives and old ladies coming in with their handbags. It's really sick. Elvis probably digs it. That's his good fortune if that's the way he wants it. Not me. I don't," he said unequivocally, "want to be a rock-and-roll singer my whole life."

Everyone knows everyone is basically bisexual.

—MICK

◆　◆　◆

*You can't say he's homosexual, or even bisexual.
He's beyond that. Mick Jagger is the world's greatest
practitioner of cosmic sex.*

—BEBE BUELL, MICK'S LONGTIME LOVER

◆　◆　◆

*I don't promote the image of being an eternal twenty-year-
old. That's a very dangerous thing to do.*

—MICK

His marriage to Bianca didn't change things at all.
He'd still drive around picking up girls.
The younger the better.

—RODNEY BINGENHEIMER, FRIEND

◆　◆　◆

Reporter: How many children do you have?
Mick: I don't know. Not many.

6

◆ ◆ ◆

"Oh, Shut Up, Keith. Don't Be Stupid"

*B*ianca was unhappy—even more than usual. And she let Mick know it. "Mick and Bianca fought *constantly*," a former personal secretary said. "You couldn't be around them for two minutes without both of them erupting like Vesuvius."

Her main complaint? That her famous husband was ignoring her. To be sure, he had bought yet another lavishly appointed property— this one in Ocho Rios, Jamaica—but Mick made no secret of his general disdain for married life. For her part, Bianca was not about to become a hausfrau in a rump-sprung bathrobe.

Capitalizing on her newfound visibility, Bianca set out to make a name for herself in the rarefied world of fashion. Yves Saint Laurent remained a personal favorite, available at the drop of a rhinestone-embroidered cloche to design a white sheath for her and a matching white satin suit for Mick. Bianca soon spread her fashion wings to include Halston, Ossie Clark, Calvin Klein, Bill Blass, Ralph Lauren, and others—all eager for the exposure that only the wife of the world's biggest rock star could give them.

Bianca also added touches of her own to the mix: feather boas, transparent blouses, fur wraps, lace mantillas, and a collection of gold-, ivory-, and silver-tipped walking sticks that would become her trademark. Bianca, hailed as a bona fide fashion original, soon joined her husband on best-dressed lists around the world.

As 1972 drew to a close, the battling Jaggers agreed to put their differences aside, if only to make the holiday season bearable for Jade. Everyone seemed headed for a memorably happy Christmas when, on December 23, a devastating earthquake struck Bianca's hometown of Managua, reducing a sizable portion of that city to rubble and killing six thousand people.

Unable to locate Bianca's family by phone or even determine if they had survived the quake, Mick chartered a private jet and filled it with medical supplies. Once in Managua, Bianca faced the sobering possibility that close members of her family—including her mother—may have been killed. Where her mother's lunch counter had been, there was now only rubble.

Bianca searched for days before finally tracking down both her parents in a nearby village. Incredibly, they had managed to survive the ordeal unharmed.

At Bianca's urging, the Stones raised $787,500 for earthquake relief with a single benefit concert at the Los Angeles Forum. Such altruism was apparently of no consequence to the Japanese government. Within days of the concert, authorities in Tokyo decreed that Mick would not be allowed to enter the country because of his 1967 drug conviction—a major blow to the Rolling Stones' upcoming tour of the Far East. It was a sign of things to come for Mick and his fellow Stones; for the next forty years, their arrest records would complicate the process of obtaining the visas they needed to work abroad.

In the short term, Mick hoped to use his Nicaraguan relief efforts to drum up a little good will in Washington. He also hoped to get his name removed once and for all from some of the airport watch lists he had been added to over the years.

Although the United States had not yet made the decision to follow Japan's lead and bar the Stones from entering the country altogether, Mick had been placed on the Immigration and Naturalization Service's roster of potential undesirables following his drug arrests in the mid-1960s. The US Customs Service also red-flagged Jagger, as did both the CIA and the State Department after he joined the 1968 march on the US Embassy in London. It didn't help, of course, that Mick was also an outspoken supporter of the Black Panthers—a black nationalist group FBI director J. Edgar Hoover had vowed to destroy—or that at various times Jagger described himself as an anarchist, a socialist, a communist, or a Maoist.

As one might have expected, Hoover took an interest in Mick that bordered on obsession. Under direct orders from Hoover, more than a dozen FBI agents posing as drug dealers, hippies, and bikers mingled with the crowd at Altamont. By 1970, several paid informants had infiltrated the Stones organization and were reporting back to J. Edgar with stories of drug abuse and orgies.

Mick was under constant surveillance. The phones in his hotel rooms were tapped. The director also had very personal reasons for hating Jagger. Hoover, whose tough crime-fighter persona had been nurtured to combat whispered rumors that he was gay, often ordered agents to uncover evidence of homosexual activity. He then used the information—whether it was accurate or not—to either blackmail his political enemies or ruin them.

In Mick, Hoover saw nothing less than a vile and wanton corruptor of America's youth. Clearly, the man whose mask of machismo rarely slipped found Mick's androgynous appearance and bisexual bravado unnerving. "Hoover hated Jagger," one former FBI agent said, "probably more than any other pop culture figure of his generation."

Hoover was certainly not alone. At the height of his 1972 reelection campaign, President Richard Nixon saw a photograph of Mick in *Life* magazine singing "Jumpin' Jack Flash" in an Uncle Sam top hat and, according to his then press secretary Ron Ziegler, "went completely nuts." Nixon ordered that Jagger be officially added to his famous enemies list.

Still, Washington rolled out the red carpet when Mick and Bianca arrived to present their $787,500 donation to the Pan American Development Foundation. Several prominent lawmakers and members of the diplomatic corps crowded the halls of the Senate Office Building to catch a glimpse of the Jaggers, and the habitually restrained *Washington Post* breathlessly described Bianca as "the newest superstar of the family, his wife and twin in sullen-lipped looks, darling of the social and fashion worlds."

The ploy worked. According to Bianca, Mick was told that his efforts on behalf of Nicaraguan earthquake relief would result in his being granted a permanent visa. All he had to do was ask for it.

But according to Bianca, the idea no longer appealed to Mick. Being harassed by the FBI or immigration authorities was one thing, but running afoul of the Internal Revenue Service was something else entirely. "Mick said to me that since he was trying to avoid paying United States income taxes, he did not want and would not apply for a permanent visa . . . He told me many times that he wanted to give the impression that he was not recording in the US, when he actually was." The ruse worked; inexplicably, the IRS was one of the few government agencies that expressed no interest in pursuing Jagger.

The same could not be said for Marsha Hunt, who was finally fed up with trying to chase down Mick for the occasional handout so she could feed and clothe their daughter. She filed for support in July 1973, and immediately newspapers around the world were filled with stories about the home-wrecking gold digger claiming to be the mother of Mick's love child.

Jagger, furious with the woman he had called Miss Fuzzy, insisted that he was not Karis's father and offered to take a blood test to prove it. That never happened. Instead Mick offered to set up a $25,000 trust fund for Karis and to pay just $20 a week for nanny care—but only if Hunt signed a sworn affidavit stating that Mick was not Karis's father. She agreed. But it wasn't, Mick should have guessed easily, the last he'd be hearing from Marsha Hunt.

Mick did not pretend to be much of a father, period. When Bianca slammed him for not spending enough time with Jade, he made no excuses. "It's my own choice," he admitted, "but I'm fucking negligent. I just am."

Jagger had more pressing issues on his mind: namely, the release of the Stones' new album, *Goats Head Soup,* on August 31. To give their latest effort the proper send-off, Mick invited Princess Margaret, Lord Lichfield, all the relevant Ormsby-Gores, several members of parliament, and the movers and shakers of the music industry to a launch party at Blenheim Palace, the eighteenth-century seat of the Dukes of Marlborough and birthplace of Winston Churchill.

With Sir Winston's ancestors gazing down at them from the walls, Mick and Bianca held court until a strung-out Anita Pallenberg marched in looking for Keith. After showering Bianca with blistering expletives, she grabbed Richards, and the two headed out the door looking for drugs. Although Keith claimed he was only joking when he told reporters two weeks later that he was going to get his blood supply replaced ("like a vampire in reverse"), he did check into a Swiss clinic where such treatment was offered. Whatever the specifics, he emerged clean enough to join the other Stones on their next British and American tours.

Goats Head Soup, with its cover image of a very feminine, pink-hued Mick gazing open-mouthed through layers of gauze, was an immediate success both critically and commercially. Yet only two songs from the album were hit singles—a gritty urban tale of guns and drugs called "Doo Doo Doo Doo Doo (Heartbreaker)," and a simpering, slightly off-key lament that bore little resemblance to the Stones' usual throbbing fare but nonetheless zoomed to number one: "Angie."

As might have been expected, speculation ran rampant as to the inspiration for "Angie," which held on to the number one spot for an impressive thirteen weeks. According to one version, Keith's main contribution to the lyric was suggesting the middle name of his newborn daughter, Dandelion Angela Richards, as the title. Another, more widely held belief was that the song was about Angela Bowie, David's wife. Neither was true. Mick was not inspired by David Bowie's wife but by Bowie himself.

Among practitioners of the new musical subgenre called glam rock, no one—not even Liberace imitator Elton John—pushed the limits faster or further than David Bowie. As an aspiring rocker growing up in working-class South London, David Jones (Bowie's real name) wanted to combine the nonthreatening pop appeal of the Beatles with the shock value of Mick Jagger. "I used to dream of being Mick Jagger," he said, "but not just because he was a sex symbol." To Bowie, Mick was "more of a mother image."

As it happened, this desire to follow in Jagger's footsteps would even influence his choice of a stage name. Mick had often stated in interviews that, in Old English, a "jagger" was a knife. The bowie knife, named after American pioneer and folk hero Jim Bowie, had the added benefit of beginning with a *B*—his nod to the Beatles. Hence, David Bowie was born.

Mary Angela Barnett had just been expelled from Connecticut College for Women for having a lesbian affair when a mutual boyfriend introduced her to Bowie. "We were both laying the same bloke," Bowie recalled. Another mutual friend, a young woman named Clare, slept with the couple on the eve of their 1970 wedding, then served as a witness at the ceremony the next morning. During the course of their ten-year marriage, David and Angie would have sex together and separately with both men and women.

"Like everyone else on the planet, we were blown away by the chances Mick took," Angie said. "He was wearing full makeup and dresses by Michael Fish." But Angie pressed David to take bisexual chic as far as it could go. Soon Bowie's plastic disco boots, Day-Glo orange hair, Kabuki makeup, and painted fingernails made his Ziggy Stardust alter ego the incontestable king of androgynous rock.

The two fascinated each other, both as stars and as men. Jagger was just four years older than Bowie, and yet Bowie was now being hailed as the hot new star. Ziggy, in spandex and gold body paint, hugged Mick when Jagger paid him a backstage visit in the spring of 1973. When Bowie and his companion Scott were invited to a Stones concert a few months later, Mick not only paid for the couple's hotel room but sent along roses and champagne with a note signed "Love, Mick."

Where Jagger was still coy about his own sexual preferences, Bowie made no effort to conceal the fact that both he and his wife were bisexual and often shared partners. "Mick looked at David and wondered if maybe this was the wave of the future," said Leee Black Childers, former executive vice president of MainMan, the management firm that handled Bowie. "Mick was very conscious of doing whatever it takes to stay hot, and David was the hottest thing around at the time."

"It was the glitter era, and everybody wanted to be part of the bisexual revolution," explained singer Chuckie Starr, who ran into Mick at a party in Beverly Hills the week that "Angie" hit number one. "Mick was no different. He was wearing rhinestones, blue eye shadow, and platform shoes." Why the offstage getup? Starr asked. "Because," Mick answered, "I have a lot of respect for David Bowie."

Keith Richards, for one, was mystified by his friend's apparent obsession with Bowie. "The fact is," Keith said, "Mick could deliver ten times more than Bowie in just a T-shirt and a pair of jeans. Why would you want to be anything else if you're Mick Jagger?"

Angie Bowie also looked askance at the blossoming relationship between Mick and David, but for very different reasons. She thought her husband had nothing to gain from cozying up to Jagger, and that such a friendship might even cost him credibility with his hip, young fan base. Bowie, who called Jagger Mike—never Mick—thought differently. Not only was he in awe of Mick's ability to electrify audiences year after year, but he also respected the veteran rocker's songwriting talent and business savvy. "He thought Mick was a financial genius," Angie said. "We all did."

Bowie and Jagger were soon spotted everywhere together without their wives: sitting ringside at the Muhammad Ali–Ken Norton bout, hanging out at the London disco Tramp, yelling and stomping their approval at a Diana Ross concert, or just cuddling up together on a hotel room couch. Neither superstar complained when one enterprising photographer snapped the two men in a moment of repose, Bowie tenderly cradling Mick's head in his lap. Bowie also took Mick to gay films. "David," said British TV producer Kevin Kahn, "is a born proselytizer."

By October 1973 the Bowies were living on Oakley Street, just a stroll from Cheyne Walk. Angie had been out of town for a few days when she returned home one morning and went straight to the kitchen to make some tea. The Bowies' maid, who had arrived about an hour earlier, approached the lady of the house with a peculiar look on her face. "Someone," she told Angie, "is in your bed."

Angie went upstairs to her bedroom, slowly pushed the door open, and there they were: Mick Jagger and David Bowie, naked in bed together, sleeping. Both men woke up with a start. "Oh, hello," said Bowie, clearly taken by surprise. "How are you?"

"I'm fine," Angie replied. "Do you want some tea?" Mick, blinking awake, remained silent. Angie returned a few minutes later with tea and orange juice on a tray. While it was not a case of catching them *in flagrante,* Angie "felt absolutely dead certain that they'd been screwing. It was so obvious, in fact, that I never even considered the possibility that they *hadn't* been screwing."

Angie was upset at the time, unsure if David was serious about Mick—and, if he was, how she could ever compete with him. "Even though I cared," she said, "there wasn't much I was going to do about it . . . Maybe," she tried to joke later, "they were writing 'Angie' when I caught them in bed together." She left to do some errands, and when she returned that afternoon, Mick had already left.

Oddly enough, while she attempted to discourage David from having an affair with Mick, Angie herself was vying for Jagger's attention. "I wish it had been me with Mick," she said. "I've always thought Mick must be a wild man in bed. He is a very sexy guy." In truth, she had her chance and blew it. When he did try to seduce her, Angie inexplicably "could not stop giggling." Mick's former love Marianne Faithfull had no such difficulty: she and Bowie carried on an affair in late 1973, arguably when his relationship with Mick was at its most intense.

Indeed, none of these dalliances seemed to have an effect on the feelings Bowie and Jagger had for each other. Ava Cherry, a black backup singer who lived with the Bowies for a time, reportedly told a friend that "Mick and David were really sexually obsessed with each other. Even though I was in bed with them many times, I ended up just watching them have sex." According to Cherry, the relationship was more than just sexual. The two men became "very close" emotionally and "practically lived together for several months." Shrugged Leee Childers: "Everyone knew what was going on between them. It wasn't something either one of them was trying to hide."

LA disc jockey and music industry insider Rodney Bingenheimer scoffed at later attempts to downplay the relationship between Jagger and Bowie. "Mick and David were lovers, of course," he said. "They didn't exactly make a secret of it."

Jagger and his pansexual pals—particularly Bowie and Nureyev—found a kindred spirit in Andy Warhol. Like Mick, described by his longtime friend Liz Derringer (the then-wife of rocker Rick Derringer) as "chatty, bitchy . . . a real girl's guy," Andy thrived on gossip. One of Jagger's and Warhol's favorite pastimes was sizing up other celebrities and rating their sex appeal. "Mick was always pointing out cute men," said Warhol confidante Christopher Makos. "He would say to me, 'Wow, look at that good-looking guy over there.' But I really think he was more heterosexual than bi."

Nevertheless, Makos and others in Andy's circles believed that Jagger and Warhol were involved as well. Mick would "get drunk and dance with Andy at Max's Kansas City," Makos said. "Andy claimed that he had slept with Mick. He told me that several times, and I believed him." Adding to Jagger's bisexual credentials were his Andy Warhol phallus paintings: graphic depictions of male genitalia by the artist, for which Jagger paid thousands. Over the years, these would go on and off the walls of Jagger's homes, depending on who was visiting.

Perhaps no one was in a better position to assay the relationship between Bowie and Jagger than Bebe Buell, the tall, stunning *Playboy* centerfold who conducted affairs with both men that lasted several years. She didn't stop there. Over time, Buell's amorous escapades involved Elvis Costello, Rod Stewart, Jimmy Page, Aerosmith's Steve Tyler, Todd Rundgren, and Prince. (She claimed that Prince wrote the song "Little Red Corvette" about her.)

Buell was just eighteen and dating Rundgren, whose biggest hits were "Hello It's Me" and "I Saw the Light," when she caught Bowie's eye at the club Max's Kansas City in New York in 1973. David quickly seduced her. Not long after, she met Mick at an Eric Clapton concert. At the postshow party, Mick seemed to be reconnecting with his old friend Clapton while at the same time doing his best to lure Buell into bed. "He was flirting outrageously," she recalled. "He kept coming over and telling me to ditch Todd."

Rundgren "hit the roof" when he watched Jagger follow his girlfriend into the kitchen. "We're going home *now,*" Rundgren told Buell, and on the way home, he gave her a stern lecture about "guys like Warren Beatty and Mick Jagger."

Eventually Mick talked her into joining him for dinner. "Here is a man who can go slumming downtown with the gutter pigs and have high tea with Baron so-and-so," she said after he introduced her to her first taste of sushi. "Mick is very versatile, very multifaceted. I was impressed."

Finally, he convinced her to join him at his suite at New York's Plaza Hotel. Mick wasted no time stripping off his clothes and climbing into bed. "I was very, very shocked by his smallness, his fragility," she recalled. "Such tiny little bones. But Mick was not fragile or demure as a lover. Being with him was not like sleeping with a bag of bones. He was very aggressive as a lover, very strong and confident." As for the part of Jagger's anatomy Keith would later describe as his "tiny todger," Buell was more charitable. "I'd say he was more than adequate in that department."

Once Bowie and Jagger realized that they were both carrying on affairs with Buell ("*Nobody* was monogamous. Everybody was sleeping with everybody," she said), the two stars teamed up to lure her into an orgy or two. "I used to get some pretty strange phone calls from Mick and David at three in the morning," she said, "inviting me to join them in bed with four gorgeous black women." Or, she added, "four gorgeous black men."

"Sexually, Mick pushes himself to the limits—sampling all colors, all classes," Buell concluded. "He loves blondes. He loves blacks. He loves Indians, Latins, and Asians. There is no stopping him."

Still, in the end, Buell insists that their relationship had less to do with sex than it did with romance. Mick showered her with expensive gifts and thought nothing of flying her in on his private jet so that they could have a quiet candlelit dinner for two. As with all the other women in his life, Buell had to live up to Mick's high standards. "He demanded a certain chic of his women," she said. Before each date, he had to look Buell over. "If he didn't like what I was wearing, he would send me back to put on another outfit." Buell implied that Mick was also something of a shoe fetishist; he often showed up for dates with a shoe box under his arm. Inside was always "the perfect pump, the perfect stiletto, the perfect pair of platform heels."

Mick was also an expert, as one could easily imagine, on makeup and skin care. "Mick's a genius with skin. He told me how to steam my face, what herbs to use," Buell said. "No woman on earth knows more about cosmetics than Mick."

Despite all the cheating with a cavalcade of women and men, Mick remained emotionally attached to only one person: Bianca. "He loved her so much more than he admitted," said Buell, who called Jagger a "traditional Englishman" in the sense that he felt his wife should stay home with the kids while he did what he wanted. "Mick was madly, passionately in love with Bianca," Liz Derringer agreed. "We all thought he loved her and she didn't love him."

Once the prototypical jealous wife, by this point Bianca was plainly no longer interested in staking her claim to Mick's affections. She began treating her husband's lovers not only with respect but also with a curious affection. She called Buell, who at five feet eleven towered over both Jaggers, "Mick's little friend."

"Bianca was very sweet to me," remembered Buell, who said that Mick's wife always complimented her on her hairstyle or what she was wearing. "She tried to make you feel like a million bucks." Buell also felt that Mrs. Jagger was trying to send her husband a message. "She would clutch my hand and ask me to sit next to her at parties"—Bianca's way, Buell surmised, of telling Mick that she simply no longer cared what he did.

He cared deeply, however, when Bianca turned the tables. Suddenly her name was being linked in the papers with, among others, actors Helmut Berger, Elliott Gould, and Ryan O'Neal. Mick was especially incensed by Bianca's on-again, off-again romance with O'Neal, which began in 1974 while he was filming director Stanley Kubrick's *Barry Lyndon* and stretched over several years. In O'Neal, Jagger recognized a worthy adversary. Long before falling for actress and original *Charlie's Angel* Farrah Fawcett, the young star of *Love Story* had had well-publicized affairs with actresses Joan Collins, Anouk Aimée, and Ursula Andress, as well as Barbra Streisand and Diana Ross—just to name a few.

Their marriage would technically drag on for another five years, although Mick would later pinpoint its end as 1973, the year they separated. It remained for Bianca to fire the first salvo in their divorce wars, with an offhand comment in *Viva* magazine. "If someone I care for lies to me, I can't forgive lies," she said. "Lies are offensive to the intelligence." Showing more vulnerability than she ever had in public, Bianca speculated that "perhaps Mick isn't attracted to me anymore. When I first met him, I knew who he was. But I don't know now."

Mick wasted no time firing back. "I've never been madly, deeply in love in my life," he confessed blithely. "I'm not a very emotional person." And, he added defiantly, "I'm not the least bit domesticated."

Mick took another swipe at his wife in the title track for his next album. For years, Bianca had been pressuring Jagger to move on to more "adult" pursuits such as acting or even politics. He answered her by writing, in the LP's title track and first single, "I know it's only rock 'n roll / But I *like* it!"

Since the Stones were prohibited from staying in either the States or the United Kingdom for more than ninety days without paying income tax, they recorded the new album in Munich. To add insult to injury, Mick barred Bianca from the studio, but he called in his other love interest, David Bowie, to sing background vocals on "It's Only Rock 'n Roll (But I Like It)." Hyped by a Michael Lindsay-Hogg–directed pre-MTV video of the Stones cavorting in sailor suits before being engulfed in a sea of soap suds, the album soared to number one.

Mick returned the favor when he showed up to cheer on his friend at the opening of Bowie's spellbinding Diamond Dogs show at Madison Square Garden in July 1974. Although Bianca was a no-show, Angie Bowie and Nureyev mingled with Mick and other guests during the after-party at the Plaza Hotel. Everyone took notice when Mick, Bowie, and Bette Midler locked themselves in a bedroom closet. They stayed inside for over an hour, during which, according to other guests, they did little to disguise what sounded like a spirited ménage à trois. "It was pretty obvious," recalled one record executive. "There was moaning and moving about. Naughty giggles, too." When the trio emerged, they were "a tad disheveled, but all smiles."

Not everyone was enjoying life at the top. In mid-December, just one day before he was to join his fellow Stones in Munich to begin work on the group's *Black and Blue* album, Mick Taylor called it quits. Once a nonsmoking teetotaler, Taylor had developed such a serious cocaine problem that he'd burned a hole in his septum. Now that he was using heroin, Taylor felt he had to bail out of the Stones—or risk the same fate as the seemingly hopelessly addicted Richards and Pallenberg.

After a Scarlett O'Hara–like talent search for Taylor's replacement, Jagger was about to give the job to Alabama-born session musician Wayne Perkins when someone mentioned that Rod Stewart's group the Faces might be on the verge of breaking up. Mick had long admired the Faces' gaunt, raven-haired lead guitarist Ron Wood, and jumped at the chance to hire him to tour with the Stones in 1975.

Wood, who accepted Mick's offer even though he also remained with the Faces until the group dissolved a year later, was in Munich recording with the rest of the Stones when word came that police had raided his mansion in the tony London suburb of Richmond looking for drugs. What they found was Wood's then wife, Krissy, in bed with another woman. The subsequent scandalous headlines only confirmed Jagger's conviction that he had made the right choice.

Just before the Stones embarked on their most ambitious tour ever—twenty-nine western hemisphere cities followed by the Middle East and Asia—Mick was leaving a restaurant when he mistook a plate glass window for a revolving door and wound up with a seven-inch-long gash running up his arm. Photographer Annie Leibovitz, who was assigned to cover the tour for *Rolling Stone,* convinced him to let her shoot the gory wound—which he agreed to only if it were in color.

By the end of three months on the road with the Stones, Leibovitz was shaken by what she had witnessed—and the life she got sucked into. "People always talk about the soul of the sitter," said

Leibovitz, who became seriously addicted to drugs and eventually went into rehab. "But the photographer has a soul, too. And I almost lost it."

Once again, the show was an over-the-top spectacle designed to shock. At the start of each show, the stage—a giant metal "flower" with bulletproof petals—opened to reveal the band inside. Mick, more dolled up than ever, seemed determined to out-camp Bowie. In singer-keyboardist Billy Preston, he had a willing accomplice. The two men grabbed each other by the hips and ground their pelvises together suggestively.

The show's most visually striking moment came when a forty-foot-long inflatable phallus unfurled from the back of the stage. Mick climbed aboard and then stroked it as he belted out his X-rated ode to groupies, "Star Star." (Since the song's lyrics mention Steve McQueen receiving oral sex, Jagger was required to obtain a signed release from the actor himself. McQueen happily obliged. The song's title, before the record company forced Mick to change it, was "Starfucker.")

"Kevin" is the alias of a New York fashion designer who was a Stones groupie in the 1970s. He recalled that Mick was a regular at Manhattan's gay nightclubs, including the 82 Club, Les Mouches, the Gilded Grape, and Galaxy 21 on West Twenty-third Street, where gay porn films were shown in the pillow room. At the Gilded Grape, Kevin remembered watching David and Angie Bowie, Mick, and Queen's bisexual lead singer Freddie Mercury "whooping it up with a bunch of transvestites."

Returning to the Plaza Hotel late one night, a seriously stoned Mick spotted Kevin in the lobby and invited him upstairs for a drink. Once upstairs, Jagger began quizzing the skinny twenty-year-old, who was wearing "seventy percent" women's clothing, about his wardrobe.

1

Notwithstanding his ersatz
cockney accent, Michael Philip
Jagger (shown right at age two)
grew up solidly middle class in the
London suburb of Dartford and
was even captain of the Dartford
Grammar School basketball team.
Jagger (standing at right) bit off
the tip of his tongue during a
game, changing his speech forever.

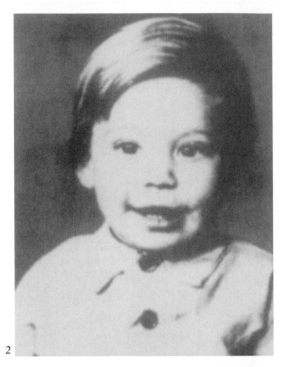

2

3

4

Mick and Keith—the Glimmer Twins—destined to spend the next half century locked in a volatile love-hate relationship that even their wives described as "a marriage."

The original, nonthreatening Rolling Stones. Back row, from left: Bill Wyman, Charlie Watts, Ian Stewart. Front row: Brian Jones, Mick, and a surprisingly nerdy Keith Richards. Stewart, whose stalwart look was deemed unsuitable, was soon shoved into the background.

6

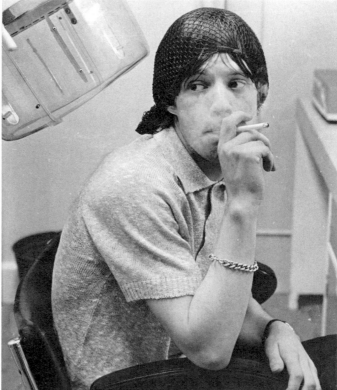

Mobbed by fans at London's Heathrow Airport, Mick was a star on both sides of the Atlantic even before the Stones first set foot on American soil in 1964. An expert on cosmetics, hair care, and fashion since childhood (Mick's mum was an Avon lady in postwar Britain), Mick primps in the dressing room before a Stones concert.

7

Mick and Marianne Faithfull in 1967, before her abrupt slide into heroin addiction. This photograph of Mick being whisked off to jail in handcuffs following the scandalous Redlands drug trial ignited an international outcry.

In *Performance,* Jagger shared a bath with actress Michele Breton
and Keith's then love Anita Pallenberg. Jagger's offscreen affair with
Pallenberg enraged Richards. Mick and Marianne (below) were back in
court on drug charges in the summer of 1969, just seven months after
she miscarried their baby.

Just two days after Brian Jones's mysterious death in July 1969, Mick, wearing his "party dress," performed with the other surviving Stones at a free Hyde Park memorial concert that drew a crowd of more than 250,000. Five months later, nearly twice as many fans showed up at Altamont (below)—a dark and bloody spectacle chronicled in the documentary *Gimme Shelter.*

12

13

"You look *ravishing*," Mick told Kevin. "Where did you get those shoes? Where did you get that shirt?"

After he'd picked the young fan's brain ("He was superobsessed with appearance, with style. He was like a sponge"), the two started kissing and eventually wound up in bed. "Mick took the active role sexually. Basically he overpowered me in bed."

After they woke up, Mick ordered up room service, and the two lay naked in bed eating from silver trays while, Kevin recalled, "people knocked on the door all morning long." Whenever they bumped into each other after that encounter, Jagger "just stared blankly," Kevin said. "Mick always pretended not to notice me."

Jade was beginning to feel unnoticed by her parents. Mick and Bianca had both made it clear that they had lives of their own, which meant that their child would be left for long stretches of time in the care of nannies and housekeepers.

In the beginning, their mutual love of Jade held Mick and Bianca together as a couple. Mick was still willing to carry on the sham of a loveless marriage if it meant sparing their daughter the trauma of divorce. For a time, the two of them struggled to keep up the charade. Every summer, they spent time together as a family at the oceanside retreat in Montauk, Long Island, that they rented from Andy Warhol.

Situated at the easternmost tip of the island, Montauk was, unlike the socially souped-up Hamptons, a sleepy fishing village devoid of trendy restaurants, shops, or clubs. The Jaggers made do by flying in friends like Clapton, Bowie, John Lennon and Yoko Ono, John Phillips of The Mamas and the Papas, Jack Nicholson, and Warren Beatty—and turning Andy's charming shingled "cottage" into a pulsating beachfront nightspot. Their neighbor Dick Cavett remembered how, aside from the noise, he knew when the Jaggers were in residence from the haze of pot smoke that settled over that end of the island. "Sometimes," Cavett said, "it smelled like a brushfire in Sonora over there."

Cavett discovered quickly that Mick's circle of friends was not confined to drug-abusing rock stars and womanizing Hollywood actors. The talk show host was riding his horse along the beach when a dark-haired woman walked out of the Jaggers' house and asked him to stop.

"As she came closer," Cavett said, "I realized it was Jacqueline Onassis." Jackie, an accomplished horsewoman in her own right, walked around his horse and checked it out before returning to Jagger's compound.

Among those who witnessed the interaction between Mick and Jackie, there was the inevitable speculation that theirs might be more than just a casual friendship. According to Cavett, Jackie was certainly "intrigued" by Mick, and "of course Mick was sort of in awe of Jackie, like everybody else."

Jackie's interest in Mick was, in fact, more than just social. In her role as an editor, first at Viking Press and then at Doubleday, the most famous woman in the world actively courted celebrities in hopes of snagging their memoirs. Over the years, she would aggressively pursue her old friend Frank Sinatra, Marlon Brando, Michael Jackson, Princess Diana, the Duchess of Windsor, Elizabeth Taylor, and Queen Elizabeth.

Jagger was no exception. When she failed to convince him to write his autobiography for Viking, Jackie asked Mick to intercede with another famous person she'd been trying to land: his good friend Princess Margaret. "Jackie could be very flirtatious and very coy when she wanted to be," said Kennedy confidante and former presidential press secretary Pierre Salinger. "It's not hard to imagine her working her magic on Mick Jagger."

After JFK's assassination and the death of her second husband,

Aristotle Onassis, in March 1975, Jackie gravitated toward younger men like journalist Pete Hamill and documentary filmmaker Peter Davis. "There was a period when she seemed to be interested in men who were a little younger, more exciting," Salinger observed. "But Jackie had incredibly high standards. Jagger is the biggest rock star in the world, a huge sex symbol. He is also a very bright, very sophisticated, very worldly guy." He also, Salinger said, "had a lot in common with Jack Kennedy when it came to women, apparently."

The Jackie-Jagger flirtation was apparently short-lived. So, too, was the strange exchange between Bianca and the son of a sitting American president. That spring Bianca, who had begun contributing pieces to Warhol's glitzy celebrity journal *Interview,* managed to land Jack Ford, the twenty-three-year-old son of then president Gerald R. Ford.

Their interview took place inside the White House, and soon photographs taken by Andy Warhol of Jack Ford with his arm around Bianca in the Lincoln Bedroom triggered the usual round of newspaper stories speculating on the nature of the relationship. Adding fuel to the fire was Jack's claim that, as a young man craving a normal life, he felt trapped inside the executive mansion and would trade his life with anyone else's "for a penny." In order to expose Jack to a world he might never have seen otherwise, Bianca and Andy took him to Manhattan's legendary nightclub El Morocco and the gay disco Le Jardin.

When it came to pure, unadulterated decadence, nothing compared to the Jaggers' home away from home: Studio 54. Dubbed "the New Oz" by the *New York Times,* Manhattan's Studio 54 was the pulsating epicenter of the celebrity universe—a place where the famous, the notorious, and the just plain curious mingled, drank, danced, and made love in the shadows. Many of them also consumed copious amounts of drugs—a fact the club itself scarcely tried to conceal. Throughout the course of any given evening, the crowd roared its approval as a neon man in the moon swung down from the ceiling and snorted coke from a glowing spoon.

By the midseventies, Bianca was on the short list of the world's most glamorous women. She was not about to let down her public. Studio 54 had been open only a few days when, at a thirtieth birthday party thrown in her honor, Bianca made her club debut astride a white stallion. To make her entrance even more memorable, the horse was preceded by a six-foot-five-inch-tall black man whose evening attire consisted of nothing but gold glitter.

When it came to over-the-top spectacle, club owners Steve Rubell and Ian Schrager credited Bianca with setting the bar high. In 1980, at the premiere party for the film *Raging Bull,* near-naked trapeze artists swung overhead, while at a bash for wildlife photographer Peter Beard, an African elephant almost managed to upstage guests Jackie Onassis, Elizabeth Taylor, and Elton John.

Even in this environment, Bianca and Mick operated independently. Whenever he dropped into the club, Mick invariably headed straight for the VIPs-only basement room. Bianca preferred to survey her domain from a steel catwalk that dangled high above the club's enormous banquette-lined dance floor.

In what would become a fairly typical scene, both Jaggers attended a party for Elizabeth Taylor. Each entered through separate doors with their respective entourages and, in the crush of bodies, managed to avoid making contact altogether. "She was definitely the queen at Studio 54," a mutual friend said of the competition between Bianca and her husband, "and Mick resented being upstaged."

Outside of the Studio 54 cocoon, upstaging Mick was something that was virtually impossible to do, although there were certainly times when Mick craved a little anonymity. That was certainly the case when, just minutes before the Stones were to perform in Paris, a jealous boyfriend threatened Mick with a loaded pistol. Security managed to subdue the would-be assailant, and the show went on as planned.

As for Jade, with her mother reigning over New York's nightlife and Dad on the road earning millions, it was difficult to see where the girl fit into the Jagger family equation. She was occasionally left in the care of her Jagger grandparents at their home in Kent. For the most part, however, she was looked after by nannies in New York or London.

Those times when she was around both parents, they often quarreled bitterly—with Jade caught in the crossfire. Still, those who came in contact with the Jaggers' pretty, chestnut-maned daughter found her charming, if a tad precocious.

Warhol was a particular favorite of Jade's—and vice versa. "Jade's more my speed," Andy allowed. "I taught her how to color, and she taught me how to play Monopoly. She was four, and I was forty-four." Two years later, when Andy and a friend dropped by and asked for two vodkas on the rocks, Jade called for the Spanish-speaking maid and ordered up *"dos vodkas con hielo."*

For the only child of one of the world's most famous and volatile couples, the psychological pressures were incalculable. Although adult friends of the couple such as Dick Cavett, Halston, and Warhol continued to be charmed by the littlest Jagger, Jade was far from perfect.

When Mick took her to an Easter egg hunt in the home of a wealthy British socialite, Jade quickly grabbed most of the eggs and promptly smashed them on the parquet floor. At the Garden House School, which she attended whenever her parents were in residence in London, Jade frequently disrupted class, in what her teachers saw as an obvious cry for attention.

Mick doted on Jade when he was with her, but those moments

were increasingly rare. And Jagger never failed to find time for his favorite pursuits. While weighing film offers—among the many he turned down was the lead opposite Barbra Streisand in a remake of *A Star Is Born* (the role went to Kris Kristofferson)—Mick joined John Lennon and Keith Moon for a game of pool with veteran Hollywood actor Peter Lawford. A fellow British expatriate, Lawford doled out copious amounts of cocaine to his famous guests. Lawford's widow, Patricia Seaton, was amazed at how well all four men seemed to tolerate the drug. "It was remarkable to watch these great stars," she said, "shooting pool while high on cocaine."

There was an added treat for Mick that evening. JFK in-law Peter Lawford invited a stoned Jagger to sit in one of the late president's favorite rocking chairs. "Mick just sat there cross-legged in Kennedy's rocking chair," Lawford's wife said, "loving every minute of it."

If anything, things got even more out of hand during the Stones' 1976 European tour. Writer Nick Kent, who traveled with the group, recalled that "Jagger, Wood, and Richards were all going off and doing vast amounts of drugs . . . it was really just incredible."

Real life intruded occasionally. The Stones were about to go onstage at Les Abattoirs in Paris when the call came that Keith's two-month-old son Tara—named after the doomed Guinness heir Tara Browne—had died, presumably of sudden infant death syndrome. Richards had decided to bring his seven-year-old son Marlon on the road with him and leave his two younger children—four-year-old Angela and Tara—home with their mother, Anita Pallenberg. In the wake of Tara's death, Marlon took on the heavy burden of essentially babysitting his heroin-dependent dad. But there was nothing that he—or for that matter, Mick—could do to prevent Keith from sinking even deeper into the abyss.

Grief quickly turned to rage. While Jagger was photographed frolicking with the glitterati in New York and Los Angeles, Richards—the original punk rocker—seethed over what he saw as Mick's unseemly social posturing. Keith told anyone who would listen that his fellow Stone was a sellout, and went about proving his own commitment to the cause by starting bar fights, taunting the police, squabbling with the vexsome Pallenberg, and passing out behind the wheel of his Bentley.

If the amount of drugs being consumed defied belief, so did Mick's stamina. That August, the Stones gave their first free concert since Altamont, this time at Knebworth House in Hertfordshire. The band Utopia was also on the bill, and once again its leader, Todd Rundgren, brought along his girlfriend, the indefatigable Bebe Buell.

While Bianca watched from the wings, Mick flirted outrageously with Buell. "Todd was frustrated and angry," Bebe recalled. "Then Mick started playing his favorite game: 'I'm going to steal you from the rock star you're already with.'"

"I'm a bigger star than you are, Todd," Mick told Rundgren. "I'll nab her."

Unbeknownst to Jagger and Rundgren, Buell had already been "nabbed" by someone else—Jagger lookalike Steve Tyler, Aerosmith's scrawny, lush-lipped lead singer. Buell and Tyler had managed to keep their affair under wraps. But when Bebe confided to Mick that she was cheating on Rundgren with the front man for one of rock's wildest groups, Jagger was even more determined to get her into bed. "It was just twice as enticing for Mick," she said. "He'd be stealing me away from not one but *two* big rock stars."

Pointing out that Tyler was often described in the press as the poor man's Jagger, Mick offered an argument that was as predictable as it was compelling: "Why go with him," Jagger asked, "when you can have the real thing?"

By the time Buell became pregnant that autumn, Mick had forgotten about her affair with Tyler and believed that the baby was either his or Rundgren's. Buell's daughter, Liv, was born on July 1, 1977, and the next day, Mick called. "I'm coming over to see *my* child," he told Bebe. Within hours, Mick and Ron Wood were at Buell's side—the first to visit mother and child.

Since Steve Tyler was battling heroin addiction, both he and Buell agreed that it was in Liv's best interest for her to be raised as the child of Todd Rundgren. Since not even industry insiders were aware of Buell's clandestine affair with Tyler, "most people," Bebe said, "thought she was Mick's baby." It was a role Mick seemed perfectly willing to play. For years, he would introduce Buell to friends as "the mother of one of my illegitimate children."

Liv, raised as the daughter of Todd Rundgren, was eight years old before she finally got the truth out of her mother. It would be several more years before Buell went public with the fact that Steve Tyler was Liv's dad. "I think part of Mick was a little jealous," Bebe said. "There were a lot of shocked people when it turned out that neither Todd nor Mick was the father, but Steve Tyler." Mick was certainly one of them. Liv Tyler became a top teen cover girl, then went on to achieve the film stardom that eluded Mick.

As 1976 wound to a close, the Jaggers refused to acknowledge that divorce was inevitable. They moved into a stately townhouse on New York's East Seventy-third Street and celebrated Christmas by proclaiming that their union was stronger than ever. "We have no intention of splitting up," Mick insisted.

As long as Bianca—who was now rumored falsely to be seeing Warren Beatty—felt unthreatened by the women Mick slept with, it seemed entirely possible that their marriage might survive. "Mick screws many," she acknowledged publicly, "but has few affairs."

One of the new women in Mick's life who did give Bianca some cause for concern was a rock star famous for her many and varied liaisons. Linda Ronstadt already had a half dozen platinum albums and a string of hits such as "You're No Good," "When Will I Be Loved," "Long Long Time," "Tracks of My Tears," and "Blue Bayou" to her credit when she and Mick got together in the late 1970s. She was also known for the men in her life: rocker Jackson Browne, singer-songwriter J. D. Souther, comedians Steve Martin and Albert Brooks, Pete Hamill, and then-and-future California governor Jerry Brown, to name just a few. Ronstadt didn't regard her romantic life as anything out of the ordinary. "I wish I had as much in bed," she claimed, "as I get in the newspapers."

With Mick's help, Ronstadt, who had a difficult time mastering the lyrics to "Tumbling Dice," recorded her own version of the song. Her countrified take was one of the rare covers of a Stones tune ever to make it into the Top Ten.

It was only a matter of time before Bianca learned that her husband was spending quality time with Ronstadt at the singer's oceanfront home. Although she flew straight to California and confronted Mick—effectively bringing an end to the affair—Bianca admitted that she actually liked Ronstadt; the only woman she really felt threatened by was still Carly Simon.

There was someone on the horizon who would make Bianca forget all about Simon. But in the interim, Mick's wife simply shrugged off the gossip about the women who moved in and quickly out of Jagger's life. Among these were the exotic model Apollonia van Ravenstein ("Apples" to Mick), British actress Carinthia West (daughter of NATO general Sir Michael West), and his old flame Sabrina Guinness.

It had been nearly six months since all five Stones had been together in the same room—until now, their longest stretch apart. Determined to escape the media glare and get back to work, they agreed to record parts of their upcoming *Love You Live* album before an audience at the El Mocambo club in Toronto.

On February 20, 1977, Mick arrived in Toronto to find all hands accounted for—save one. Keith, strung out on cocaine and heroin, had yet to leave London. After five days of frantic phone calls and telegrams ("WHERE ARE YOU? Mick"), Richards finally flew to Toronto—only to have customs officials seize a heroin-encrusted spoon from Anita's luggage. Three days later, police busted Keith at his Harbour Castle Hilton suite. This time Mounties found over an ounce of heroin, enough to warrant a charge of possession with intent to traffic. Richards now faced the possibility of a life sentence—a likely deathblow for the Stones. Undaunted, Keith was released on bail and went straight to the El Mocambo, where, Mick said, "he played his fucking heart out—better than I'd heard in years."

All hopes of containing the scandal went up in smoke when, at this delicate moment in the Stones' history, Margaret Trudeau decided to escape the pressures of being Canada's first lady by hanging out with the band. At twenty-nine, the wistfully beautiful "Maggie" Trudeau was twenty-nine years younger than her husband, flamboyant Canadian prime minister Pierre Trudeau. With her husband and their three young children waiting at home in Ottawa, Maggie's abrupt decision to spend time with the notorious bad boys of rock made international headlines for months. It also threatened to bring down Trudeau's fragile government.

Mrs. Trudeau took a room next to Ronnie Wood's at the Harbour Castle, and Mick escorted her each night to the El Mocambo. For several days, she reportedly wandered the Harbour Castle hallways in her hotel bathrobe, popping in and out of Mick's suite. When it was time for the Stones to decamp for the United States, Maggie canceled her official schedule and joined them. On the Trudeaus' sixth wedding anniversary, the prime minister seethed while his flighty young wife partied with the Stones in New York.

Mick would later deny that he'd ever had an affair with Maggie Trudeau. "I wouldn't touch her with a barge pole," he insisted. "She was just a very sick girl in search of something. She found it—but not with me." She found it with Ronnie Wood, who conceded that he and Canada's runaway first lady "shared something special for that short time." Richards's take on the entire affair was less charitable: "She was a groupie, that's all she was, pure and simple."

Bianca agreed. "It's very strange, the mystique of women feeling they've made it if they've slept with Mick," she observed. "It shows such a lack of respect for themselves. He finds it repugnant."

So many classically beautiful, witty, and refined young women floated in and out of Mick's life that Bianca was scarcely intimidated by the horsey, blonde, six-foot-tall Texas model whose name began popping up in gossip columns alongside her husband's.

Jerry Fay Hall grew up the youngest (with her twin Terry) of a truck driver's five girls in Mesquite, just outside Dallas. Nicknamed "Tall Hall" by her classmates, the gawky teenager never dated in high school but made the decision at fifteen to lose her virginity. While working at the local Dairy Queen, Jerry and a girlfriend asked the town's champion bull rider if he would do the job. He obliged ("in the hayloft, in the rain"), never bothering to take off his boots.

Hall was injured in a car accident the following year, and she used the insurance money to pay for rhinoplasty and a plane ticket to Paris. Soon she and her pal, the Amazonian singer and actress Grace Jones, were performing a raunchy cabaret act at private parties. An early fan: the Shah of Iran, who was so taken by the lanky Texan with the down-home drawl that he flew her to Tehran and entertained her at his palace.

Hall soon moved in with fashion illustrator Antonio Lopez, and was an established model by the time that Bryan Ferry of the rock group Roxy Music spotted her on the cover of Italian *Vogue* in 1975.

Six months later, they were engaged.

Unfortunately for the debonair Ferry, they were in no rush and postponed the wedding for over a year. It was while Ferry was touring Japan in early 1977 that Jerry was seated at a dinner party between Mick and his frequent love rival Warren Beatty. Driven by the obsessive desire to abscond with yet another rock star's woman, Mick soon tired of competing with Beatty for Hall's attention. He called another model, arranged for Beatty to meet up with her, and then took off with Hall for Studio 54.

It was just after four o'clock in the morning when Jagger offered to give Hall a ride home. Instead she found herself with Mick at the Jaggers' East Seventy-third Street townhouse. "The next morning," Jerry recalled, "I was thinking, 'Oh no, what have I done?'"

Ferry was understandably livid, and he knew just how to exact sweet revenge on his high-fashion ex. Instead of removing Hall's clothes from the London home they shared and shipping them to her in New York, Ferry simply kept them.

Hall had plenty of notions about how to hold on to a man, and fashion had nothing to do with it. "There are three secrets that my mother taught me," she said. "Be a maid in the living room, a cook in the kitchen—and a whore in the bedroom. So long as I have a maid and a cook, I'll do the rest myself." Her most treasured piece of advice did not come from Mom: "Even if you have only two seconds, drop everything and give him a blow job. That way he won't really want sex with anyone else."

If another girl got too close to her man for comfort, Hall let her know it. Even at the most elegant affairs, she was not above jabbing, poking, or even kicking other women until they finally backed off.

One of Hall's most formidable rivals during this period was

another tall, outspoken model named Janice Dickinson. "There were fifty thousand phone calls day and night," she recalled, "from places all around the globe. He became obsessed with me. He was filling my room with pink roses and signing the note 'Love, Prince Philip.'" It was then that Mick used one of his tried-and-true lines: "Will you have my baby?"

"How seductive is that?" Dickinson asked. "But it was never going to happen. However, Mick Jagger is the best of the best of the best of lovers bar none." Less charming, perhaps, was Mick's post-coital behavior. After they made love for the first time, Jagger threw $400 on the bed and said, "There, buy yourself a new frock."

"Sex with Mick," Dickinson continued, "for me was like a boxing match. The ring was my queen-sized mattress. He'd flip me over and then I'd flip him over—which wasn't hard because he only came up to my shoulders if we were standing. In the throes of passion, I thought about my ideal man—who was not Mick Jagger. My dream was a Jewish Jim Morrison. Mick was more like the Dutch boy you see on paint cans. He wasn't at all my type. But then again, it didn't matter—because he was Mick Jagger."

Dickinson took issue with Mick's reputation for being a tightwad. For Christmas he gave her a heart-shaped ruby brooch with a diamond-encrusted arrow through it. "It was huge," she said, "as big as my fist, and it must have cost a fortune." She was dancing at Studio 54 two months later when she looked down and realized it was gone. "Oh, well," Mick replied when Janice told him she had lost the brooch, "girls will be girls."

Mick was less offhand about the other men in Dickinson's life, especially other rock stars. When he spotted a poster of Rod Stewart on the wall of her apartment, Mick asked Janice if she had slept with Stewart. She said no, but Jagger was not satisfied. "He just stood there," she recalled, "and ripped the poster off the wall."

At one point, Dickinson decided to try her hand at singing and landed a gig at Studio 54. Although Keith Richards and Ronnie Wood showed, Mick didn't. After Dickinson's singing debut was panned by critics the next day, Jerry called her. "Ha, ha, ha, I heard your show was a flop," she said. "Good. Now keep your hands off my man." Then Jerry warned her, "I've got a gun in my purse and know how to use it."

"I got the message," Janice said of the confrontation. "I kind of freaked out at that."

Not long after, Dickinson was talking to Mick on the phone when she could hear Jerry's voice in the background. "She wants me," Mick told Janice, "to break it up with you." Then he hung up.

Most of Mick's friends—particularly the British ones—were charmed by Hall's warmth, candor, and bombastic good humor. "She will magically lift everyone's spirits," said the Irish author and brewery heir Desmond Guinness, "just by walking into the room." Concurred Keith Altham: "Jerry is sweet, kind—and extremely patient."

Mick could also be patient, at least when it came to handling his Glimmer Twin. As Keith waited for his narcotics case to go to trial in Toronto, the guitarist was permitted to seek treatment in the States for his heroin addiction. While Keith and Anita received mild electroshock therapy in Philadelphia, Mick drove the tapes of the group's *Love You Live* concerts down from New York so that the two men could get to work.

Richards admitted later, "I have to say that during the drug bust in Toronto—in fact, during all busts—Mick looked after me with great sweetness, never complaining. He ran things; he did the work and marshaled the forces that saved me. Mick looked after me like a brother."

For the moment at least, the Glimmer Twins had managed to

put their differences behind them. Of course, that didn't keep Richards from needling Mick about his latest attempts to stay young-looking now that the years of partying and overwork were taking their toll. Jagger considered plastic surgery to smooth out his crow's feet and the deep grooves in his cheeks, but rejected that in favor of enhancing his famous smile with a bit of bling.

First he had a Cartier emerald placed in his upper right incisor, but Keith said that it looked like he had a piece of spinach stuck between his teeth. When Mick replaced the emerald with a ruby, Richards pointed out that it looked like a speck of blood. Jagger finally settled on a diamond. The folks at Cartier, he remarked, "were very nice about it."

That autumn of 1977, the Stones were back at the Pathé Marconi studios in Paris working on their next studio album, *Some Girls*. Facing the grim possibility that Keith might go to prison and the Rolling Stones might cease to exist, Mick poured his creative talents into the album as if it were the group's last.

"A lot of it was, 'We've got to outpunk the punks,'" said Richards, who like other established rock musicians may have felt somewhat threatened by such hard-edged pioneers of the punk rock movement as the Sex Pistols, the Clash, and the Ramones. With that in mind, Keith used his "little green box"—an MXR reverb-echo pedal—to give the cuts on *Some Girls* a ramped-up sound. But Mick, having been exposed for endless hours to the relentless "four-on-the-floor" dance beat at Studio 54, was determined to record a disco hit.

Upon its release the following year, *Some Girls* sold seven million copies and spawned several hit singles: "Beast of Burden," "Shattered," and the song that Richards at first described disparagingly as "Mick's disco shit": "Miss You." In fact, "Miss You"—inspired by Mick's Studio 54 nights with Jerry, not Bianca—would make it all the way to number one.

Mick returned to London for the holidays, but he didn't spend them with Bianca and Jade. Instead he and Jerry Hall checked into the Savoy Hotel on Christmas Eve and, three days later, jetted off to Barbados with the press in hot pursuit. On New Year's Eve, he hurled a beer bottle at one photographer; several days later in Paris, another scuffle with the paparazzi ended with Mick spread-eagle on the sidewalk.

By the time Mick returned to New York in March 1978, it was clear to everyone—including Bianca—that their marriage was over. Liz Derringer was visiting Mick and Jerry at their Carlyle Hotel suite when Jagger was served with divorce papers. Bianca was suing in London on grounds of adultery, naming Jerry as correspondent. "Can you believe she served *me*?" he asked Derringer. Then he added, apparently in all seriousness, "In all those years, have you ever seen me in the paper with another girl?"

Although Bianca had been strong-armed into signing a crude prenup right before her chaotic Saint-Tropez wedding, she was not about to walk away empty-handed. With California palimony pioneer Marvin Mitchelson and New York shark Roy Cohn as her lawyers (Cohn was best known as red-baiting Senator Joe McCarthy's chief counsel during the infamous 1954 Army-McCarthy hearings), Bianca tried to get the case moved to California, where community property would entitle her to $12.5 million—half of Mick's fortune.

Jagger responded with a flat offer of $100,000. In the meantime, he cut off Bianca's charge cards and moved her furniture out of 48 Cheyne Walk.

"Jagger is completely, totally ruthless," said Stones publicist Keith Altham. "He doesn't have much loyalty. People come and go swiftly, and are decimated." This applied to his treatment of longtime employees. "Mick is cowardly—he gets somebody else to fire you." Not even those who were instrumental in the Stones' success—like

Decca chairman Sir Edward Lewis—were immune. When Altham asked Mick for a public comment on Sir Edward's death, Mick said, "Tell them I said it was about time."

As the Stones dashed from one US stadium to another during the 1978 Some Girls summer tour, everyone went back to their on-the-road ways. "Drugs were always around," said Daniel Stewart, who was one of the supervisors of tour security. "There were literally mountains of dope, and Jagger wouldn't pass it up."

Nor would Keith, even though the Canadian drug charges still hung over his head. On October 24, 1978, Richards's case finally came to trial in Toronto. Just like a decade before when Keith was hauled up on drug charges alongside Jagger in the wake of the infamous Redlands bust, hundreds of fans stood outside the courthouse shouting, "Free Keith! Free Keith!" Inside, the judge made it clear that he was not going to send Keith to jail for "addiction and wealth." Instead, in exchange for pleading guilty, the trafficking charges were dropped and Keith was sentenced to a year's probation. Inspired by a blind fan named Rita who followed the band everywhere, Keith also agreed to give a concert for the Canadian National Institute for the Blind.

Mick breathed a sigh of relief. For the moment at least, the moneymaking machine known as the Rolling Stones would remain intact. He returned to New York and—usually with Hall but sometimes solo—hit the club scene with a vengeance.

"Wherever he went, women and men were still throwing themselves at him," Altham said. "Jerry was patient—to a point." It was easier for Mick to operate when Jerry was on a shoot at some exotic, faraway locale. But even when they were both checked into the Carlyle under the alias "Mr. and Mrs. Phillips," Mick could always find what he wanted at his old stomping ground, the Plaza.

Aware that Jagger could show up at any time, there were Stones groupies who knew how to circulate at the Plaza without being tossed out by hotel security. In late 1978, there was a new face in the crowd: a short, dark-haired, gum-snapping twenty-year-old who, like Kevin the New York fashion designer, had briefly been a junior dancer with the Alvin Ailey troupe.

The young woman with a fondness for animal prints and leggings was also very loud, and had no qualms about suddenly bursting into song. "I thought, Get me away from this obnoxious girl!" said Kevin. "She's blowing my cover!" He quickly determined that the only Stone this new groupie was interested in was Mick, and that she "thought he'd help her with her career."

For whatever reason, Mick was instantly taken with the brash newcomer and invited her upstairs on several occasions. "She was wild, and that appealed to him," Kevin said. Or maybe it was her name that caught his attention: Madonna.

Of course, no groupie appealed to Mick as much as the girlfriend of another rock star. Unless, perhaps, it was the teenage daughter of another rock star—Mick's longtime friend and Keith's fellow heroin addict John Phillips of The Mamas and the Papas.

"I grew up knowing Mick—from the time I was eight, he and Keith were always hanging out with Dad," said Phillips's daughter Mackenzie, who at sixteen would achieve fame in her own right as one of the stars of the hit TV sitcom *One Day at a Time*. "I was a child, but I was incredibly attracted to Mick. He was like a cat. He curled and moved and was so attractive and sensual."

Sadly, Phillips introduced his daughter to pot when she was ten, and cocaine four years later. He got her hooked on heroin by shooting her up himself when she was seventeen. Mackenzie later revealed that she and her father had a long-running incestuous relationship.

Given this grotesque family dynamic, what happened between Mick and Mackenzie in 1978 seemed only logical. At the time, John

Phillips lived on the same New York block as Mick, and Jerry was out of town on a modeling assignment. "We'd all been to a party, and Mick suggested we go back to his place for a tuna sandwich," said Mackenzie, who was eighteen at the time. When they arrived, Mick realized he didn't have any mayonnaise. "Dad said he thought we had some, so he went off—and then Mick flicked the lock on the door."

Mick swept Mackenzie up in his arms and led her toward the bedroom. "I've been waiting for this," he said, "since you were ten." A few minutes later, Phillips returned with the mayonnaise and, Mackenzie recalled, "started hammering on the door, but Mick and I were already in the bedroom. He was a fantastic lover, everything I'd imagined and more."

The next morning, Mick was serving Mackenzie tea, toast, and strawberries when the phone rang. "Have you got my daughter in there?" John Phillips asked.

"Yes," replied Mick, who a decade earlier had also slept with Michelle Phillips, John's second wife and Mackenzie's stepmother. "But I am treating her well."

Mackenzie would continue to hold a grudge against Keith for introducing her father to hard drugs, but she had nothing but warm feelings toward Mick. "Mick is many things," she said, "but he's not a pervert. When he said he'd been waiting for me, he meant he'd been waiting for me to be legal. He slept with me as a woman. And it was wonderful."

Mackenzie wasn't the only teenager in Mick's life around this time. He would soon begin spending time with Natasha Fraser, grandchild of Britain's Lord Longford and the daughter of bestselling author Lady Antonia Fraser. Far from being outraged, the family later invited Mick to attend the wedding of Lady Antonia and playwright Harold Pinter.

Mick's own daughter was not faring so well. Eighteen-year-old Karis Hunt was living in Los Angeles on welfare, and her mother had grown tired of pestering Mick for money. Borrowing a page from Bianca, Marsha Hunt hired Marvin Mitchelson and sued for a mere $2,190 in monthly child support payments.

Pointing out that Jagger had energy and money enough for other women "but none for his daughter," Hunt also wanted Mick to formally acknowledge paternity. "Mick's there every time you turn on the radio or see a magazine cover," Marsha said. "If Karis has to suffer that, I don't think she should also have to suffer being poverty stricken."

Jagger eventually relented, but only after Mitchelson got a court order blocking him from receiving his share of the proceeds from two concerts in Anaheim, California. Mick, forced to shell out less than $25,000 a year to support his eldest child, wasted no time in branding Marsha a "hustler" and a "lazy bitch."

Mick was more diplomatic about Bianca, but the sentiment was similar. Their divorce, like their marriage, was a three-ring media circus. Starting out in LA, where the judge claimed to have never heard of Mick Jagger ("I'm strictly a Lawrence Welk man"), the proceedings moved to London. There the case dragged on for months, until a property settlement was reached in a single eighteen-minute meeting. Bianca was awarded custody of Jade and $1.4 million. Eventually Bianca's lawyers convinced the UK courts to raise the figure to $2.5 million. "She just wanted the divorce to drag on so long so she could get her name in papers," Mick said. "She has been so difficult, that I'll never be friends with her again."

It would take something pretty shocking to blow the Jaggers' messy divorce off the front page—like a suicide involving the long-time girlfriend of another Stone. Months before, on Saint Patrick's Day 1979, Keith had met striking blonde supermodel Patti Hansen at Studio 54 and fallen in love with her. Anita Pallenberg, left to her own devices, took up with a seventeen-year-old high school dropout named Scott Cantrell.

In late July, while Pallenberg was passed out on the bed of her Westchester County home, Scott Cantrell lay beside her playing Russian roulette with Pallenberg's .38-caliber pistol. Tragically, Cantrell lost. Police arrived to find a hysterical Pallenberg covered in the dead teenager's blood. Once the inevitable scandal about Pallenberg's drug-taking and satanist past quieted down, she was charged with possession of an unlicensed handgun.

As it turned out, things could have been much, much worse. While Mick continued to entertain at the Montauk beach house that summer, plans were allegedly afoot to attack the house commando-style and murder all its inhabitants. According to an FBI informant, several Hell's Angels, still vowing revenge on Jagger for not helping in their defense against murder charges in the Altamont case, climbed into a raft in a remote spot along Long Island's South Shore and made their way under cover of darkness to the house Jagger rented from Andy Warhol. The raft was loaded with plastic explosives—enough, the informant told a US Senate Judiciary Committee, "to blow the whole band and everybody in the party up."

The alleged scheme came frighteningly close to being carried out. Just minutes before landing on the beach, the raft sprang a leak and took on water, leaving the would-be assassins to swim for their lives. According to the informant's sworn testimony, all the weapons on board—including firearms and the explosives that were to be planted beneath Jagger's house—went down with the raft.

Although the Hell's Angels organization formally denied there ever was such a plan to kill Jagger, the talkative former Hell's Angel identified in Senate documents as "Butch" insisted that there were still bikers determined to get even. "Whoever does it, well, it will be quite a trophy," he said. "They swear they will do it . . . This has been discussed many times . . . Eventually it will happen."

Not long after, Jerry and Mick moved into a townhouse at 135 Central Park West, just around the corner from John and Yoko's sprawling triplex in the fabled Dakota. Earlier in the decade, when Lennon was living with his mistress May Pang on East Fifty-second Street, the two rock icons often spent time together. "Mick would drop by our apartment," Pang said, "and the two of them would talk about who was the hot new guitar player, or they'd just sit on the floor eating Chinese food and watching television."

Now that John and Yoko were back together, Mick almost never saw his old friend. "I like John really a lot, you know?" said Mick, who was turned away by the doorman every time he dropped by the Dakota. "He's just kowtowing to his bleedin' wife, probably." Still, he often left a "Mick was here" note for John at the front door. "I know you don't want to see anyone," one of these read, "but if you ever do, call me." Later Jagger would note wistfully, "He never did."

Not that Mick was sitting home twiddling his thumbs whenever he was in Manhattan. Although it was still generally agreed that the night's revels at Studio 54 had not begun until Bianca arrived, Mick and Jerry continued to spend plenty of time there.

Mick claimed in a New Year's Eve interview to *High Times* magazine that he "very rarely" took drugs. However, celebrity photographer David McGough got a different impression when he sat just a few feet from Mick and Jerry in the Studio 54 balcony. "Mick and Jerry just sat there, taking drugs from anyone who came up to them," McGough said. "People just wanted to say they turned Mick Jagger on."

What increasingly turned Mick on—in addition to sex, drugs,

rock and roll, and money—was real estate. Jagger also realized that, given Bianca's claim during their divorce trial that her husband was trying to avoid paying US income taxes, he needed more far-flung residences to prove his nontaxable "wandering minstrel" status.

To the homes in London and New York, he added a gracious apartment on Paris's Isle de la Cite and a spectacular seventeenth-century Loire Valley château. Designated a historic monument by the French government, La Fourchette ("the Fork") boasted its own vineyard and cave, twelve bedrooms, and a private chapel where Mick and Jerry slept during the three-year, $2 million renovation.

Then there was Mick's comparatively modest cottage on L'Ansecoy Beach in Mustique, a remote and very private island paradise in the Grenadines. Mustique (a variation of the French word for *mosquito*) was acquired in 1958 by British real estate tycoon Colin Tennant (later Lord Glenconner). Determined to transform this tiny spot in the Caribbean into the world's most exclusive retreat, Tennant built a scaled-down version of the Taj Mahal for himself and gave his friend Princess Margaret property on which to build her own hideaway. She called it Les Jolies Eaux: "the Beautiful Waters."

The high-living Margaret, whose affair on the island with landscape gardener Roddy Llewellyn—eighteen years her junior—would effectively end her marriage to Lord Snowden, invited her pal Mick to build his own house there in 1971. Eventually Stargroves—named after the country manor he had purchased for Marianne Faithfull—would consist of a series of Japanese pavilions housing guest rooms, a bathhouse with hot tub, separate children's quarters, a teahouse, a moon deck, and a game room where the teak floor was inlaid with thousands of red-and-white Contac capsules.

Cold medicine wasn't enough to get Mick through the party thrown at New York's four-floor nightclub Danceteria to mark the release of *Emotional Rescue* in June 1980. According to writer Victor Bockris, who witnessed the episode, Mick headed straight for the men's room and, with his bodyguard standing by, "proceeded to snort a half gram of coke, smoke a big joint, and bolt a half bottle of whiskey in order to become 'Mick Jagger' for forty-five minutes."

Emotional Rescue, with Mick's falsetto-driven title track, was the Stones' first hit album of the new decade, soaring straight to number one and staying there for seven weeks. Keith, as always, was eager to hit the road again to promote the record. But Mick's new strategy was to limit the Stones to touring every three years, allowing demand to build. Knowing that this would not go over well with Richards, Jagger waited until he was vacationing with Jerry in Morocco to telex the Stones' office in New York that there would be no 1980 tour.

It was during this period, Keith recalled, that he and Mick "almost came to blows—or worse." Mick had, Richards observed, "fallen in love with power while I was being 'artistic.'" Before Keith had a chance to convey an idea in business meetings, rehearsals, or even at parties, Mick often blurted "Oh, shut up, Keith. Don't be stupid."

"It was so fucking rude," Richards recalled. "I've known him so long he can get away with murder like that. But you think about it. It hurts."

By this time, Keith noticed a change in his old friend. Jagger, convinced that everybody wanted something from him, had grown cold. "He used to be a lot warmer," Keith said. "He put himself in the fridge." Mick had long been known in rock circles as famous for his imperious attitude toward staff and crew members—the very people on whom the success or failure of a concert, a tour, or recording hinged. He never bothered to learn his employees' names or even to acknowledge them. "You could say hi to Mick, and nine times out of ten he'd walk right past you," Altham said. "He did that to the other Stones: Charlie Watts, Bill Wyman, Ronnie Wood. He even started ignoring Keith." Jagger had grown so suspicious of other people's motives that eventually not even his spiritual brother was immune. "He closed the circle," Keith said, "until I was on the outside too."

This cool air of detachment served Jagger well in the boardroom. Arthur Collins, who took over from Earl McGrath as head of Rolling Stones Records, was "amazed" by Jagger's hands-on approach to running the Stones brand. "He's a very global guy, detail oriented," Collins said. When Jagger asked for sales figures, "he expected you to have those figures at your fingertips . . . You had to be very precise, or he'd just walk away." Jagger also wanted up-to-date intelligence on rival artists: just how many records Michael Jackson, Elton John, Bruce Springsteen, and even Barry Manilow were selling. "Mick," Collins added, "is very much a bottom-line guy."

Nothing could have prepared Mick—or, for that matter, the world—for what happened on December 8, 1980. Without warning, a deranged fan named Mark David Chapman confronted John Lennon outside the Dakota and shot him to death. Mick's friend was only forty.

Mick made no public statement at the time, but he was deeply shaken. When he first heard the terrible news, Jagger "went absolutely white," his driver said. "His eyes were red, he was shaking." Jagger was in a state of shock and disbelief, in part because—unlike the Stones—Lennon was hardly known for stirring up feelings of anger or resentment among his fans.

The gruesome murder of John Lennon left Mick shaken for months—and with reason. It was later discovered that Jagger had also been on Mark David Chapman's hit list. With Jerry's help, Mick began looking for a new apartment on a quiet Upper East Side block—and he started carrying a gun. He had no qualms about pulling the trigger. "There'd be no point in carrying a gun," he said matter-of-factly, "if you wouldn't use it."

*Mick is one of the sexiest men in the world and the best lover
I've ever had.*

—JERRY HALL

◆　◆　◆

*You can't keep it up with sixteen-year-old girls forever.
They're very demanding.*

—MICK

◆　◆　◆

It's love-hate all the way with those two. Constant friction.

—JANE ROSE, LONGTIME FRIEND AND STONES STAFFER, ON THE
RELATIONSHIP BETWEEN MICK AND KEITH

I weaned him off drugs, but he replaced them with sex.

—JERRY HALL

◆　　◆　　◆

I suppose I can imagine myself doing it at fifty, though it seems a crazy thing to say.

—MICK, ON HOW LONG HE COULD SEE HIMSELF PERFORMING
WITH THE ROLLING STONES

7

• ◆ •

Steel Wheels, Voodoo, and Four Thousand Women

"*A*re you absolutely sure," actor Jason Robards asked Mick, "that you want to do that?" The two men had already spent several months on the banks of the Amazon River making German director Werner Herzog's *Fitzcarraldo,* the preposterous-sounding but true story of a man obsessed with building an opera house on a mountaintop in Peru. Exhausted, and perhaps more than a little disoriented, Mick was about to try an ancient Amazonian marriage ritual designed to enlarge the penis.

"It involved putting bamboo over the male member and filling it with stinger bees," said film director Julien Temple, a friend of Jagger's who later made the Stones' video for the song "Undercover of the Night" in Mexico. "So the member attained the size of the bamboo." According to Temple, Mick confirmed that he gave the painful procedure a try. "Mick spent months in the jungle in Peru," Temple said. "He was going mad out there, I think."

Mick conceded that at this point he was "cold, wet, tired, scared, and fed up" with the intolerable conditions on the set. Midway through filming, Robards was diagnosed with amoebic dysentery and quit. Mick soon followed suit. Although the entire film was reshot with Klaus Kinski in the lead, Herzog believed that only Jagger could do justice to the supporting part he'd been hired to play: that of a dimwitted actor.

Undeterred by the punishing conditions on the set of *Fitzcarraldo,* Mick continued to seek movie roles—but, as with all things in his life, on his own terms. He turned down a flat $2 million offer to play Rooster in the film adaptation of *Annie*—a part that went to *The Rocky Horror Picture Show*'s Tim Curry—opting instead to audition for the role of Mozart in *Amadeus*. The job went to a young unknown named Tom Hulce.

Mick was not about to let the part he was born to play—that of rock deity—go to a younger performer. Holing up at a training camp in the Berkshire Mountains of Massachusetts for six weeks, Mick "worked out like a fuckin' dog" in preparation for the Stones' upcoming ten-week, twenty-eight-city fall 1981 tour. He described the ordeal as "hours of torture every day . . . it's much harder as I get older." As the tour approached, Mick had a 27-inch waist and tipped the scale at 125 pounds.

Not all of the demands on Mick were physical. As always, the rest of the Stones sat back and let their leader take charge of virtually every detail, from the finances and publicity right down to costumes, staging, travel, and hotel arrangements. "No one else," he carped, "lifts a finger."

For Mick, there could be no more fitting anthem than "Start Me Up," a gentle reggae tune refashioned in the studio into the sort of hard-driving number that put the Rolling Stones on the map in the first place. Released in August 1981, "Start Me Up" was an instant classic, propelling the group's new *Tattoo You* album to number one and setting the stage for its most successful tour ever.

The stage was also set for more conflict between Jagger and Richards. Once the guitarist learned that $1.2 million of the band's money was being spent on staging—including a cherry picker to lift up Jagger so that he could toss carnations into the crowd—Richards railed against Mick for turning the tour into "a fucking sideshow." Mick's sideshow wound up being seen by two million people and grossing more than $50 million, making it at that point the richest concert tour in history.

There were plenty of tense moments along the way. In New Orleans, thirty handguns were confiscated from audience members. In Seattle, a woman carrying a revolver walked up to within feet of Mick before being apprehended. While filming an HBO special during the final stop of the tour in Hampton Roads, Virginia, a fan jumped onstage and headed straight for Mick before security could stop him. Keith acted swiftly, taking off his guitar and smashing it over the man's head.

There were times when Richards felt like doing the same to Mick. Ironically, the rift between them was wider than ever around the release of their hit single "Waiting on a Friend," Jagger's trea-cly celebration of his friendship with Richards. When there was a song that Keith took seriously, Mick would camp it up outrageously, mincing about the stage with a purse dangling from his wrist while Richards fumed. Richards retaliated by commandeering the stage with endless guitar solos that left a frustrated Mick seething in the wings.

It was a feeling that was all too familiar to Jerry Hall, who put on a brave face while Mick misbehaved with a whole new crop of worshipful teenagers—namely, the children of his contemporaries. Jagger partied at Manhattan clubs like Xenon and Regine's with eighteen-year-old "Deb of the Decade" Cornelia Guest, the comely blonde daughter of social lions Winston and C. Z. Guest. David

McGough recalled how Mick "kicked and shrieked" at photographers when they caught the couple in the lobby of the Carlyle Hotel at five thirty in the morning. (Later, while Guest looked in her closet for something to wear, a friend pulled out a black lamé jacket and tried it on. "It's spectacular!" the friend gushed. "It should be," Guest replied. "It's Mick's.")

Jagger was equally perturbed when paparazzi snapped him in the clinch with another eighteen-year-old, Gwynne Rivers, on the Studio 54 dance floor at four in the morning. Gwynne was still in diapers when Mick first got to know her father, the noted artist Larry Rivers. Understandably, Mick continued to lash out at the photographers who were making his pursuit of young women increasingly difficult. McGough was waiting at Kennedy Airport to shoot the arrival of Paul McCartney when he spotted a clearly inebriated Jagger emerge from a plane and head for his waiting limousine. Even though McGough and fellow photographer Ron Galella assured Mick they were there to shoot McCartney and not to bother him, Mick shouted back, "Well, *fuck* Paul McCartney. Paul McCartney is nothing but a fucking asshole!" With that, he kicked at the photographers, smashed Galella's camera, and lurched toward his car.

Finally fed up hearing the reports of Mick's compulsive skirt-chasing, Hall took her revenge, trotting off into the sunset with married forty-six-year-old horse breeder Robert Sangster. "Where would I go after Mick?" Jerry tried to explain. "Robert can buy him out ten times over." She was right on the, well, money. With a stable of three hundred thoroughbreds in England, Ireland, and Australia, Sangster had accumulated a net worth estimated at $400 million, which at the time dwarfed Mick's $40 million fortune.

Mick was hurt—and humiliated. He got on the phone to Jerry and, according to Sangster, "cried like a baby." They would reconcile only after Mick promised one thing: that they would start a family of their own.

But six weeks later, Mick was at it again. This time he was attending a Tina Turner concert at New York's the Ritz, where a VIP table had been reserved for him upstairs. Jagger, recalled photographer David McGough, was sitting with a "gorgeous Asian woman. He's just sitting there with his dark glasses on, and she's got her hands down his pants. Everyone in the room was staring at them."

Mick's decision to have children with Jerry did have one unexpected result: he reached out to his daughter Karis, phoning her on her twelfth birthday. It signified, a tearful Marsha Hunt said, that he wanted to be part of Karis's life.

In 1983, only weeks after Mick's much-ballyhooed and overanalyzed fortieth birthday (the *New York Times,* the *Washington Post,* the *Times* of London, and even the *Wall Street Journal* devoted columns of ink to this cultural milestone), Jerry informed him that she was pregnant. She had become pregnant by Bryan Ferry years earlier, and had an abortion that left her traumatized. This time, pregnancy occurred only after six months of trying and visits to fertility experts in Manhattan, Paris, and London. On hearing the news, she called a friend of Mick's in Paris and asked if he could help her out with a new wardrobe. The friend, Yves Saint Laurent, offered to design a line of maternity wear exclusively for Jerry.

Now that Jerry was expecting his child, Mick was telling reporters that he wanted to have two more with her. Marriage? Not so much. "It gives me claustrophobia," he said, adding that he considered the institution "legalistic, contractual claptrap." He allowed privately, however, that he might be willing to wed if Hall signed a prenup. But unlike Bianca, Jerry was not—for the time being, at least—willing to sign away her marital property rights.

Mick was, in fact, on the verge of ending another marriage—

to Ahmet Ertegun's Atlantic Records—and taking a bombastic wheeler-dealer named Walter Yetnikoff as his new bride. As president of Columbia Records (later to be acquired by Sony), Yetnikoff had championed the career of Bruce Springsteen and, most important of all, Michael Jackson's monumental 1982 album, *Thriller*.

The Stones' last four albums had all been worldwide monster hits, but none came close to matching *Thriller*'s numbers. With seven smash singles, thirty-seven weeks at number one, and forty million copies sold, it was far and away the biggest-grossing album of all time.

Mick respected Jackson's work. But he also knew that in the hands of the wrong record company, *Thriller* never would have become the colossal success it turned out to be. In dealing with Yetnikoff, Mick enjoyed a unique position of strength. As a performer, he was unparalleled; twenty years after meeting Keith on that railway platform in Dartford, Mick was still striking fear, love, anger, loathing, and lust into the hearts of trembling teens—and their baby boomer parents. More than anyone, Mick had made shock chic.

He was also a shrewd, calculating, no-nonsense businessman, and more than a match for any "suit" in the entertainment industry. That soon became apparent during a meeting between the Stones and Columbia Records executives held at the Ritz Hotel in Paris. At loggerheads with Yetnikoff over whether the Stones would have the right to choose which cuts on an album would be released as singles, Mick jumped up. "You fat, fucking record executives!" he yelled. "What do you know?" Yetnikoff screamed back, "Fuck you!" Incredibly, Keith remained seated, calmly taking it all in.

At three in the morning, Mick and Yetnikoff signed the richest deal in record history: $28 million for the Stones and, unbeknownst to his bandmates, Mick's first two solo albums. When he found out later about Jagger's separate deal, Keith was livid. "I wanted to rip his fuckin' throat out . . . I don't care who you are," he said. "You don't piggyback on a Rolling Stones deal . . . Everybody felt betrayed. What happened to the friendship?"

Mick chalked up the criticism to "petty jealousy" and promptly lined up some major names—Herbie Hancock, Pete Townshend, Jeff Beck—to appear on his first solo album. *She's the Boss* would take six months to record at studios in Jamaica, New York, and London.

Work took a backseat to the birth of Elizabeth Scarlett Jagger at New York's Lenox Hill Hospital on March 2, 1984. Jerry proudly declared that the eight-pound, two-ounce infant "has the cutest lips, just like her daddy."

Back at the couple's new five-story townhouse on West Eighty-first Street—where *MICK* was spelled out in blue letters on the white marble floor and a Union Jack covered an entire wall—Mick made it clear that he had no intention of changing diapers. Nor would he allow Jerry to bring the child into their bed for midnight feedings. The smell of Hall's breast milk, Mick said, made him nauseous.

When he shared these tidbits with Michael Jackson at Jackson's Helmsley Palace Hotel suite in mid-April, the Gloved One was clearly taken aback. Yet he still desperately wanted to work with Mick. Jackson had recorded two hit duets with Jagger contemporary Paul McCartney—"Say Say Say" and "The Girl Is Mine"—and felt that Mick would add street cred to an edgy new song he had written called "State of Shock."

At first Mick played hard to get. "You've got your family," he told Jackson. "You don't need me." But Michael persevered, and when it was released on June 5, their "State of Shock" duet shot straight to number three—a much-needed boost of confidence for Jagger, who had begun to doubt whether he could forge a career outside the Stones. As for the collaboration itself, neither star was impressed with the other. Jackson accused Jagger of singing off-key

("How did *he* ever get to be a star"), and Mick dismissed Michael's talent as "very lightweight—like froth on a beer."

Convinced that he no longer needed his fellow Stones, Mick was even more arrogant than usual when the band members met in Amsterdam that October to sort things out. After a night on the town with Keith, Mick rang up Charlie Watts's hotel room. "Is that my drummer?" he told Watts. "Why don't you get your ass down here?" The always dapper Watts put on a tailored Savile Row double-breasted suit, carefully knotted his Hardy Amies tie, slipped on his handmade shoes from Lobb in St. James's, then went to Mick's room and punched him in the face.

"Charlie went boom," Keith said. "He dished Mick a left hook that knocked him into a plate of smoked salmon. He almost floated out of the window and into the canal outside."

"Don't you *ever* call me 'my drummer' again," Watts fumed. "You're *my* fucking singer!"

Although he often felt like taking a swing at Mick, Keith never did. "There's no joy," he explained, "in punching a wimp." Most of the time, he was content simply to mock Jagger. After stumbling upon a book written by a woman named Brenda Jagger, Keith discovered that he could infuriate Mick simply by calling him Brenda.

There were moments, however, when things between the two men got physical. While they were working on the group's new *Dirty Work* album in Paris, it was clear to everyone that Jagger, distracted by his solo career, was simply going through the motions. At one point, Keith grabbed Mick by the throat and screamed, "I'll kill you! One day I'll wipe you clean away!"

Jagger took it all in stride. "Oh, that's just Keith," he calmly told a shocked record company executive who witnessed the incident. "He's always stomping about acting all pissed off, but he wouldn't hurt a fly."

The same could be said for Mick, although it was the last thing he wanted his daughters' boyfriends to know. "When she's older," Mick once said, "I'll tell Jade to watch out for men like me." Now that Karis was fifteen and Jade fourteen, he enjoyed terrorizing their dates whenever the girls visited him in New York. "I think it's important to encourage the ones who are interesting," said the man who was once every parent's nightmare, "and discourage the ones who are jerks." Jade, mortified by her father's public remarks, vowed to get even by turning Mick and Bianca into Grandpa and Grandma.

She's the Boss, released in March 1985, instantly went platinum, spinning off the hit single "Just Another Night." In a ninety-minute video released to promote the album, Mick plays (what else?) a spoiled-rotten rock star who is assaulted by three transvestites. In the process, he somehow manages to camp it up in full drag: wig, heels, and fire engine–red dress. Retitled *Running Out of Luck,* the Julien Temple–directed film bypassed theaters and went straight to video—much to the relief of Mick's costar Rae Dawn Chong. "I'm not against love scenes as long as they are tasteful," she said of her racier on-screen moments with Jagger. "The scenes in this video are not tasteful."

On July 11, 1985, he would silence all critics by turning his twenty-five-minute portion of the historic Live Aid event into a tour de force. The concert, organized by Bob Geldof, lead singer for the Irish band Boomtown Rats, took place at Philadelphia's JFK Stadium before a live audience of 90,000 and a worldwide TV audience of 1.6 billion. With Daryl Hall, John Oates, and their band playing backup, Mick and Tina Turner sang "State of Shock," then segued into a sweaty chorus of "It's Only Rock 'n Roll." The steamy duet, perhaps most memorable for the climactic moment when Mick ripped off Tina's leather skirt to reveal a corset and sheer black stockings beneath, was in sharp contrast to Live Aid's other Jagger offering: the world premiere of Mick's hammy, eyebrow-raisingly camp "Dancing in the Street" video with David Bowie.

Drawn together by the success of their video, Jagger and Bowie were once again a fixture on the club scenes in New York and London. After a messy divorce from Angie, Bowie had managed to shed his glam-rock image and even make a name for himself as a serious actor (in the film *The Man Who Fell to Earth* and on Broadway in *The Elephant Man*). Now Jagger and Bowie—both of whom now insisted they had never *really* been bisexual—were nonetheless contemplating a remake of *Some Like It Hot,* a film that required them to do virtually their entire parts in drag.

As strange as the Jagger-Bowie alliance seemed to those on the outside, Jerry was not threatened by it. On the contrary, Bowie took up time that Mick would otherwise be spending with other rock stars' girlfriends or the teenage daughters of his peers.

What Hall wanted desperately was to become Mrs. Jagger. For years now, she never traveled without packing a plastic ring and an orange blossom corsage in her suitcase—just in case the mood suddenly struck Mick. Hall was now even willing to sign away her marital property rights in a prenup, if that's what it took.

Apparently, it would take more. "Monogamy," Mick shrugged, "is not for me." Hall resolved to bide her time. "I'm not unhappy about the way we are," she said. "It's just that I'd rather be married."

She gave Mick another reason to consider matrimony on August 28, 1985, when, after twelve hours of labor, she gave birth to seven-pound James Leroy Augustin Jagger. Mick held Jerry's hand through much of the ordeal, but, suddenly feeling faint, he faced the wall rather than witness the actual delivery. "I love my daughters," Dad said, "but there's nothing like having a first son."

Several months later, there would be another first that seemed an incongruously long time in the making. In all their years, the

Rolling Stones had never received a Grammy—until Mick's old pal Eric Clapton presented them with a Lifetime Achievement Award in early 1986. Jagger worried at first that the award made the Stones look like fossils, but it did give them a chance to debut their new video before a huge TV audience. "Harlem Shuffle," a remake of the 1964 Bob and Earl song, was a hit, and so was the new *Dirty Work* album from which it came.

To keep up the momentum, Richards and the other Stones were eager to tour. Noting that this was the first album in their new contract with Columbia, Keith said that they would be *"idiots* not to get behind it."

Mick claimed that his fellow band members were in no shape physically to tour, scoffing, "They couldn't walk across the Champs-Élysées, much less go on the road." But if Mick was considering a solo tour, Keith had a clear message for him: "If Mick tours without this band," he told a reporter, *"I'll slit his fuckin' throat."*

As it turned out, even without a tour of any kind, Mick seemed to be everywhere—nearly always in Bowie's company. They performed "Dancing in the Street" for Princess Diana and Prince Charles at the Prince's Trust Concert in London's Wembley Arena, caused a stir at Prince's Madison Square Garden opening, and chatted up Madonna after her Wembley concert. (She presumably did not remind him that they had once spent time together at the Plaza, after which he had walked away thinking she was a "thimbleful of talent thrown into a sea of ambition.")

Mick's famous friends were making it easy for him to believe that he no longer needed the Stones. When Jagger turned forty-three, Sting, Tina Turner, Eric Clapton, actress Faye Dunaway, Michael Caine—and, of course, David Bowie—were just a few of the celebrities who turned up at his birthday party in London.

It was all adding up to an exciting new life for Mick sans the

Stones. "I'm not nineteen anymore," he said. "The Rolling Stones are not my only interest in life." In January 1987 Jagger took Jerry and their kids to Barbados to splash in the surf while he was at the island's Blue Wave Recording Studios working on his next solo album, *Primitive Cool*. In two of the album's tracks—"Shoot Off Your Mouth" and "Kow Tow"—Mick unloaded on his estranged buddy Keith.

Once again, Mick's concentration would be interrupted by another drug sting—only this time the target was Jerry, arrested and falsely accused of trying to smuggle $60,000 worth of pot into Barbados. The charges were eventually dropped, but not before Jerry blasted the local authorities for trying to set her up because she was "an American, female, famous, and rich."

Despite glowing reviews ("While the Rolling Stones simmer on the back burner, Mick Jagger is at full boil," proclaimed *USA Today*), *Primitive Cool* topped out at forty-one on the album chart. It was a huge disappointment for Mick, but not enough to send him crawling back to Keith and the boys. If anything, Mick was more convinced than ever that his solo career was suffering from his association with the other Stones. "I can't go onstage with them," Mick said, hinting strongly that his days with the Stones might soon be over. "I don't need this bunch of old farts."

He had a point. Although Mick's face had more grooves than his records, he had worked hard to keep fit; as a result, he was the only Stone who was not gray, haggard, or stooped.

Mick's manic energy left an impression on even the youngest Jagger. Glued to a Tarzan movie on television, twenty-month-old Jimmy Jagger brightened when Cheetah swung into view and began screaming, mugging, and hopping about. "Dada!" Jimmy squealed, pointing to the screen.

Primitive Cool wasn't the only disappointment Mick had to contend with during this time. There would be other setbacks in the coming months, not the least of which was the cancellation of a planned US solo tour due to sluggish advance ticket sales. Mick bounced back in April 1988 with his first-ever tour of Japan—a country the Rolling Stones had been banned from for a quarter century because of their collective history of drug abuse.

The 170,000 fans who came to see his eight solo performances were not disappointed. Aware that he had to deliver a concert experience on par with that of the Stones, he was backed by forty dancing girls and sang "Satisfaction" against a backdrop of fiery, lava-spewing volcanoes. Mick's total take for the tour: $8 million. His next solo outing, this time a series of concerts in Australia, would rake in $20 million.

While Mick was performing to sold-out crowds in Sydney and Melbourne, Richards's own solo album for Richard Branson's Virgin Records, *Talk Is Cheap,* was released to critical raves. The song "You Don't Move Me" addressed the Glimmer Twins' feud, but the title cut was an out-and-out rant against "greedy, seedy" Mick. Hurt by Keith's attack, Jagger sat down and wrote "Mixed Emotions," which found its way onto the next Stones album and into the Top Five.

In the meantime, Mick wasn't the only Jagger with an eye for the bottom line. That spring, Jade announced her intention to drop out of school and sign a $1 million modeling contract. When both Mick and Bianca put their feet down, Jade struck back. She was expelled from her tony English boarding school for climbing out of her bedroom window at two in the morning to meet her twenty-one-year-old boyfriend. "My dad," Jade told school officials, "will kill me!"

Not exactly. After summoning Jade to the family château in the Loire, Mick and Jerry kept close watch on her there until finally letting her take an art history course in Florence, Italy. On the plane,

Jade met a young art student named Piers Jackson and—much to Dad's chagrin—promptly fell in love.

Mick had other, equally pressing problems on the home front. Now that they were about to mark their tenth anniversary as a couple, Jerry wanted a marriage proposal. The milestone passed, and Hall, remembering how Mick had reacted when she ran off with Robert Sangster, took matters into her own hands. She signed a $1 million deal to endorse her own swimwear collection—a reminder that she was, to say the very least, financially independent—and began dating several high-profile English aristocrats.

Mick pretended not to care. When Jerry was offered a small part in the blockbuster *Batman,* he urged her to take it. It remained to be seen whether Mick took secret pleasure in seeing Jack Nicholson, playing the villainous Joker, douse Jerry's face with acid.

It seemed at times that Mick was trying to make amends. When Jerry made her stage debut in a Montclair, New Jersey, production of William Inge's *Bus Stop,* Mick was in the opening night audience. It also happened to be his forty-fifth birthday. Bored, Mick turned to his friend Liz Derringer and asked if she had any pot. "No," she said. Any coke? No. He paused for a moment. "How about a blow job, then?"

It was, Derringer said, "vintage Mick." Later at the cast party, someone loudly asked the couple if they were going to marry. "The *M* word," Hall groaned. "Golly, I'm tryin'! Y'all quit rubbin' it in!?" Mick merely shook his head and smiled.

Jerry was not the only significant other Mick would have to deal with during this critical period. With the announcement that the Rolling Stones would be inducted into the recently established Rock and Roll Hall of Fame on January 18, 1989 came renewed speculation that the Jagger-Richards partnership was damaged beyond repair. If that were true, then what better time and place to announce the band's demise than at the Hall of Fame ceremonies? "Obviously," Mick said, "it was not something any of us wanted to see happen."

In an eleventh-hour effort to iron out their differences, Jagger and Richards agreed to hold a summit meeting in Barbados. The two men exchanged perfunctory greetings, and within minutes were screaming insults at each other. But by the end of the day, Richards said, "It was like old times." Sharing a joint and taking swigs from the same fifth of Jack Daniel's, the Glimmer Twins shrieked with laughter over the nasty things they'd said about each other in their songs—and in the press. A particular favorite of Mick's:

Reporter to Keith: "When are you two going to stop bitching at each other?"

Keith to reporter: "Ask the bitch."

After the Hall of Fame induction ceremonies, all the Stones convened in Barbados. From beginning to end, it would take only ten weeks for them to record and mix their first album in three years, *Steel Wheels*. "It was remarkably smooth, really," Mick allowed. "I wouldn't say *easy*—it's never that—but things just sort of flowed."

More daunting was the prospect of another world tour. Eventually they settled on a 115-concert tour spread out over thirteen months. In July 1989 the Rolling Stones took over Wykeham Rise, a former girls' school in the tony Connecticut hamlet of Washington, and began rehearsing. Locals soon became accustomed to the sight of Mick running backward along remote country roads—a new trick he'd learned to develop endurance and agility—and Keith dropping into the local grocery store for cigarettes.

More than three hundred reporters were on hand when the Stones rolled into Grand Central Station aboard an antique caboose and announced their upcoming Steel Wheels tour. What about the epic Jagger-Richards feud? "We gave up masochism," Keith answered. Finally, it fell to Mick to signal an end to the press conference. "Just one more question," he said. "My mascara is running."

Fans had never seen anything like it. Toronto promoter Michael Cohl was guaranteeing the Stones an unheard-of $70 million up front—their projected $50 million take from ticket sales plus another $20 million from merchandise. This time fans would be able to buy more than just T-shirts and souvenir catalogues, and they'd be able to make their purchases at major department stores as well as the concert sites themselves. Rolling Stones "boutiques" in Macy's and JCPenney offered sweatshirts, skateboards, $450 bomber jackets, and Converse sneakers—all bearing the Steel Wheels or Rolling Stones logos.

With his eye for detail, Mick approved every item that went on sale. His main concern, of course, was that when it came to the show itself, fans got their money's worth. Nearly four hundred technicians had been hired to operate the two 100-foot-high "industrial holocaust" sets, while four generators put out the 2.4 million watts needed to power the lasers, strobes, and fireworks—not to mention ignite a 300-foot-wide wall of flame. On billboard-sized screens overhead was the image of Jagger, mugging, prancing, jumping, and springing from one end of the stage to the other. Three hours and twenty-seven songs later, Mick was drenched in sweat—and grinning from ear to ear.

With good reason. Commercially, Steel Wheels was a stunning achievement for Mick and the Stones. The US tour took in $140 million—twice the guarantee—while the album went double platinum. Mick and Keith gladly posed for the cover of *Forbes* magazine, which asked the simple question, "What Will They Do with All That Money?"

The rock purists who made up *Rolling Stone*'s readership were equally impressed. By an overwhelming margin, they voted the Stones

Artists of the Year and Band of the Year, and Steel Wheels the Tour of the Year. A TV broadcast of the final stop in Atlantic City, New Jersey, was watched in 13.5 million homes—the biggest pay-per-view audience in history. "The Rolling Stones are back, all right," Jay Cocks wrote in *Time*'s cover story on the band's rebirth. "Just look at these guys! Giants. Golems. Geezers . . . and they can still rock the boat."

No one knew this more than Jerry, who kept an eye on Mick during the tour. It didn't seem to help. Even though Hall was standing just a few feet away backstage with little Elizabeth Scarlett and James, Jagger couldn't resist making a play for Eric Clapton's eighteen-year-old girlfriend of the moment. "As soon as Clapton turned his back," a crew member said, "Mick was flirting with the girl outrageously. Jerry just ignored it, but you couldn't help but feel sorry for her."

Renaming Steel Wheels the Urban Jungle tour, the Stones, no longer persona non grata in Japan, played for two straight weeks at Tokyo's Korakuen Dome—a gig for which they were paid $30 million. Then it was on to thirty-seven cities in Europe.

By the time it was all over, Mick had barely seen Hall for eighteen months. When he celebrated their twelfth anniversary by building a $100,000 heart-shaped pool at Jerry's Texas ranch, she wasn't sure what to make of it. "I'm sure," she said, "he must have done something . . ."

What he hadn't done yet was propose. This time when Jerry threatened to leave, Mick took the threat to heart. He ordered his lawyers to draw up an ironclad prenuptial agreement, and then jetted off with Jerry and their children for a six-week holiday in India, Nepal, Bhutan, Thailand, and Indonesia.

Around six o'clock in the evening on November 21, 1990, Mick and Jerry were wed at the hilltop home of a friend on the exotic Indonesian island of Bali. The ceremony was conducted by a Hindu priest who read prayers in Sanskrit and dabbed saffron on their foreheads. Afterward, while Jerry dressed for bed, Mick allegedly went after their host's wife. "He *jumped* me, can you believe it?" she told a friend. "Mick tried to make love to me on his wedding night!"

At Stargroves, their posh beachfront retreat on Mustique, Mick made it abundantly clear to his bride that nothing had really changed. As usual, days were spent as a family, frolicking in the surf or picnicking with the locals at Macaroni Beach. But evenings were often wiled away at Mustique's one nightspot, Basil's Bar, and there Jagger made no effort to conceal his interest in other women. Just weeks after their wedding, Hall and their guests watched while Mick danced suggestively with one island girl after another. "Jagger flirts outrageously," said writer Stephanie Mansfield, an eyewitness. "It's embarrassing, but Jerry is obviously willing to put up with it."

Hall was also willing to put up with the arrival of David Bowie and his new wife, the African-born model Iman. Unfazed by gossip that continued to swirl around Jagger's curious friendship with the former Ziggy Stardust, she now saw Bowie, who seemed very devoted to Iman, as having a positive effect on her husband. "Maybe Mick will look at how happy those two are together," she confided to one of her Mustique neighbors, "and stop foolin' around."

Not likely. But for a time, it did appear as if Mick was more interested in getting his stalled film career off the ground than chasing other women. Jagger and Bowie tried to sell themselves as the new Bing Crosby and Bob Hope, auditioning for the leads in the comedies *Dirty Rotten Scoundrels* (the roles went to Steve Martin and Michael Caine) and *Ishtar* (Dustin Hoffman and Warren Beatty). Eventually Mick landed a part as the villain in *Freejack,* a science-fiction thriller set in the not-so-distant future: 2009. The movie, which also starred Emilio Estevez and Rene Russo, turned out to be a *Ned Kelly*–sized bomb, earning back only half its $30 million budget.

Ironically, while Mick's acting career sputtered, Jagger and the Stones were a hit on the big screen—the *really* big screen. The IMAX film of their Steel Wheels/Urban Jungle tour, shot in Berlin, Turin, and London, thrilled critics and audiences alike when it was released in 1992.

It seemed fitting, then, that their new $45 million, three-album record deal with Virgin would be the biggest in history. "Mick is a brilliant businessman who knows more about the industry than anyone," said Ahmet Ertegun, who could not come close to meeting Virgin's offer. "He is tough, shrewd, and analytical. Any record company executive who underestimates him—and there have been a few—is a damn fool."

Jagger was, to be sure, a master of multitasking. At the height of the Urban Jungle tour the year before, he had spotted his old pal Eric Clapton with a twenty-three-year-old model named Carla Bruni. An heir to the Pirelli tire fortune, Bruni had all the qualities he looked for in a woman: jaw-dropping beauty, youth, money of her own ($4 million a year in modeling fees, plus her inheritance), and, most important, a rock star boyfriend.

"I knew Carla would appeal to his eye," said Clapton, who remembered all too well how Jagger had tried unsuccessfully to steal his ex-wife, Pattie Boyd Harrison Clapton, away from him. He begged his friend to stay away from Carla.

"Please, Mick," Clapton pleaded, "not this one. I think I'm in love." But within days, Jagger and Bruni began what Clapton called their "clandestine affair. After Carla stood me up a couple of times, I got a call from the girl who had introduced us, telling me Carla was seeing Mick, and it was serious."

Clapton was devastated. "The obsession with Mick and Carla gripped me for the rest of that year," he said. "It took some grisly turns when I found myself guesting with the Stones on a couple of shows, knowing she was lurking in the background." (Clapton soon sank far deeper into despair when, in March 1991, his four-year-old son Conor plunged to his death from the fifty-third floor of a New York City apartment building. The tragedy inspired Clapton's Grammy Award–winning "Tears in Heaven.")

Jerry had also been aware of the rumors during the Urban Jungle tour and dismissed Carla as just another camp follower. But when stories surfaced in the press indicating that the affair was still going strong after a full year, Hall ordered him to end it. Instead Mick flew out the door in a rage.

Worried that she had pushed Mick too far, Jerry dashed off a letter begging him to forgive her. The ploy worked. Three days later, a tourist spotted Jerry and Mick sharing a quiet drink at the Crane Beach Hotel bar in Barbados. They kissed and then got up to leave. When the tourist noticed that they had left an envelope on the table, he decided to take a peek at the contents:

Oh, my darling Mick . . . I'm truly sorry I was jealous . . . you're all that matters to me in the world . . . Please don't take your love away.

I want you to have your freedom and I won't mind if you fuck other girls. I'll do it with other girls and you too . . . I respect, admire, trust, need, and love you all through my being. I think you're a genious [sic] . . . I love to fuck you . . . I just want to be your #1 girl. I LOVE YOU.

Your Baby, Jerry

Apparently touched by Jerry's heartfelt apology, Mick plunked down $4 million for Downe House, a twenty-six-room white Georgian mansion overlooking the Thames in the leafy London suburb of Richmond. While Jerry, now expecting their third child, set about redecorating the couple's latest acquisition, Mick took Hall up on her offer to look the other way.

Still, Bruni, confronted with the distinct possibility that Hall might ultimately prevail, began to hedge her bets. Having just ended a separate affair with Crown Prince Dimitri of Yugoslavia, she was now also spending time with brash New York real estate tycoon Donald Trump. Although Trump would later concede that Bruni was "desperately stuck" on Jagger, Carla reportedly offered to end her affair with Mick if Trump dumped his fiancée, Marla Maples. Carla's "constant calling became a total pain in the ass," Trump said. "She was trying to get me to leave Marla, something I had in mind anyway, and she was using every psychological trick in the book. In the end, Carla became a woman who is very difficult to even like."

On January 12, 1992, Jerry gave birth to seven-pound, thirteen-ounce Georgia May Ayeesha Jagger. The next morning, Mick was on a plane bound for Thailand, where he and Bruni checked into villa 15 at Phuket's luxurious Amunpuri Hotel using the tongue-in-cheek (and vaguely Thai-sounding) name "Someching."

Jerry managed to get through to Mick. "Who are you with?" she demanded to know. "Are you with Carla?" He denied it, but that hardly explained why Mick was not by Hall's side. "A man is supposed to be with his woman," Hall said, "when she has just had a baby!"

Mick thought otherwise. Over the next several days, he and Carla strolled on the beach, swam in their villa's private pool, and prowled Phuket's nightclubs. "They danced and kissed," one club bartender recalled. "There was a lot of touching going on. They weren't hiding anything."

Satisfied that Hall was no longer a problem, Bruni bragged to her friends that forty-eight-year-old Mick ("my boyfriend") was "incredible in bed. He is a wonderful lover—for an old man." To the press, she lied with alacrity, protesting, "I hardly know the man. It's completely impossible. I can't understand it. Perhaps someone's pretending to be me."

Not that Bruni had ever shied away from controversy. On one occasion, a young male reporter sent to interview Bruni knocked on her door only to have her answer it topless. For the remainder of the lengthy sit-down interview, Bruni made a half-hearted attempt to cover her breasts with one or the other of two purring Siamese cats, Betty and Mitzy. "I bore myself with monogamy," she told another journalist. "I prefer polygamy and polyandry." Polyandry is the female equivalent of polygamy.

Jerry, left alone in England to care for little Georgia May, regretted that she had ever given Mick carte blanche to cheat. At one point, Hall intercepted a written message from Bruni and showed it to Keith. It was written in code, albeit not a very sophisticated one; all Jerry had to do was hold it up to a mirror. The note from Bruni read, "I'll be your mistress forever."

"I almost had a nervous breakdown . . . I cried myself inside out when Mick went off with Carla Bruni," Jerry later said. "I felt sick. It was unforgivable." When Hall demanded an explanation from Mick, he stormed out again. Hall then phoned Bruni. "Leave my man alone!" Jerry told Carla, who promptly slammed down the phone.

Bruni apparently did not get the message. Jerry was breast-feeding Georgia May one afternoon when the phone rang again. This time, Hall tried to reason with her husband's paramour of the moment. "There's a family," Jerry explained, "and there are three children involved."

Jerry was "absolutely heartbroken," she said later, but she was determined not to let on that her marriage was falling apart. "Making love is by far the best way for me to keep my figure," she blithely told one French reporter even as she and Mick began seeing a marriage counselor. "That is why I hate those times when Mick is far from me. But when we are back together, we make up for lost time, believe me."

The only party who seemed unaffected by all the drama was Mick. Finally reunited with Hall in France, Jagger spent the next several months hosting weekend house parties at La Fourchette for his aristocratic pals. In addition to the hot air balloon rides that had become fashionable in recent years, the Jaggers offered their guests horseback rides through the French countryside and catered lunches on the banks of the Loire River.

There were also parlor games like backgammon and charades, although none of these matched the popularity of simple dress-up. "Everyone comes down to dinner in drag," one guest said, "and it's just huge fun." No one enjoyed cross-dressing more than Mick, who was dolled up one evening as Madonna in black mesh stockings, a blonde wig, and cone-shaped bullet bra.

That June, Mick and Jerry returned to the States to attend Karis's graduation from Yale University. Then, on Hall's birthday, Mick reached another milestone when twenty-year-old Jade, living on a farm in England with her boyfriend Piers Jackson, gave birth to a girl at home. They named the newest Jagger Assisi.

A grandfather at forty-eight, Mick showed no signs of slowing down. Now that the Rolling Stones had left Sony to sign with Virgin, Mick chose to go back to Ahmet Ertegun's Atlantic label for his next solo album. Off to LA to work on *Wandering Spirit,* Jagger continued to prove that he was just that: a wandering spirit. Within days, Mick was photographed at a club cozying up to another model—this time petite twenty-two-year-old Californian Kathy Latham. But it turned out that Mick was even more beguiled by Latham's friend Melissa Behr, a tall twenty-seven-year-old blonde in the Jerry Hall mold. What made Behr even more attractive to Mick was that she was already the girlfriend of rocker Charlie Sexton.

Jerry wrote off Latham and Behr, but not the dark-haired "mystery woman"—widely believed to be Carla Bruni—who was once again keeping company with Mick in California. Things between Hall and Bruni came to a head that fall, when the two models—both on assignment in Paris—crossed paths in the lobby of the Ritz Hotel. Hall reportedly called Bruni a tramp, then shouted, "Why can't you leave my husband alone?"

"Tell your husband," Bruni replied haughtily, "to leave *me* alone!" As for her opinion of Jerry, Carla sniped, "I think people should learn not to wash their dirty linen in public. Maybe in Texas they think this shows class, but I think her behavior shows a big lack of discretion and elegance."

By the time a reporter for London's *Daily Mail* cornered her at the Thierry Mugler fashion show where she was modeling, Hall was ready to throw in the towel. "Yes, it's true," she admitted. "We are separated, and I suppose we'll get a divorce. I'm in too much pain for this to go on any longer. I'm hoping for a quiet life." Later she would confess that looking the other way in hopes Mick would change had taken an emotional toll. "There's nothing more humiliating," she said, "than loving him so much you can forgive his infidelities."

Keith, whose marriage to Patti Hansen was still going strong after ten years, publicly urged Mick to "come to his senses. You know—the old black book bit—kicking fifty, it's a bit much, a bit manic." He had a point. Mick reportedly told Carla Bruni that he had slept with four thousand women.

His friend's advice aside, Mick chafed at the prospect of a costly divorce. True, the legality of his marriage had been in question almost from the start; shortly after the ceremony in Bali, the Hindu priest who performed it said that it wasn't valid because he had not received the proper paperwork. Mick himself was unsure. When asked if he was legally married, Jagger replied, "Depends what you call married . . . I *think* so."

Nevertheless, Mick knew that at the very least, he and Jerry had had a common-law marriage and that it was unlikely she would walk away from their fifteen-year relationship with anything less than eight figures. Four days after news of their split hit the papers, Mick was on the phone to Jerry, pleading with her to take him back. She did—although it was a decision that she would soon regret.

Back in Paris, the normally resilient Bruni was inconsolable. "I thought I would never get over it," she recalled. "I used to wake up every morning in despair. I thought I would never fall in love with someone else. When your heart is broken, you think the pain is never going to stop." Carrying on with a married man, she concluded, was "terrible, awful. It's a ticket to pain, and it leaves you very bitter."

His marriage woes momentarily behind him, Jagger was wrestling with doubts of his own, wondering after the *Primitive Cool* debacle if he really had what it took to make it as a solo artist. On *Wandering Spirit,* which featured a guest vocal by Lenny Kravitz and the Red Hot Chili Peppers' Flea on bass, Mick decided to return to his rock and R & B roots. The strategy worked. Not only was Mick's third solo album a commercial hit, but critics were hailing it as the best work he'd done in years. *Wandering Spirit,* gushed Karen Schoemer in the *New York Times,* had "more gusto than the Stones have cooked up on record in years. It's as if Mr. Jagger is willing to admit his long past."

His confidence restored, Jagger agreed to get back to work with the Stones. Once again, Keith and Mick decided that Barbados—the spot where they had called a truce that lasted long enough to record

Steel Wheels—would be the perfect place to iron out their differences. They would also get a name for their next album out of their brief stay on the island. While on a run to the local market to pick up cigarettes, Keith rescued a scraggly stray kitten from a drainpipe. Impressed with the cat's ability to survive, Richards named it Voodoo, and the terrace where the kitten slept the "Voodoo Lounge."

In recording their *Voodoo Lounge* album, the Stones would face a new challenge: at fifty-six, bass guitarist Bill Wyman had decided to leave the group. In searching for Wyman's replacement, Jagger was careful, said one longtime Stones staffer, not to pick "someone who had too much rock-star potential, who might upstage him, or make the other Stones look old." They settled on Darryl Jones, a stocky African American bassist who had apprenticed with jazz great Miles Davis and went on to tour with, among others, Madonna, Peter Gabriel, Cher, Eric Clapton, and Sting. Jones, also known as "The Munch," was not made a full-fledged Stone, but instead was hired as a salaried employee and would remain so for the next two decades.

The Stones began working on *Voodoo Lounge* at Windmill Studios in Dublin, but it wasn't long before Mick and Keith were back at each other's throats. One fight began when Keith jokingly scolded Mick for playing some riffs on a guitar. "There's only two guitar players in this band," Richards cracked, "and you're not one of them." With that, the two men screamed at each other about every conceivable issue they'd had over the years—Keith's drug use, Marianne Faithfull and Anita Pallenberg, Mick's secret solo deals and how Keith felt betrayed—while the other musicians, sound technicians, and crew members cringed on the sidelines.

It was left to producer Don Was to broker an uneasy peace. Over the six months it took to make the *Voodoo Lounge* album, Mick and Keith spoke outside the studio only once—when Keith thought he was ordering up ice from room service but accidentally speed-dialed

Mick instead. "You think they have this whole big relationship when they're not working," Was said. "But they don't. They just don't talk to each other if they don't have to, which comes as a shock."

Mick and Keith did come together halfway through the making of the album, when they were inducted into the Songwriters Hall of Fame. As soon as the ceremonies in New York were over, they returned to their separate corners.

Mick and Keith would reunite that July for Mick's fiftieth birthday bash. This time Jerry, more determined than ever to make it appear as if all was well in the Jagger household, took over a suburban London teaching college to throw her husband a costume banquet with a Bastille Day theme. More than three hundred of Mick's closest friends showed up dressed as everyone from the fictional Madame Defarge to Robespierre and Marie Antoinette.

With the exception of this and two other fiftieth birthday celebrations rumored to cost a total of $500,000, Mick tried to downplay the significance of turning fifty. "I don't put a lot of store in these supposedly great milestones," he said. "There's a danger in making too much of it. I mean, as long as you can deliver the goods . . ."

The Glimmer Twins were both in LA to share another memorable moment. On the morning of January 17, 1994, the Northridge earthquake struck Southern California, killing 57 people, injuring another 8,700, and causing $20 billion in damage.

That May the Stones sailed up to New York's Pier 60 aboard the *Honey Fitz,* JFK's mahogany-hulled presidential yacht, and unveiled their Voodoo Lounge tour plans. "Are you doing it just for the money?" one reporter asked. "What about all the beer you can drink and all the girls down in front," Mick replied, flashing that face-enveloping grin. "I mean, there's other things than money."

Jagger was, in fact, growing weary of stories in the press that revealed him to be the savvy businessman that he was. "I think people have a hard time accepting that you can be both a great performer and someone who's also good on the business end," Mick once told Ertegun. "I want people to think of me as a fucking great performer. I mean, Keith doesn't have to worry about this shit. I'm Ebenezer Scrooge, and Keith's the pure *artiste*. Everybody *loves* Keith."

The Stones spent most of that summer rehearsing at a private boys' school on the outskirts of Toronto. For the first time in years, Keith and Mick were getting along famously. "To me, Mick seems ten times happier than I've seen him," Richards said, "and he's really into the band. You know, he's lost some of that star-trip thing that was really pissing me off."

Jagger was glad to hear it. With even bigger cyber-industrial sets than those built for the Steel Wheels/Urban Jungle tour and more complicated special effects (one gargantuan screen integrated with the main stage action instead of two huge screens on either side, for example), Voodoo Lounge was a daunting operation even for the seasoned likes of the Stones.

Yet Mick eagerly embraced the challenge. "I *love* putting the biggest show on," he explained, "but contrary to what people say, I'm not interested in the business side of it—only as an adjunct to getting the show up. To get it *up there*—to me, *that*'s a business achievement." Of course, it didn't stop there. "And then the stage design spills over into everything: T-shirts, merchandising, so that the merchandising looks good. You know, if you *don't* get involved, then you're stuck with some company in Vancouver doing a lousy job. 'Like the T-shirt, Mick? Black T-shirt with a tongue on it.'"

Sponsored by Budweiser and hyped relentlessly on VH1 and MTV, the Voodoo Lounge tour opened on August 1, 1994, at Washington, DC's RFK Stadium. Against the now-familiar urban-surreal backdrop of inflatable leviathans, blinding pyrotechnics, and sets right out of the post-apocalyptic world depicted in the 1982 sci-fi classic *Blade Runner,* the fifty-year-old Grandfather of Rock led the Stones through twenty-seven numbers—beginning with "Not Fade Away" ("I start out slow, because if you don't watch out, it's dangerous, and you can hurt yourself") and ending with "Jumpin' Jack Flash." Over the next thirteen months, Mick and the Stones did 123 more shows, working their magic on six and a half million people in eighty-six cities spread across six continents. The Voodoo Lounge gross of $320 million was the biggest in concert history—a record that stood until the Stones themselves broke it several years later.

For someone who professed not to be really all that interested in the money side of things, Mick showed his business acumen once again when Microsoft chairman Bill Gates called with an unexpected offer. Microsoft's new Windows 95 software featured a Start button, and Gates, an ardent Stones fan, wanted to use "Start Me Up" in commercials to promote the product.

So, Microsoft asked Mick, how much did he and the tune's coauthor, Keith Richards, want for the song? Half in jest, Mick threw out an absurd figure—$10 million—confident that Gates would back away. He didn't. To Keith, it was just another example of how royalties from the songs he wrote with Mick "make me money while I'm asleep." Much more money, certainly, than if Mick wasn't handling such matters. "Oh, he's a smart bastard," Richards allowed. "You'll get no argument from me there."

Incredibly, Mick still found time to pursue his other favorite activity—much to Hall's horror. On October 10, 1994, while the Stones were finishing their gig at New Orleans's Louisiana Superdome and getting ready to move on to Las Vegas, a fax meant for Mick wound up in Jerry's hands. It was from Carla Bruni and read simply, "See you at the MGM Grand."

Hall was on the next plane to Nevada.

Although Hall had believed that she was rid of Bruni, the persistent Italian would continue her on-again, off-again affair with Mick for several more years. "It was a fling," Bruni eventually admitted. "I was in my twenties, so I wasn't thinking about a relationship." As for her "fling" with Clapton as well as Jagger: "It was fun and emotional," Bruni said. "I learned from them, or rather absorbed things. If I had not learnt from them, I would have been no better than a groupie."

From Hall's perspective, this was a minor distinction. Yet Bruni believed that she was not the sole cause of the Jaggers' eventual breakup. "There were so many other women with Mick," Carla said. "I don't think I was responsible . . . There were maybe ten other women."

And counting. In March 1995, on the Japanese leg of the Voodoo Lounge tour, Mick was in his suite at Tokyo's Hotel Okura sipping champagne with twenty-two-year-old British model Nicole Kruk when a bodyguard rushed in to say that Jerry was on her way up. Panic-stricken, Mick hurriedly checked the room to make sure that there were no telltale signs he'd been there with a woman, then slipped down a back staircase with Kruk just as Hall stormed in. "I was panicking too," Kruk said. "I wouldn't like to bump into Jerry Hall in an angry mood."

Nicole was in Japan on a six-month modeling assignment. One of the designers she worked for told the stunning brunette that Jagger was intent on "meeting" some attractive young women. She volunteered, but not because she was a Stones fan—her mother was.

At the hotel where Jagger was staying under the alias "Mr. Brook," Mick spoon-fed Nicole crème brûlée ("It was very sexy, no one but my mother had ever fed me before") while they lounged on the couch watching a DVD of *Mrs. Doubtfire*. At one point in the film, star Robin Williams is being made up to look like an older woman and complains that his skin looks "saggy—like Mick Jagger's." Kruk laughed at the line, but Mick was clearly agitated and started biting her—hard.

"He was pretty rough," Nicole said. "It was like I was a piece of meat." When she looked in the mirror the next day, she was "horrified. I looked like I'd been in an accident, and my nipple was bleeding and sore." Kruk conceded that although she told him to stop, she found the whole experience "exciting."

It was at that point that he pulled her into the bedroom. "The thing I most remember about making love with him was his face," she said. "He has such saggy skin that when he makes love, his mouth goes slack like an animal's . . . but he was a good lover."

The next morning, Nicole called Mick and told him that she looked like she'd been "dragged through a hedge backward." He laughed and promised to be more gentle, but when the model jokingly threatened to sell pictures of her bruised and bloodied body to the papers, he suddenly turned quiet.

The affair lasted a week, with Kruk dropping by his hotel each night and leaving the next morning. At the time, she was well aware that he was sleeping with other women in Tokyo. "He went into hostess bars, picking up girls everywhere," she said. "Mick is incapable of being faithful. If I hadn't been with him when Jerry turned up, it would have been someone else."

Once the Voodoo Lounge tour finally ground to a halt at the end of August, Jerry hoped that Mick would start spending more time with his family. He also had a new grandchild to dote on: Jade's infant daughter, Amba, named after the Indian god of motherhood. The following spring, Mick made a special effort to spend time with eleven-year-old James, showing up to cheer him on at a school cricket match and watching him win a goldfish playing ringtoss at a country fair.

Paterfamilias was a far cry from the screen role he was playing that July—that of Greta, a drag queen whose nightclub is raided by the SS in *Bent,* the film adaptation of Martin Sherman's controversial 1979 play about Nazi persecution of gays during World War II. The movie, directed by Sean Mathias, also starred Sir Ian McKellen and newcomer Clive Owen.

During filming in Scotland that July, Mick was called upon to slip into a satin evening gown slit to the thigh, fishnet stockings, diamond necklace, and wig, then dangle from the ceiling on a swing while singing avant-garde composer Philip Glass's haunting "Streets of Berlin" a la Marlene Dietrich. True to form, Mick, whose character becomes "George" to avoid being sent to a concentration camp, had definite ideas about how he was to look as a woman. Jagger claimed he spent "hours" arguing with the director about the floor-length gowns he had been told to wear. "I looked far better," Mick insisted, "in short dresses."

Although he found this latest movie experience "satisfying" and would pursue other roles, Mick no longer harbored any illusions about big-screen stardom. He did, however, see a future for himself behind the camera.

In August 1996 Mick and his partner, former production executive Victoria Pearman, announced the formation of Jagged Films, a London-based production company that planned to roll out thirteen films over the next five years at a cost of $350 million. Jagger quickly made his presence known in Hollywood, snatching up the rights to Robert Harris's best-selling World War II spy thriller *Enigma* and hiring celebrated British playwright Tom Stoppard to adapt it. He also courted Antonio Banderas to play the role of Che Guevara in the love story *Tania,* and tapped old pals such as Jack Nicholson, Warren Beatty, and Harrison Ford for projects and ideas.

Mick's avowed goal as a filmmaker was to make "smart" films— "intelligent movies without what my children call 'splosions' in them." He was particularly excited by the prospect of making a British film that didn't involve Hugh Grant. "Hugh Grant," sniggered Jagger, who made no attempt to conceal his contempt. "It's very hard to make a film about England if it doesn't have special effects or a very famous actor. So you're stuck making comedies with—ugh—*Hugh Grant*."

With Mick pouring so much time and energy into his own performance in *Bent,* his new film company, and plans for the Stones' next album, it seemed inconceivable to Jerry that he'd find time to pursue other women—certainly not to the extent that he had before. Jerry's friends weren't so sure. "Jerry is a wonderful woman," one said, pointing to a prevailing concern that she was sinking deeper and deeper into depression. "It's impossible not to like her, and, frankly, we were all just very upset at the way she was being treated. She deserved to know the truth."

Toward that end, and without Jerry's knowledge, they banded together to pay for a private investigator. Within weeks, he came back with a thick dossier detailing Mick's nocturnal activities in and around London, including nights spent holed up with yet another model in the aptly named Halcyon Hotel.

"We didn't want to see her hurt again," said one of the friends who hired the detective. "But I suppose this has backfired."

It was in Hollywood, however, that Mick's exploits would make the biggest splash. For several weeks in the fall of 1996, Mick carried on a torrid affair with actress Uma Thurman, who at twenty-six was twenty-seven years Jagger's junior. Thurman had been briefly married to actor Gary Oldman and linked to actors Robert Downey Jr., Richard Gere, Nicolas Cage, and Robert De Niro. When she began seeing Mick, Thurman had just wrapped up work on the film *Batman & Robin*. She played the seductive supervillain Poison Ivy.

Somehow the high-profile couple managed to fly below the radar, confining themselves to out-of-the-way restaurants and clubs. Late one evening at the notorious Viper Room on Sunset Boulevard, Mick and Uma were in a dark corner booth while the Wallflowers, a group fronted by Bob Dylan's son Jakob, played onstage. When Hollywood photographer Russell Einhorn happened in, he was taken aback by what he saw.

"I couldn't believe my eyes," Einhorn said. "He was kissing her—a real, hot heavy kiss, like in some film with the stars overacting—and he had his hands all over her. His leg was cocked over hers." For Einhorn, it was "too good an opportunity to miss."

The instant Einhorn's flash filled the room, he was tackled by Mick's hulking bodyguard. "I was really hit hard," recalled Einhorn, who tossed the camera across the club. "I hit the ground with a big thump, and it hurt like hell." For the next several minutes, he was pinned down while everyone fished around in the dark for the camera with its incriminating picture of Mick and Uma locked in a passionate embrace. Once Mick's bodyguards found the camera, they ripped out the film and threw Einhorn out of the club and onto the street.

Einhorn sued both Jagger and the club, claiming that he could have sold the photos for $1 million or more. Mick forked over a reported $350,000 settlement to keep from having to testify in court as to what went on that evening. The Viper Club, however, maintained its innocence and went to trial. The jury ruled in favor of Einhorn, awarding him an additional $600,000 and bringing him very close to that million-dollar payday.

Mick's fascination with Uma did not end there. Several months later, when Thurman and her future husband Ethan Hawke were expecting their first child, Jagger called late one night, hoping to pick up where they left off. Hawke answered the phone.

"He was looking for her!" said Hawke, who eventually saw

the humor in Mick's persistence. "Remember that old saying, 'You wouldn't kick Mick Jagger out of bed?' It was tense!"

If the Viper Room incident wasn't enough to push Jerry over the edge, what happened the very next day certainly was. After papers carried a photograph of twenty-nine-year-old Czech-Polynesian model Jana Rajlich leaving Jagger's Beverly Hills bungalow early in the morning, Hall was shattered. Mick and the six-foot-tall Jana had reportedly been carrying on an on-again, off-again affair for years. Not only had she stayed with Mick at the Ritz-Carlton in Atlanta when he was recording there, but during one three-week stretch, Jana and Jerry both stayed at New York's Carlyle Hotel while Mick—obviously unbeknownst to Hall—shuttled between them.

Jana sneaked past the paparazzi planted on the front lawn of her LA home and joined Mick in London. "It's been so blown out of proportion, it's a joke," she told a friend. "To me, it's funny. It's ridiculous." But for the first time in years, Jagger worried that he'd gone too far. They should keep their distance, he suggested, until the press cooled down. Jana finally said of her years-long relationship with Mick, "It's just over, the whole thing." Paraphrasing a Stones classic, "Mother's Little Helper," she declared their affair to be "a drag."

Hall couldn't have agreed more. She hired Anthony Julius, the British divorce lawyer who had just landed a $26 million cash settlement for Princess Diana, and told Mick that their marriage was over. "Being a single parent is not what I would choose," she said wistfully. "I like a proper home life."

Ironically, when news of the split hit the papers, it happened to be one of those rare times when Mick was in charge of the children. While Jerry was in the south of France filming *RPM,* a caper comedy starring David Arquette, Dad holed up with thirteen-year-old Elizabeth, eleven-year-old James, and three-year-old Georgia at Desmond Guinness's spectacular Leixlip Castle near Dublin.

Watched over by their nanny, the children rode horses and explored the castle grounds, leaving Jagger to weigh carefully the possible outcome of his latest indiscretions: namely, that Jerry might walk away with a sizable chunk of his fortune, now conservatively estimated at $200 million.

Keith had long pondered what it was that made his friend so reckless in his pursuit of women. Now, for the first time, Richards felt compelled to urge Jagger to seek professional help for sex addiction. "I sometimes see what the old bugger wants in life," Keith said. "He's intent on being Casanova or Don Juan. He's always looking for it, which is a little cruel on his loved ones. But he's always been like that." The trouble with that, said Keith, is that you "end up alone. It's all pretty pathetic, if you really want to know."

Over the next several months, Mick bombarded Jerry with tender love notes, flowers, and expensive gifts. Incredibly, Jerry ("I don't remember anything bad for very long") agreed to take him back again, but this time only after he agreed to seek therapy for sex addiction. "I had hoped he would outgrow these things," she said, "but that didn't happen." As for the chances that Mick intended to hold up his end of the bargain and get counseling, Jerry waxed philosophical. "I'll believe it," she sighed, "when I see it."

As they had so many times before, and primarily for the sake of the kids, Mick and Jerry set out to prove that all was well in the House of Jagger. The family spent the holidays together at the house in Richmond, then Mick joined the other Stones back at Ocean Way Recording in LA. Once again, tensions arose when Mick unilaterally hired several cutting-edge producers to work on different album tracks. The result was chaos. "We ended up for the first time almost making separate records," Richards said. "Mine and Mick's."

They resolved their differences, along with an unforeseen problem with one of the cuts on the LP. While the record was being mastered, Keith's daughter Angela noticed that the new song "Anybody Seen My Baby?" bore a strong resemblance to k. d. lang's 1992 hit "Constant Craving." To head off a lawsuit, Mick suggested that they just share credit with Lang and her songwriting partner, Ben Mink. Lang was delighted.

At this late stage in the process, Mick still had no idea what to call the album and the tour that would accompany its release. "We still hadn't settled on any kind of theme," Mick said, "and I was banging my head trying to find one. I have always been obsessed with bridges . . ." In the end, Mick came up with a name that both catered to his obsession and conveyed that touch of malevolence for which the Stones were famous: *Bridges to Babylon*.

Now Mick could concentrate on a name for his next child. That spring, Jerry, who had just turned forty-one, informed Mick that she was expecting their fourth child. "We were all very surprised, to say the least," a Richmond neighbor said. "Given all that had been going on between them, another baby just didn't make any sense."

With their usual flair, on August 18, 1997 the Stones climbed into a red Cadillac and drove it over the Brooklyn Bridge. Waiting on the Manhattan side beneath the bridge was the usual contingent of several hundred reporters, this time eager to hear details about the Stones' Bridges to Babylon world tour.

The next day, the Stones started filming the video for "Anybody Seen My Baby?" The set: a seedy burlesque house where Mick sits in the audience ogling the scantily clad dancers onstage.

From the moment she stepped onto the set, the lushly beautiful unknown hired to play the "baby" Mick is missing seized his attention—and everyone else's. Her name: Angelina Jolie.

Mick: great guy, lousy husband.

—JERRY HALL

◆   ◆   ◆

Obviously, I'm no paragon of virtue.

—MICK

8

◆ ◆ ◆

The Final Straw:
"Angelina, It's Mick. Call Me!"

*a*ngelina Jolie made it perfectly clear to everyone that she didn't want to be playing the part of a stripper in a Rolling Stones video. "I can't fucking sing, and I can't fucking dance!" she said, tossing an angry look at the director. "What the fuck am I doing here?" The daughter of Academy Award–winning actor Jon Voight had just finished portraying doomed model Gia Carangi in a television film of the same name, and the part had left her physically and emotionally drained—and, like Gia, who died of AIDS at just twenty-six, addicted to heroin.

Angie's mother, actress-producer Marcheline Bertrand, was behind Jolie's decision to appear in the Stones video. Although Angelina was already married to British actor Jonny Lee Miller of *Trainspotting* fame and carrying on an affair with actor Timothy Hutton, Marche felt that her daughter needed a man like Mick. "Marche loved Mick for Angie," said Marcheline's friend Lauren Taines. "She felt that he could teach her about fame and how to handle it."

Right now, all Angelina wanted was to get through the video

shoot. At one point, Jolie whipped off her blonde wig to reveal her bald head, shaved for her role in *Gia*. Then, clad in a fur coat opened to reveal a gold lamé bustier beneath, Angelina brought traffic to a standstill as she strolled down a midtown street with Mick in hot pursuit.

Beyond her obvious physical attributes and the fact that she was the daughter of a bona fide Hollywood star (Mick was just four years younger than Voight), Jolie offered something extra: an element of danger. She was high-strung, foul-mouthed, and given to dark moods and fits of temper. She used hard drugs. She had a fondness for tattoos, piercings, and S&M ("It's a weird cleansing of self"). She was a self-confessed "cutter"—someone whose self-esteem was so low that she coped by making small cuts in her arms and legs. As an actress, she totally immersed herself in her characters, sometimes disappearing for days or weeks at a time.

Unbeknownst to Mick, Angelina was also prone to bouts of suicidal depression—a condition aggravated by the fact that she had not yet managed to get her acting career off the ground. At one point, she even contacted a contract killer and asked how she might go about hiring him to end her life. After she'd overcome these demons, Jolie would admit that her suicide-for-hire scheme was "very weird."

For Mick, a large part of Jolie's appeal was her wild streak. "She scares me a little," he said. "I like that." Encouraged by Marcheline, who was determined to see her mercurial daughter marry him, Mick wasted no time pursuing Jolie once the cameras stopped rolling. At first she refused to return his phone calls, and the messages began to pile up on her machine: "Angelina, it's Mick. Will you please, please call me?" "Miss Jolie, why aren't you returning my calls?" "Angelina, I have *got* to speak to you. Call me."

Eventually she did accept an invitation to spend time with Mick in Palm Beach, Florida, during a break in the *Bridges to Babylon* tour that fall. The weekend left Angelina unimpressed and Mick wanting more.

After another flurry of pleading calls went unanswered, Mick switched to a more indirect approach. He knew that Angelina and Jonny Miller were amicably separated, and that if Miller were cast in Jagged Films' upcoming *Enigma,* Jolie would almost certainly visit him on the set.

When Angelina learned of Mick's machinations, she phoned him and unleashed a torrent of expletives. She did not want to see him again, and she did not want him leaving her any more plaintive messages.

But the messages continued, each sounding more desperate than the last. Taines, who listened to the new batch, described them as "astonishing." After all, here was Mick Jagger, "virtually sobbing" over the phone. Angie, added Taines, was doing a marvelous job of "messing with Mick's head." Jagger's stop-and-go romance with Angelina Jolie lurched on for another two years—and even that was not the end of it.

None of this distracted Mick from the business at hand: putting on the most exciting stage show audiences had ever seen. Starting in Toronto on September 9, 1997, the yearlong Bridges to Babylon tour included 108 shows seen by 4.58 million people on four continents. They would pay $339 million for the privilege, enabling the group to best its own record-smashing take for the Voodoo Lounge tour.

This time, veteran set designer Mark Fisher borrowed from epic filmmaker Cecil B. DeMille to create an immense main stage with a Babylonian motif. In keeping with the tour's theme, $1 million was spent on building a 150-foot-long telescoping cantilevered bridge that extended out over the first rows to a "B" stage.

At first there was real concern that the bridge might collapse on the audience. "They were yelling 'Only one person at a time!'" Jagger recalled, "and 'Not too fast, Mick!'" But after fifty shows, things had loosened up to the point where "there we all were, running along and banging across the bridge."

The Stones were about to take the stage in Atlanta on December 9, when Mick left another message for Angelina, beseeching her to join him. The call was interrupted by Jerry, phoning from London with the news that Mick was a father for the sixth time. Hall had just given birth to their fourth child and second son together: Gabriel Luke Beauregard Jagger. Unfortunately, any father and child meeting would have to wait. The Stones had a concert in St. Louis before Mick could fly home on December 13 to lay eyes on his newborn son for the first time.

There would be other firsts for Mick and the Stones in the coming months. Resuming the Bridges to Babylon tour in January, Mick opened his mouth during a microphone check in Syracuse, New York, only to have nothing come out. Because of his laryngitis, three shows had to be canceled and rescheduled—the first time a show had ever been canceled because of Jagger. Later the European leg of the tour was postponed a month. The reason: Keith, reaching for a book in his Connecticut home, fell off a library ladder and cracked three ribs. "Ah," he said at the time, "all part of life's rich pageant."

Changes in Britain's tax laws forced the Stones to cancel shows there as well, but Mick came across one easy way to make up for lost revenue. For a reported $2 million fee, the Stones took time off from their February concert at Honolulu's Aloha Stadium to perform for four thousand Pepsi employees celebrating the company's centennial. "I did coke for twenty years," he announced at the start of the show, "and now I'm doing Pepsi!" The crowd roared its approval.

As the band headed to South America that spring, Mick seemed more obsessed than ever with persuading Angelina to join him. By March, he'd turned to Charlie Watts for help. Jolie had been learning to play the drums, as both an artistic outlet and a form of therapy. In the process, she had become friends with Charlie. Now Watts was interceding on Mick's behalf, telling Jolie that she really should return Mick's calls.

When Jolie finally called Mick back, he invited her to join him in Rio de Janeiro on the Brazilian leg of the tour. This time she had a solid reason for not accepting. She was filming the part of a sociopath in *Girl, Interrupted*—the role that would win her an Academy Award for Best Supporting Actress.

Mick sought companionship elsewhere. One night in April, wearing a maroon blazer and tight white trousers, he strolled into a party at the villa of Brazilian oil and gas tycoon Olavo Egydio Monteiro De Carvalho. Although he danced happily with a number of young women there, one in particular caught his eye: a six-foot-tall, chestnut-haired beauty named Luciana Gimenez Morad.

The daughter of a nightclub impresario and an actress, Luciana started modeling in her native São Paulo at age thirteen, and three years later was discovered by Elite Model Agency founder John Casablancas. After a decade spent walking the runways of Paris, London, Milan, and New York, Luciana had grown tired of the grind. For a time, it looked as if Rod Stewart might come to her rescue. Their affair lasted for nearly a year before it became clear to Luciana that Stewart was not quite ready to leave his wife, model Rachel Hunter (in the end, it was Hunter who would dump Rod).

Since Luciana was one of the few attractive young women at the party who spoke English (in addition to Portuguese, Spanish, German, Italian, and French), Jagger wound up spending much of the evening whispering into her ear. At one point, Mick told his hosts that he and the young lady were headed for the villa's gardens to "meditate." Instead, they began an affair that would have earth-shattering consequences for Jagger's family life. At three o'clock the following morning, Mick left in a black Mercedes.

Mick had not given up on Angelina, but for now, Luciana would do nicely. "I just love sex," she had once blurted out to a startled reporter. "I have had intercourse on a deserted beach, an airplane, and even in a nightclub."

She was certainly eager to please Mr. Jagger—a man who was several years older than her own father. "All Mick had to do was call her up," said her friend and former roommate Lars Albert, "and within minutes she would be on her way to the airport." According to Albert, this occurred at least once a month, and each time Luciana paid for her own plane tickets. Once, she flew from Hamburg to Denmark to spend a single night with Jagger.

On another occasion that summer, she flew into Hamburg from a photo shoot in Paris and asked Albert if he would pick her up at the airport. He met Morad in his battered VW and drove her to Hamburg's Atlantic Hotel, where Mick had reserved a suite in her name. "We rolled up in my rusty old car among a queue of limousines waiting for the Rolling Stones," Albert said, "and were ignored completely. They probably thought we were the cleaners arriving for work." Luciana was able to slip into the hotel for her rendezvous with Mick completely unnoticed. The next morning, Albert returned to pick Luciana up and drive her back to the airport.

"That's the way it often went," said a security guard who worked the European leg of the tour. "Mick had girls at every stop on the tour, some flying in from other cities, but it was rare that reporters ever got wind of them."

Early in the relationship, Luciana told Albert that she practiced safe sex with Jagger. "I am very careful with Mick at the moment," she said. "We always have safe sex. I am in control of that. It would not happen unless I wanted it to."

Albert believed that is exactly what she wanted from the very beginning. "Luciana was totally besotted with Mick," he said, "but she knew that under ordinary circumstances Mick would not leave Jerry, no matter what Luciana did to please him." So Luciana hatched a plan. "She wanted Mick," Albert said. "She decided there was only one way to get him—to trap him by having his baby. Then Jerry would kick Mick out, and Mick would come to Luciana."

Luciana did her best to keep Mick interested. Once when they were drinking Dom Perignon in bed, she poured some in her stiletto shoe. "She handed it to him," Albert said, "he drank it down and threw it over his shoulder." She also told Albert there were naked pillow fights that left them both "giggling like little kids. Luciana loved all this; it was great fun for her."

By July, Luciana had stopped using contraception—information she apparently neglected to share with Mick. "It was her dream to have children," Albert said, "so now she tried to achieve this dream with Mick, with or without his consent. She is the one who controlled what happened between them."

Not all of Jagger's conquests during this period were leggy models. Mick also allegedly had time for the help. Claire Houseman had already worked as a nanny for Dire Straits' Mark Knopfler as well as for Sting when she was hired in June 1998 to care for Gabriel. But from her first meeting with Mick and Jerry on tour with the Stones in Brussels, Houseman realized that nothing had prepared her for the Jaggers.

Jerry was lying on a bed with baby Gabriel when Houseman, thirty-two, was ushered into the room carrying her suitcase. Within seconds Mick popped out of the shower—"stark naked. I didn't know where to put my eyes," said Houseman, who recalled dropping her bag. "The next thing I knew he put out his hand and said, 'Hi, I'm Mick.' He didn't seem embarrassed . . . it was all so unreal." As for Jerry: "She didn't say a word."

The next afternoon, Houseman was making coffee in the kitchen when Mick sidled up next to her. "We were laughing and joking together," she said. "I must say, he is a real charmer. The kitchen was so small, we kept bumping into each other." Mick began stroking her hair, and moments later lifted her up onto the kitchen counter and pulled down her pants. "We kissed passionately," the nanny said, "my head was swimming. The next thing I remember, he was making love to me."

It was over in a flash. "The earth didn't move or anything like that," Houseman said. "I just thought to myself, 'God, is that it?'"

Mick zipped up his pants, helped the nanny down off the counter, and kissed her on the nose. "Okay, babe," he said. "And," Houseman said, "that was it." Incredibly, the entire time, Jerry was just thirty feet away in the bedroom with little Gabriel. "It all seemed like a blur to me," Houseman recalled. "Mick went back to his wife, while I carried on making the coffee. It was very strange."

Now that he was fifty-five, Mick at least seemed to have graduated from teenagers to twentysomethings and even thirtysomethings. One particular twenty-six-year-old, however, was of particular concern. Now split from Piers Jackson, the father of her two daughters, Jade decided to move from the million-dollar mansion that Mick had purchased for her in London's Notting Hill district to a hilltop cottage on the Spanish resort island of Ibiza.

On the morning of July 12, Mick was on tour in Vienna, Austria, when someone handed him a copy of one of London's biggest tabloids: "Exposed: Jagger's Daughter Jade in Sex Film Scandal." As a favor to friends who owned one of the island's wildest nightclubs, Manumission, Jade had posed for a series of X-rated posters promoting the club as well as a line of porn videos. Under the heading "pink pussy," Jade wore nothing but a cat mask and was trussed up with white rope. In another, she posed with a naked couple—both were daubed with ketchup, her legs are spread, and he's biting her knee. The posters were slapped up all over the island for everyone to see—including Mick's grandchildren, their playmates, other parents, and visiting British tourists. Many were shocked. "It is sleazy and tasteless," one said. "I found the images offensive and shocking. It's hard to imagine her father wouldn't as well."

Jade's friends, Manumission owners Mike McKay and Claire Davis, regularly had sex onstage in front of thousands of cheering patrons. Their lucrative side business involved producing videos featuring drag queens, strippers, and dwarves engaging in a variety of graphic sex acts.

"Jade's a good friend. She wanted to do those pictures," McKay said. "She didn't get paid. If she wants to take part in a porn movie or the live sex shows, that's up to her."

What about Mick? "Her dad wouldn't give a toss," McKay answered. "Who's he to moralize, anyway?"

Mick and Bianca had kept their distance since the divorce, but when it came to their daughter, they often put up a united front. They also realized that there was not much they could do to influence the headstrong Jade once she'd made up her mind. "Mick's very old-fashioned when it comes to the children," Jerry said. "He's always said he's exactly the kind of person he'd tell Jade to stay away from."

Jade wasn't the only Jagger child giving Mick cause for concern. That summer, fourteen-year-old Elizabeth had been strutting the catwalks and appearing alongside her mom in photo shoots—all designed, it was suggested, to boost forty-two-year-old Jerry's flagging career.

At the Thierry Mugler fashion show in Paris, Jerry and Elizabeth created a sensation swanning down the runway in matching gowns. They later did the same at Vivienne Westwood's Paris show, and in the fall, famed fashion photographer David Bailey shot mother and daughter for the cover of *Harper's & Queen* magazine.

Jagger called home to let Hall know that he did not want Elizabeth modeling under any circumstances. "Mick is furious about it," Jerry conceded. "He says it's silly, because she doesn't need the money. He wants Elizabeth to concentrate on her schoolwork." Hall, who coached Elizabeth for each of her modeling assignments, disagreed. "I tell him almost every schoolgirl wants to be a model," she said. "Elizabeth is very grown-up, polite, and mature, and she's only doing it in her summer holidays . . ." But, Hall added, "I'd never let Elizabeth work with an agency that takes young girls off to Milan and encourages them to go out with playboys. Ugh!"

Mom found ingenious ways to showcase other Jagger children as well. That spring, Jerry was photographed by Annie Leibovitz for *Vanity Fair,* bearing her breast to feed Gabriel as she struck a regal pose in fur coat, evening dress, and high heels.

No one seriously believed that Jerry wanted to stop working entirely or, for that matter, give up life in the public eye. But she realized that her days as a runway model were numbered. To make way for new blood—namely, Elizabeth—Hall announced in *Harper's & Queen* that she was retiring. "I don't need the money either," said Jerry, whose own fortune from modeling and endorsements was estimated at more than $7 million. "I just want to be a housewife and mother." She also couldn't resist taking a very public swipe at one of Mick's lovers—a certain model who "doesn't know I know she slept with Mick, but I do, and she's just a little tramp."

At the time, she had no idea that the "little tramp" was about to cause big trouble. Luciana found out she was pregnant that November while on a modeling assignment in Paris. She called Mick with the news. "I broke down in tears and told him over the phone," she recalled. "I think he cried too. He was really understanding. I told him I had already heard the baby's heartbeat, and abortion was not an option. I really wanted to have my baby. He was fine; he was rather nice."

Understandably, Jagger took a different tack with Hall. Jetting home to London in mid-November, Mick broke the news to Jerry that Luciana Morad was pregnant—and claiming the baby was his.

"Well?" Jerry asked.

"I don't think so," Mick replied.

Jerry had at last reached the breaking point.

"You're driving me crazy!" she screamed. "You're trying to make me go mad, like the woman in *Gaslight*." She bundled up one-year-old Gabriel and left the next morning for New York. Mick, meanwhile, headed for the Jaggers' Loire Valley château. Along the way, he stopped off at Carla Bruni's Paris apartment for dinner and left shortly before midnight.

The next morning, Carla made no effort to conceal the fact that she had been with Jagger. "Who wouldn't love Mick?" she told a photographer. "He's very charming." Moreover, she admitted that she dreamt of becoming Mrs. Jagger. "If I'd met Mick before he was married, I would have loved to marry him," she said. "Mick would make a fantastic husband."

Bruni then took aim squarely at Jerry: "Jerry Hall has problems with her husband, but she doesn't blame them on herself. She blames them on him and me," Bruni said. "She's looking for sympathy, but I think it's a pretty pathetic thing to do in public."

If he had intended to hurt Jerry by "visiting" with Bruni in such a public manner, Mick succeeded. Yet it was nothing compared to the humiliation she felt when, on November 27, the *Sun* broke the news that Luciana Morad was pregnant with Jagger's baby.

It was now clearer than ever to Hall that Mick would "never change. It's like an addiction he can't stop. He is a sexual predator," she added, "who can't help indulging himself with other women."

What really pushed her over the edge this time was the children's attitude toward Dad's womanizing and, more important, Mom's willingness to look the other way. "The final straw," she said, "was when my children began to take on a mocking, disrespectful tone. Then I thought, 'Uh-oh, I'm setting a terrible example.' I was to blame because I tolerated a bad situation . . . It was my fault too. Every week it was in the papers. Public humiliation, private heartbreak. It's not easy for any woman."

Once again, Jerry turned to Princess Diana's divorce attorney, Anthony Julius of the prestigious London law firm of Mishcon de Reya. On January 15, 1999, Hall filed for a divorce on the grounds of "multiple adultery" and demanded $50 million worth of satisfaction.

Mick was in San Francisco rehearsing for the Stones' No Security tour—a scaled-down version of Bridges to Babylon playing at smaller venues—when he got the news. Obviously, his lawyers had already been briefed on what to expect and wasted no time in answering Jerry's complaint. Simply put, Mick was contesting Jerry's divorce petition on the grounds that their Hindu wedding on Bali was not valid; according to Jagger, they were never married in the first place.

Not that Mick and Jerry would let a little thing like divorce get in the way of their friendship. While their lawyers sparred over technicalities in England's High Court, the couple agreed that it was in the best interest of the children for them to be civil toward each other. In fact, that February Mick rented a $7,500-a-day chalet in Aspen for a family ski vacation. On Valentine's Day, Mick and Jerry even shared a cozy candlelit dinner for two. "For a couple who are supposed to hate each other," a friend said, "they are being remarkably friendly. They clearly still have very deep feelings for one another."

The togetherness would continue for months: whenever Mick had a break in the tour, he spent time with Jerry and the kids, taking them to the park, shopping, splashing in the surf in the south of France. "He's a wonderful person. He's not a mean person," said Jerry, who had nonetheless resumed her smoking habit under the strain. "He's a good father, he's clever, he's funny, he's attractive, he's great to be with. We are always laughing . . .

"It's funny," she went on, "I think we're more comfortable with each other than we've been in years, now that we know it's over." So comfortable, in fact, that Mick moved into the house next to Jerry's in Richmond and knocked down a dining room wall for easy access between the two buildings. "I really don't see," said their friend and former Stone Bill Wyman, "how anything has changed at all."

Not much really had. While he was working on repairing relations with Jerry, Mick gave a $5,000 pair of earrings to Angelina Jolie. Now juggling Tim Hutton, future husband Billy Bob Thornton, Nicolas Cage, and Australian actor Russell Crowe, Jolie still enjoyed toying with Mick's affections—and needling her meddlesome mother. One evening Angie called Marcheline with the trumped-up tale that she and Mick were getting married. Marcheline couldn't wait to call Jagger.

"Congratulations, Mick!" Marcheline cooed over the phone. "Such wonderful news!"

"What," he asked in reply, "are you talking about?"

Incredibly, Angie's antics only made Mick that much more persistent. His acrimony was reserved for just one woman at the moment—the one who claimed that she was having his baby. On May 17, 1999, Luciana Morad gave birth to a baby boy in New York. She named him Lucas Maurice but left the father's name blank on the birth certificate, waiting for legal affirmation that Mick was Lucas's dad. Even before they left the hospital, Luciana noticed a family resemblance. "I'm not saying he has Mick's lips," she said, "but he has his lungs—listen to him howl!"

Like Hall, Luciana waged legal war on Mick while simultaneously trying to forge a new relationship with him. In London, Luciana sued Jagger for £5 million—then about $8 million—to settle her paternity claims. With the help of famed New York divorce lawyer

Raoul Felder, she was seeking to have a US court force Mick to take a DNA test to prove whether or not the baby was his.

Luciana was convinced that once Mick saw his son, they could be a family. "He's the sweetest little thing you've ever seen," she said. "How could Mick fail to fall in love with him? I can't take my eyes off of him, he's so beautiful. I want Mick to see him as soon as possible." The young model who had been so willing to fly anywhere for a tryst with Jagger now said that she would drop everything to show Mick his newborn son. "If he can't come to America, then we'll fly to him," she said. "Wherever he wants to meet in the world, we'll go. I want Lucas to know his daddy."

The feeling was not mutual. Convinced that Luciana had tricked him into fathering her child, Mick blamed her for destroying his marriage—assuming, of course, that Jerry was willing to tolerate his infidelities forever. A month after Lucas's birth, Mick was performing with the Stones in London and singing the lyrics to "Some Girls"—*Some girls give me children/I never asked them for*—with an extra splash of venom. The crowd, well aware of the ongoing paternity scandal, cheered.

Even Eva Jagger, now suffering heart problems and confined to a wheelchair, was drawn into the scandal. When a reporter called and asked Mick's mum how many grandchildren she had, she paused. "I knew what they wanted," she recalled, "so I told him, 'I think it's twenty-two.' There was dead silence at the other end."

Not everyone was amused. "He's a horrible man, ugly, and a womanizer," snapped Veronica Doyle, the Scottish nanny Luciana hired to care for Lucas. Doyle had looked after Luciana as a child, and broke her customary silence to share what she thought of Jagger. "I can't stand his music. He's just an awful man."

Even before DNA tests would prove in July that Mick was indeed Lucas's father, Jerry and Mick reached a settlement in her ongoing divorce action. In exchange for not contesting his claim that their marriage was invalid, Jerry agreed to accept $15 million in cash and the mansion in Richmond, Surrey, now valued at $7 million. In addition, $1.5 million would be deposited in each of their four children's trust funds.

By agreeing to annul their marriage, Jerry and Mick instantly made their children illegitimate—the sort of niggling technicality that apparently concerned Jagger not at all. Hall felt differently. Despite dropping her action and going along with the settlement, Jerry stated for the record one final time that she believed that she and Mick were married legally.

"The marriage ceremony bore, so far as I was aware, all the usual hallmarks of a wedding," she said. "The ceremony was lengthy and complicated and was preceded by what I believed was a ceremonial conversion into the Hindu faith. Mick and I exchanged wedding vows and rings." She acknowledged, however, that she had never seen a marriage certificate.

In the end, both agreed that a quick and amicable settlement would be best for everyone. "Mick Jagger and Jerry Hall are determined that their friendship and mutual respect will endure," read a joint statement by the couple's lawyers. "They will always be linked through the great shared love they have for their four children and their determination to play their full part as parents to Elizabeth, James, Georgia May, and Gabriel."

It remained to be seen what role, if any, Mick intended to play in the life of little Lucas. Now armed with DNA results, Luciana pressed her case for a multimillion-dollar settlement in both England and the United States, all the while hoping that she might entice Mick into a longer relationship. "She knew that as the mother of his child, she had the kind of hold on Mick only a few women in the world had," a friend said. "She wanted to step in where Jerry Hall left off."

Hall herself claimed to hold "no animosity towards the baby, or towards her." She told Mick that any time he wanted Lucas to meet his half-siblings, she was happy to oblige. In the meantime, Jagger would have to deal with Luciana. "It's not my problem," shrugged Jerry. "Mick has to sort it out."

But even before Lucas's birth, Jagger had moved on to another Latin bombshell—one who, like the erstwhile Carla Bruni, had money of her own. In fact, Mick had known Vanessa Neumann since she was four; her father, Venezuelan industrialist Hans Neumann, had actually purchased the island of Mustique from Colin Tennant in the mid-1970s, and the Neumann family still owned a sizable chunk of the island. Now twenty-seven and boasting a personal fortune estimated at $200 million, Vanessa had just purchased a mansion in London's exclusive St. John's Wood neighborhood. She spent most of her time, however, in New York, studying for her PhD in philosophy at Columbia University. It was on Mustique, at a Christmas party in 1998, that they began their affair.

For Neumann, Mick's age was a plus. "I've taken toy boys on trips, bought them tickets to Paris or Mustique, bought them gifts," she said. "I was very generous, but I always got bored. I wipe the floor with men my own age."

Ballyhooed in Britain's tabloid press as the "[Fire] Cracker from Caracas," Neumann soon echoed the oft-repeated claim that Mick was "amazing in bed" and "the best lover I've ever had." Neumann brought something new to the table. In between romps, Mick and his erudite girlfriend of the moment discussed German philosophers Schopenhauer and Nietzsche, global affairs, and business.

There were other affairs as well, with Ortensia Visconti, niece of legendary Italian director Luciano Visconti, and sloe-eyed, six-foot-tall British actress-feminist-socialist Saffron Burrows. One of the stars of the Jagger-produced *Enigma,* the then-twenty-eight-year-old Burrows was ending her relationship with fifty-two-year-old film director Mike Figgis (*Leaving Las Vegas*). Burrows was also an outspoken bisexual who claimed to have a crush on Hillary Clinton—a tidbit that Burrows would later share with Bill Clinton when she started seeing the former president in 2001. For now, however, Jagger and Burrows were steaming things up in London, New York, and on the French Riviera.

Jerry, now content to watch all the bed hopping from the sidelines, sympathized with the man she once called her husband. "I feel sorry for Mick," she said. "Sexual promiscuity just leads to chaos, and you have to clear it up. I wish he'd find happiness, but I'm not churning inside about it."

As for Mick's chances of ever really changing, Hall struck a hopeful note. "I hope he changes," she said. "He probably will; he's very smart. I still have faith, but it's hard for him. He's like a Greek god—he symbolizes fertility."

There was another reason, Jerry hastened to add, for her newfound sense of inner peace. To cope with Mick's rampant cheating, she had turned to Kabbalah, a trendy form of Jewish mysticism that had been embraced by Madonna, Michael Jackson, Elizabeth Taylor, and other celebrities in search of a spiritual fix. To please his then wife, Mick not only took Kabbalah lessons but cohosted a celebrity fund-raiser for the movement in London.

As delighted as she was by Mick's newfound spiritualism, Jerry was even more impressed to learn that he was finally seeing a sex therapist—until he seduced the therapist. "He loved to spank," Natasha Terry recalled of their affair. "I started laughing because I was never into spanking." Her professional opinion: "I think he is like a sex vampire. Being with all these different people makes him feel young and gives him all this energy. He can't stay faithful to one woman. He has to get that satisfaction from bedding a lot of women at the same time."

That was never more evident than at the party record producer Richard Perry threw to watch the Evander Holyfield–Lennox Lewis world heavyweight championship fight in November 1999. Mick took Angelina Jolie as his date but wound up disappearing for a portion of the evening with a sex symbol from a different generation: Farrah Fawcett.

As 1999 drew to a close, the Stones (and Mick, individually) were offered millions to perform a single concert ringing in the new millennium. Mick accepted only one invitation—from Jerry, to spend Christmas and New Year's Eve with her and the kids. "I can't bear the thought of spending millennium night without Mick," she said. "We'll always love each other on a certain level. That doesn't change."

Another thing that had not changed was Mick's penury. "He likes going to Morocco," Hall said, "and spending the entire day arguing over the price of two carpets, and I'm saying, 'Honey, it's a poor country, just give them the money.'" Bianca was more succinct. "He," she once said of Mick, "is a penny-pinching Scrooge."

Although he remained a notorious tightwad—his former publicist Keith Altham often watched as Jagger tried to get away with tipping New York cabbies a quarter—Jagger dug into his own pocket to help build a $4 million arts center at his alma mater, Dartford Grammar School. Of course, the center was to be named in his honor.

Eva and Joe Jagger were both on hand for the opening of the Mick Jagger Centre in March 2000, but their son's reminiscences about life as a student there were hardly positive. "It really wasn't pleasant," Mick said, adding that there were teachers "who would just punch you out. They'd slap your face so hard you'd go down. Then there was the ear torture. They would drag you up to the front of the class and lecture you while twisting your ear the whole time."

Mick was at the Cannes Film Festival with Jerry when he got word on May 18 that his mother had died at age eighty-seven. "Michael," as she called him, had always been particularly close to Eva Jagger, calling her every few days from the road ("It doesn't matter where in the world he is, he'll ring to see how we are"), and frequently sending flowers, chocolates, and gifts. Five years earlier, Mick built a $400,000 "granny flat" adjacent to the Richmond house so that he could better care for his parents.

"Mick was very close to Eva," said Keith, who had known all the Jaggers since childhood. "This has hit him very hard." Devastated, Mick flew back to London to comfort his father and his brother, Chris. At the funeral, Mick's fellow Stones watched as he choked back tears singing two of Eva's favorite hymns, "Morning Has Broken" and "Will the Circle Be Unbroken." "I was standing by my window on a cold and cloudy day," Mick sang, his voice cracking, "when I saw that hearse come rolling for to carry my mother away."

Later, as the casket passed by, Mick broke down sobbing. Jerry immediately put her arm around Mick to comfort him. Once he regained his composure, it was Mick's turn to hug his father, Joe, as they left the church. "Some people may think Michael is a bad boy," Eva had once joked, "but he is a very good son."

Five weeks later, the family gathered again, but this time for a happy occasion: Karis's wedding to film production assistant Jonathan Watson in San Francisco. In a remarkable show of togetherness, four generations of Jaggers took part, including Joe Jagger, six of Mick's seven children, Marsha Hunt (now a successful writer in her own right), Jerry Hall, and all of Mick's grandchildren. (Thirteen-month-old Lucas remained in London with his mother, Luciana Morad.)

Mick, wearing a traditional black morning suit and gray waistcoat, gave away the bride. It was a far cry from the days when Mick denied being Karis's father and then waged an eight-year legal battle to keep from paying child support. "It was a shock, a total shock, when he didn't want to get involved with her," the mother of the bride said. "But we're on new ground, and it's not fair to keep rehashing what was wrong all those years ago."

Mick would, in fact, have his hands full coping with family matters in the coming months. When sixteen-year-old, five-foot-eleven Elizabeth announced that she was quitting school to become a full-time model, Mick blamed Jerry. "I was putting it off as long as possible," Mom said, "but she's thin and very pretty, so model scouts kept coming up to her in the street and giving her their cards."

"I intended that she should be raised as a normal child," Mick said, "but it is difficult, and Jerry is a famous model. We argued constantly about this." Jagger was convinced that Elizabeth, who was now smoking, had simply grown up too fast. Now when she went to parties in London or New York, Dad insisted on coming along as her chaperone. "It was very awkward and rather strange," one denizen of London's Groucho Club pointed out. "People go wild when Mick Jagger is around. Things can get out of hand. I'm not sure, in that sense, that he works well as a chaperone."

Then there was the matter of Jerry's first nude scene onstage, as Mrs. Robinson in a West End production of *The Graduate*. Jerry's mother called Mick from Texas and demanded that he stop her. "How can my daughter do things like that?" she asked. "It's so degrading. She's a mother of four, she's been to events with the royal family. Now she's going to ruin it all!"

Mick decided that it was the better part of valor not to intervene. Jerry had made it clear that Mrs. Robinson was "in a marriage where she didn't love her husband and her husband doesn't love her. She's angry," she added, "and after what I've been through, I have a lot of anger that I intend to let out."

On opening night at the Gielgud Theatre that July, Mick and several Jagger children were in the audience when Jerry dropped her towel and stood stark naked onstage. "Wham!" she recalled. "All hell broke loose. There were photographers hanging over the balcony and standing up in the stalls. It was pandemonium." Hall had turned down a $1 million offer to pose nude in *Playboy,* and now "these guys were getting the picture for free! I was annoyed."

Mick, with his eye forever on the bottom line, understood perfectly. While he juggled the Stones' finances, watched over the *Enigma* budget, and plotted his own solo career, there was still time to invest in new moneymaking schemes. In November Jagger teamed up with the rock group U2 to form a $200 million offshore real estate investment trust. Based in the Channel Islands, the new company invested in small offices and shops on the edges of London's West End and Docklands neighborhoods. It was Mick's first foray into commercial real estate, but not U2's. The Irish band had already made a huge profit expanding and then selling the Malmaison hotel chain. Members Bono and the Edge would also later buy and rebuild Dublin's landmark Clarence Hotel.

Unfortunately, the real estate deal with U2 focused even more attention on the size of Mick's fortune, which some now put at close to $300 million. To many, it seemed that Mick could well afford to pay the $8 million settlement that Luciana was demanding for Lucas.

Even as their battle raged on in the courts, Mick tried to forge a bond with the little boy. In London, he was spotted pushing Lucas through the park in his stroller, then stopping to give the toddler a wooden toy train. Moments later, Lucas squealed with delight while Daddy made faces at him.

"Lucas needs his father," Luciana said. "Mick dotes on him . . . He spoils Lucas rotten, and I think Mick wants to see more of him, too." Perhaps, but Lucas's mother had more than just a father-and-child reunion in mind. "I still believe we have a future together," she insisted. "We are good friends now, and I haven't ruled out getting back together with him."

It wasn't an idea that particularly appealed to Luciana's father. João Morad referred repeatedly to the father of his grandchild as "the dirty old man."

That was not far off from the role Mick assayed in *The Man from Elysian Fields,* the film that he started shooting in November. In the movie, which also starred Andy Garcia, Julianna Margulies, Anjelica Huston, and James Coburn, Jagger played the oleaginous owner of a male escort service called Elysian Fields. "We tend to the wounds of lonely women in need of emotional as well as spiritual solace," Mick tells Garcia's character.

"Only women?" Garcia asks.

"Call me old-fashioned," Mick replies.

"It's not just the reply," critic Roger Ebert wrote when *The Man from Elysian Fields* was released the following year. "It's the way Mick Jagger delivers it. The way *only* Mick Jagger could deliver it." Overall, the movie received mixed reviews and flopped at the box office. But that didn't prevent Ebert from naming it one of the year's ten best films, in large part because of Mick's "brave insouciance."

Notwithstanding the occasional character role, Jagger no longer coveted screen stardom. Instead he focused on his new role behind the camera.

As the coproducer (with *Saturday Night Live* creator Lorne Michaels) of *Enigma,* the true story of allied code breakers during World War II, Mick assembled a cast that included Kate Winslet, Dougray Scott, and Jeremy Northam, in addition to the colorful Saffron Burrows. (Mick made only a cameo appearance, as an RAF officer at a dance; daughter Lizzy was an extra.)

Since the plot hinges on cracking the Enigma machine used by the Nazis to send coded messages that could not be deciphered by the Allies, Jagger also bought one at a Sotheby's auction and showed it to Paramount executives. "It was a useful tool to show people," he explained, "when I was trying to get the thing off the ground. It proved that this wasn't all just theoretical nonsense. The machine really existed—and worked."

On the set, Mick the producer helped his actors get in the mood by bringing along his own mix of 1940s big band hits by Tommy Dorsey, Benny Goodman, and Glenn Miller. "Mick understood what some producers don't: that it's important for the actor to have a real sense of time and place as well as character," Winslet said. "It showed a tremendous attention to detail and meant a great deal to the actors that these were the songs that meant wartime Britain to him."

Director Michael Apted (*Coal Miner's Daughter, Gorillas in the Mist*) became accustomed to Jagger showing up at four in the afternoon—nine hours after the start of the shooting day. "Some days he was annoying, like all producers can be," Apted said. "Other days I would look at him and think, 'It's Mick fucking Jagger!'"

Mick was aware—"sort of"—that he intimidated even A-list directors and movie stars. "But I don't think about it all the time. I get to know people in their working environment, and I forget," he mused. "I mean, if I was this loudmouth guy in really sordid clothes like I am onstage, it would be a bit tiring. It wouldn't be appropriate to go on the set and shout, 'Is everybody *all right*?'"

Throwing the full weight of his considerable celebrity behind *Enigma,* Mick dutifully schmoozed studio executives at the Sundance Film Festival and shook hands with Prince Charles at the film's royal premiere in London. For all his efforts, the movie grossed under $5 million in the United States. Mick was unfazed. "It's a labor of love," he said, "which means you do it for very little money."

Money—specifically, how not to divulge how much he had of it—

it—was never far from Mick's mind. Facing the unpleasant prospect of having to spell out his finances to a New York court in the Lucas Morad paternity case, Mick finally signed off on a settlement. Although it was widely reported at the time that she received $5 million plus $25,000 a month in child support, Morad later claimed that she collected no lump sum and $12,510 in child support—a payment that would increase to $16,000 a month as Lucas grew older.

Allowed to make his New York settlement hearing appearance via conference call from London, Mick gave courtroom spectators plenty to laugh about. When asked to give his address, Mick told the judge it was Stargroves, his estate in the Caribbean tax haven of Mustique.

"Star . . . ?"

"Stargroves," Mick replied. "Would you like me to spell it?"

Was Mick under the influence of drugs or alcohol when he signed the settlement agreement?

"Noooooo," Mick answered over the phone, his voice dripping with sarcasm.

Was he under duress?

"Oh, *noooo*." Half the courtroom convulsed with laughter.

Luciana, who now hosted her own prime-time TV show in Brazil, breathed a sigh of relief. "I didn't want to go to court," she said. "To have to was very hard for me. We both feel kind of stupid, having to pay a lot of lawyer's fees. Everyone had to give in a little. Me emotionally and him financially."

Given the distance, there was no chance for Mick to be a constant presence in Lucas's life. But over the years, he would spend time with his son in London and New York, call at least once a week, and, as he did with all his children and grandchildren, shower Lucas with expensive birthday and Christmas presents. "Mick is a wonderful father," Luciana conceded. "Then again, he knows about kids because he's got so many of them!"

As for their future relationship: "I will fancy Mick forever," Luciana said. "He is a very sexy old man. I even find his wrinkles sexy. But all I want from Mick now is friendship. We have a baby together, and for his sake, things have to be friendly."

Luciana also started to echo Carla Bruni on the subject of dating married men. "Now I keep away from married men or any man who is dating anyone else," she said. "All married men should have *Married* branded on their forehead." Still, Luciana admitted that even now she could easily succumb to Mick's magnetism. "He's so sexy. Every time he talks to me, it's something," she said. "I wonder if Lucas is going to cause that much trouble with girls."

Yet the question remained: had Luciana allowed herself to become pregnant simply to entrap Mick? "It's crazy to say I got pregnant on purpose," she insisted, suddenly incensed at the mere suggestion that she might be capable of such a thing. "I'm not that kind of girl!"

As he worked feverishly to complete his fourth solo album, Mick claimed coyly that "friendships" with women were all he had. "I'm getting used to being single," he said. "I spend most nights cuddled up to my hot water bottle. I've a cashmere Burberry cover for it . . ."

It was a nice try. More than ever, Mick, still shaken by the breakup of his relationship with Jerry, was on the prowl for much younger women. "Mick doesn't like being on his own, and he never wanted to go home," said Keith Badgery, Mick's personal chauffeur for fourteen years. "He'd go out to dinner, then on to two or three different parties, and would still be on the phone at three a.m. trying to find someone . . ."

Badgery routinely picked up keys to hotel suites around the world under a variety of aliases ("Mr. Archer" and "David James" were particular favorites), then delivered Mick and his girl of the evening to a side entrance.

Even if he was staying only for the night, Mick always made

certain that the front desk had a list of his requirements. In addition to stocking four bottles of wine—two red, two white—assorted brands of beer, fresh roast java coffee, and fresh-cut flowers in every room, Mick insisted that black photographic paper be taped to the bedroom windows to block out the light. "I've always been," he explained, "a very light sleeper."

Most of Mick's conquests during this period were anonymous. Badgery remembered one girl in Chelsea, and another in Notting Hill. One of the strangest relationships, according to Badgery, was with a French woman—a total stranger that Mick met on the street. After she gave him her phone number, Jagger showed up at her West London flat for three months, bringing Chinese takeout food each time. "Personally, I thought he was quite lonely," Badgery concluded. "You can have sex seven nights a week, but something can still be missing emotionally from your life."

On those occasions when Mick failed to find someone to spend the night with, he still partied into the predawn hours. Writer Dominic Mohan remembered a typical Jagger scene at two twenty in the morning inside the Kabaret Club, a dank basement in London's Soho district. Supermodel Kate Moss was sipping champagne in one corner, and Ronnie Wood was "staggering around" when the DJ decided to put on "Jumpin' Jack Flash." It was then that Mick emerged from the shadows and began to sing along. "The world's most famous lips pouted," Mohan said, "he runs his hands through his hair and spins on his Cuban heels, flapping his arms and wiggling his snake hips . . . We've all seen drunks doing Jagger impressions at wedding receptions, but this is the real deal."

With all eyes on him, Mick spun and twirled his way through "Satisfaction" and "Brown Sugar." It was a "hilarious performance," Mohan continued, "by a wrinkled, elderly man. Hooked on attention and with a complete lack of self-consciousness, he's a walking caricature."

Jerry, who was growing tired of sharing the house in Richmond with Mick ("I told him this has got to end!") agreed with Badgery that Mick was "afraid of being alone . . . I think he's having a hard time," she said. "I mean, he's an addict. I'm sure he'll find someone else to be unfaithful to soon. Poor Mick."

That someone turned out to be statuesque blonde model Sophie Dahl, who counted among her grandparents children's book author Roald Dahl (*Willy Wonka, James and the Giant Peach*), British character actor Stanley Holloway (best known as Eliza Doolittle's dad in the 1964 movie *My Fair Lady*), and Hollywood screen legend Patricia Neal.

Mick still campaigned actively for seventeen-year-old Lizzy to give up modeling and return to school. But when Lizzy and her friend Sophie, twenty-three, got up at a karaoke bar in New York to sing Carly Simon's "You're So Vain," Daddy wasted no time in wangling an introduction from his daughter.

Another Jagger daughter, twenty-nine-year-old Jade, was less than thrilled with her father's new companion. "Don't bring home one of those younger ones, Dad," she said. "No one younger than me and no one bigger. *Please*."

Sophie had achieved notoriety as a voluptuous, 180-pound plus-size model posing in racy ads for Opium perfume. By the time she met Mick, the six-foot-tall Dahl had lost fifty pounds and transformed herself into a stunning size 8.

Soon Mick was crooning love songs to Sophie over the phone and taking her to out-of-the-way clubs and restaurants. "Mick and Sophie used to giggle a lot together in the back seat," recalled Mick's driver, Keith Badgery. "One night when he was all over Sophie in the car, I got out to let them have some privacy. The car was rocking before she got out." When Sophie had left for her flat and Badgery slid back behind the driver's seat, Mick "licked his lips and said, 'That was Sophie.'"

The fact that Sophie was thirty-four years his junior—six years younger than Jade—clearly did not bother Mick. The same could not be said for Sophie's American grandmother. An Oscar winner for her role opposite Paul Newman in the 1963 Western *Hud,* Patricia Neal was no prude; her scandalous affair with the very married Gary Cooper some fifty years earlier was the stuff of Hollywood legend. But she detested Jagger and urged her granddaughter not to have anything to do with him. "Stay away from that bastard," Neal stated bluntly. "If Sophie has anything to do with him, she is just plain crazy. She's such a sweet girl. I have told her he's no good and will break her heart. I just cannot bear the man."

Not surprisingly, Sophie's longtime boyfriend Griffin Dunne was none too pleased, either. When the American actor-director learned that Mick and Sophie had been holed up together in a $2,000-a-night suite at London's Lanesborough Hotel, Dunne dumped her.

After seven months, Dahl dumped Jagger in August 2001—but not before he took from her the inspiration for the title of his new album. To the man more than old enough to be her father, Sophie was the *Goddess in the Doorway.*

Mick wasted no time trying to replace her with an even younger model: sixteen-year-old Caroline Winberg, a Swedish beauty he met backstage at a Paris fashion show. They exchanged numbers, and for several days, Jagger bombarded Winberg with calls—a fact he later denied, claiming that she had been ringing *him,* pleading for concert tickets. "To suggest, as they do," he said, "that I pestered Caroline in any way is absolutely ridiculous."

Not so, insisted Caroline, who claimed that she called him only once and never asked for tickets. "He was the first to phone me," she said. "I found him very charming, and we got on well . . . Very often he calls and says he wants to see me. But I say 'no.' He wants me to join him on tour. I liked Mick as a friend, but he was never going to be a boyfriend. Mick is as old as my grandfather."

"He is nearly sixty," chimed in Caroline's forty-year-old mother, Camilla, "and when a man that age is after a seventeen-year-old, it is obvious what he wants. His behavior has gone too far, and it is a little bit scary. Caroline," she continued, "doesn't want him bothering her."

The last thing Mick needed now was a reminder that in two years he would be turning sixty. But that's just what he got when *Saga*, Britain's leading magazine aimed at seniors, ran him on the cover of its September issue. Inside the magazine, surrounded by ads for retirement communities and orthopedic beds, Mick expounded on everything from his music to the making of his film *Enigma*.

Although Twiggy, Goldie Hawn, and Sting were among the recent fiftysomethings who were more than happy to appear on *Saga*'s cover and pitch their latest projects to the magazine's one million readers, Jagger was singled out for special ridicule by the press. "Sittin' Jack Flash," proclaimed the *Daily Mail,* while British *Vogue* branded Mick the "pensioner's pinup."

Mick issued a public statement saying that he was "very disappointed" in the *Saga* cover story, but privately he was livid. "I think it's stupid to behave like you're seventeen," he said. "But that doesn't mean you have to be an old fart sitting in the pub talking about what happened in the sixties."

Mick was tending to the wounded Jagger ego at La Fourchette when a staff member ran into his study and told him to turn on the television set. Only moments earlier, an airliner had smashed into one of the Twin Towers of New York's World Trade Center. Like millions of people around the world, Mick sat, mouth agape, as a second airliner slammed into the other tower.

"Get me the phone," Mick pleaded. "It's Lizzy. She's in New York."

I was one of the four thousand other women.
He is, I think, like Don Juan.

—CARLA BRUNI-SARKOZY

◆　◆　◆

I've never really been deeply, madly in love. I'm just not an
emotional person.

—MICK

◆　◆　◆

Mick loves Keith, you know. They're like a married couple.

—JERRY HALL

9

◆　◆　◆

When the Moneymaker's Shaking

ick was in a panic. Lizzy lived in Manhattan's trendy Tribeca district, just fifteen blocks from Ground Zero. Jagger's seventeen-year-old daughter had been on a modeling assignment in Istanbul, Turkey, but was due back home in New York by now.

His mind was racing. Mick grabbed the phone and dialed her apartment, but he could not get through. Then he tried her cell phone, but again there was no answer. Soon he was on the phone to Jerry at the house in Richmond, outside London. Jerry was in tears. She, too, had been unable to reach their daughter, or the young, South African male model she lived with, hunky Damien Van Zyl.

For several hours, they tried and failed to reach their daughter or anyone who had seen her. "I was in a state of shock," Mick later said. "It was a terrible feeling of dread." With the phone lines in and out of New York overloaded, Jerry finally managed to get through to Lizzy via Van Zyl's family in South Africa—which, Mick conceded, was "really weird."

She was shaken by having actually witnessed the fall of the towers, as were many New Yorkers, but she was alive and unhurt.

Having resided on and off there for over thirty years, Mick felt a kinship with New Yorkers. "I have a huge sympathy for the town," he said. "I identify with it more than any other city in the US, so I know it very well. Yeah, you feel a great closeness, especially when there's trouble, you do." Like his American friends—not just New Yorkers—Jagger claimed to feel a "terrible sense of violation. It's a horrible thing to have that feeling broken—that America is this place where we all felt safe."

The feeling lingered. "People are saying to me, and I felt the same way, 'I couldn't do anything for a week. My life, all my things, feel so trivial,'" Jagger said. "But after the shock and mourning comes the adjustment to real life . . . You can't let terrorists completely change your lifestyle. They would love that. That's a victory.

"People are knocked off their feet," he went on, "but you don't want to lose hope and morale. You have to mourn, you're glued to CNN more than you should be . . . But in the end, you have to do what *you* do."

Mick and Keith brought what they did best to Paul McCartney's nationally televised October 20 Madison Square Garden Concert for New York City honoring the 343 firefighters and 87 police officers killed on 9/11. Introduced by former *Saturday Night Live* star Mike Myers (now seen and heard in movies such as *Wayne's World, Austin Powers: International Man of Mystery,* and *Shrek*), Jagger and Richards sang the two songs Mick felt seemed most appropriate: "Salt of the Earth" and "Miss You." The concert, which also featured Mick's close pals David Bowie and Eric Clapton, Billy Joel, Elton John, James Taylor, Destiny's Child, and Bon Jovi, raised more than $30 million for the victims' families. "It was something I felt close to, a good cause," Mick said afterward. "I was very pleased to do it."

Having done what he could, Mick went back to Paris, this time drumming up media interest in the forthcoming *Goddess in the Doorway* album. In the wake of the disappointing sales for his two previous solo efforts, Mick pulled out the stops to ensure the new album's success. *Goddess* featured collaborations with his old pals Lenny Kravitz, Wyclef Jean, and The Who's Pete Townshend, but also Matchbox 20's Rob Thomas, Bono, and Aerosmith guitarist Joe Perry. Mick was clearly wary of how his fellow Stones might react to calling this group of musicians a "band" per se. "I don't believe in having bands for solo records," he said. "It's pointless. I mean, I've got a very good band in the other world."

Mick was called upon repeatedly to explain why he felt the need to work without that "very good band," particularly when he was its lead singer and it was widely regarded to be the best in the world. "Because everything in the Rolling Stones is up for a vote," he said, "and democracy in music is not always a good thing."

This time, Mick packed *Goddess* with funk, dance beats, love songs, and anthemic ballads. Jerry believed all the new tunes were about her. "She always thinks that the songs are about her," Mick shrugged. "It's a very charming trait." The self-explanatory "Don't Call Me Up," however, was written about someone else: Carla Bruni, who continued phoning Mick for years after being confronted by Jerry.

By way of promoting the album to a wider audience on American television, Mick also agreed to have Oscar-winning filmmaker Kevin Macdonald film a documentary chronicling his life for one year. Much of *Being Mick* wound up being shot by the subject himself, using a handheld camera, and included, among other things: the making of *Goddess,* the premiere of *Enigma,* Mick attending a Venetian-themed costume party at the home of Elton John, Mick jumping on and off jets, Mick laying down tracks in recording studios, Mick lunching with Bono on a terrace. Perhaps most revealing were the fleeting glimpses into Jagger's family life: one minute playing with toddler Gabriel, the next concerned about nine-year-old Georgia's nail-biting. "You're worried about something," he says. "You're worried about your schoolwork?"

"Dad," Georgia replies, rolling her eyes, "I just chew my nails."

Mick conceded that, like any father, he had the uncanny ability to make his children cringe with embarrassment. "Oh, yeah, my kids find me embarrassing all the time," he said. "They say, 'You can't go out looking like that. You can't come to the school—not with *those* trousers on.' Sometimes," he allowed, "they're right. But sometimes they steal my clothes and wear them." He neglected to mention that he wore roughly the same size as his teenage son and daughters.

"I seem to have got this big, extended family," Mick marveled, as if they had all just somehow plopped onto his lap, "and I adore them."

When it aired on ABC Thanksgiving night 2001, Macdonald explained that his goal was to provide a portrait of an "enigmatic man who's also a survivor . . . The thing about Mick is that he is still going passionately and strongly."

Jagger's newest passion, as it turned out, was for a six-foot-four, thirty-four-year-old raven-haired model and stylist he met in Paris that November. The curiously named L'Wren Scott (real name: Luann Bambrough) was adopted by a deeply religious Mormon couple—her mom worked for a bank, and her insurance agent dad was for a time a Mormon bishop—and raised in small-town Roy, Utah.

"Everyone else was small and blonde with fair skin," she recalled, "and I was tall, with this long black hair and dark skin. Yes, I felt different, all right." Although Romanian Olympic champion Nadia Comaneci was her idol, L'Wren's teachers urged her to sign up for basketball instead. "How dare you tell me I'm too tall to be a gymnast!" she remembered thinking. Instead she studied gymnastics and ballet, making every effort to capitalize on the fact that her legs were an impressive forty-two inches long.

Scott had just turned eighteen when photographer Bruce Weber cast her and her high school boyfriend in a Calvin Klein ad. Weber told her, "They'll never 'get' you here," and suggested that she hop the first plane bound for France. But once in Paris, she was told that she was actually too tall for most fashion houses.

Her legs, however, were very much in demand. They were the "hands" of a clock ticking to the Kinks' "All Day and All of the Night" in a famous Pretty Polly pantyhose commercial shot by David Bailey, and featured in spreads by renowned fashion photographers Jean-Paul Goude and Guy Bourdin. She was a standout—or rather a stand-above—on the Paris social scene, and it was not long before the exotic-looking L'Wren befriended top designers such as Thierry Mugler and Karl Lagerfeld.

"I was always obsessed with what was going on behind the scenes," L'Wren said of those early days in Paris. "I became friendly with the pattern makers and obsessed with how clothes are made."

She landed back in Los Angeles in 1994, and was introduced by fellow model Helena Christensen to photographer Herb Ritts, then shooting covers for *Rolling Stone* and *Vanity Fair*. First for Ritts, and then for fellow photographers Helmut Newton and Mario Sorrenti, L'Wren was called upon to style the likes of Nicole Kidman, Penelope Cruz, Jennifer Lopez, Sarah Jessica Parker, and Sandra Bullock for dozens of fashion spreads, ads, and magazine covers. In 2000 she was hired as the style director of the Academy Awards, the first in the academy's history.

Along the way, L'Wren took advantage of her Hollywood connections to design costumes for several films, including Stanley

Kubrick's *Eyes Wide Shut* (in which Kidman starred with her then husband, the also much shorter Tom Cruise), *Diabolique,* and *Ocean's Thirteen*.

L'Wren's avowed dream was to start her own fashion house, but for now she was content to become best known as the latest in Mick's string of leggy lovers. Soon they were sharing a suite at the Carlyle and showing up together at galas and openings.

Among those old enough to know the reference, comparisons to the comic strip characters Mutt and Jeff were inevitable. Towering over Jagger by at least seven inches—there was disagreement over how tall Scott actually was—she learned, for picture-taking purposes only, to bend her legs at an odd angle when standing beside her man. But for the most part, she embraced her altitude, seldom wearing flats when she could slip into a pair of Jimmy Choos with five-inch heels. Rarely seen smiling, seemingly always dressed head-to-toe in black (black fingernail polish included) to match her long ebony tresses, L'Wren evoked another obvious comparison: to Morticia Addams.

"Height has never come into it," said L'Wren, who had a three-year relationship with five-foot-four London real estate tycoon Andrew Ladsky and was married briefly to the somewhat taller LA businessman Anthony Brand. "I would be interested to know whether Adam was taller than Eve or Eve taller than Adam."

Notwithstanding Mick's established fondness for skyscraper-tall models decades his junior, there were other things that drew this oddest of couples together. According to their friend Rachel Feinstein Currin, Mick and L'Wren shared "a love affair with the grandiose and the baroque" in art, architecture, and fashion. Even more important, said another New York friend, "L'Wren isn't needy, she isn't clingy. She is smart, very no-nonsense, and mature in a way a lot of people in the fashion industry aren't. She has no interest in being tied down by marriage, and right now that appeals to Mick. Obviously."

No less an expert on L'Wren Scott than her mother concurred. "L'Wren is very independent and would not take any nonsense from anyone, no matter how famous they were," said Lula Bambrough, whose innate sense of style as a businesswoman in Utah left a lasting impression on L'Wren. "She usually knows what she wants, and she gets it." Years later, Lula Bambrough gave her theory as to why the relationship was still going strong despite Mick's ongoing peccadilloes. "It doesn't surprise me at all that L'Wren's tamed him," Lula said. "She is very much her own woman, and it would be my guess that is why this Mick Jagger likes her." (L'Wren would ultimately reward her mom's loyalty by naming a handbag after her.)

Incredibly, when he was in England, Mick continued his next-door living arrangement with Jerry. "Mick isn't happy," Hall said. "He needs me as a kind of security blanket so he could go off and play with other women. He misses that, which is why he hasn't yet moved out of the house next door to where I live with the children. But he's got to go soon. It's getting a bit ridiculous; I can't get rid of him."

That wasn't about to happen, she added, until Mick made the conscious decision to "face his demons and stop his womanizing . . . It's a sickness. Perhaps it's a chemical thing, and he has way too much testosterone. If he doesn't admit he's got a problem, he'll never get well."

Clearly, "facing demons" was not high on Mick's to-do list. He was far too busy pushing *Goddess in the Doorway*, doing all that was asked of him and more: the prime-time TV documentary, appearances on VH1 and MTV, an unprecedented number of print and television interviews. Yet Virgin Records executives, convinced that he still had to appeal to the teenagers and young adults who made up record-buying Generation Y, wanted more.

In order to accomplish what they now called the "rebranding" of Mick Jagger, they turned to the Internet. A new Web site, mickjagger .com, was set up and made to look like the site of any teenage rock star, complete with a photo of Mick in a black shirt unbuttoned to the waist.

The marketing of Britney Spears, who at nineteen had already taken the pop music world by storm, was held up as an example for Mick to follow. Virgin executives also wanted to go after her fans. "It seems impossible, if not ridiculous," said Craig Marks, music editor of *Blender* magazine. Marks pointed out that Spears had actually recorded her own version of "Satisfaction," and that young fans would have to be convinced that Jagger wrote it. To accomplish that, Mick would have to "cover Britney Spears's cover. To think you can go online and hoodwink fourteen-year-old Melissa into buying the Jagger record," he added, "is just a waste of everybody's time and money."

Mick found Spears's pigtailed schoolgirl-vixen act intriguing. (At the time, she wore plaid-skirted school uniforms in her videos and onstage.) Once he learned that she had been dating 'N Sync's Justin Timberlake, said a longtime Stones roadie, "you could see the wheels in his head turning." Nor did it hurt that, along with Timberlake, she had once been a star of the Disney Channel's revived *Mickey Mouse Club*. "Britney a Mouseketeer?" he joked. "I wonder if she'd be willing to put on the ears?"

Over the years, Mick pursued Spears, peppering her with calls and emails from around the world. But to no avail. "He's a genius, a legend—and he's still sexy, still got the moves, you know? But," she told one of her backup singers, "he's my grandpa's age, for gosh sake!"

On a professional level, Mick found all the comparisons to Britney Spears ("What makes her voice sound like that?" he cracked at one point, "Helium?") not merely tiresome but insulting. He had actually heard Spears's cover of "Satisfaction" booming out of the bedroom of his then nine-year-old daughter, Georgia. "We quite liked the beginning of it," he said, "but it didn't seem to go anywhere."

Nor, to everyone's shock, did *Goddess in the Doorway*. Critics universally praised *Driving Rain,* a solo album released by Paul McCartney at virtually the same time, but with the exception of a five-star paean by Jann Wenner in *Rolling Stone,* many of the reviews for *Goddess* were scathing. "While Mick's new tranquility gets old fast," wrote *Time*'s Benjamin Nugent, "it turns out that Paul actually has the grit to pull it off." As for Mick's attempt to contemporize his sound, Nugent wrote, "the strongest feeling it drives home is that old guys and drum machines don't mix." New York *Daily News* critic Jim Farber branded Jagger's new songs "formulaic, confining, and aloof" but trumpeted *Driving Rain* as "McCartney at his melodic best . . . Even his silliest love songs have glorious tunes."

If he hoped for some words of solace from his spiritual other half, Mick was sadly mistaken. "What?" said Keith when asked what he thought of *Goddess in the Doorway*. "*Dog Shit in the Doorway*? I listened to three tracks and gave up on it. Sometimes you wonder. With the Stones, he's great. It's best to keep him on a short leash."

Naysayers aside, the proof was in the numbers—and the numbers were devastating. After what for solo artist Mick was an unprecedented amount of hype, *Goddess in the Doorway* sold an embarrassing 954 copies on its first day of release. In contrast, British pop star Robbie Williams's critically panned *Swing When You're Winning* sold 73,600 copies on its first day. Mick Jagger was being outsold by eighty-four other artists, including a children's group called the Tweenies and British song-and-dance man Des O'Connor.

Desperate to deflect attention from the sales numbers, Mick's publicist, Bernard Doherty, reportedly urged London's *Daily Mirror* to print a story about Jagger's alleged affair with a young British actress. Both Mick and the actress issued heated denials the next day.

The dismal sales figures "staggered everyone," one record company executive admitted. "They are just so unbelievably bad. Nothing short of disastrous."

Days before the album's release, Mick had tried to hedge his bets. "Commercial success is ephemeral," he said, "and it's a strange time. I always aim my sights low . . . I've also had a long career, so I'm not like a kid who's waiting on the sales figures every week."

But when the album failed to take off the next week, Mick was shaken. "He always says that pleasing yourself is what counts," a member of the Stones organization observed, "but I think he was totally unprepared for the solo album to be such a catastrophe. It was a real slap in the face, no doubt about it."

Mick was soon coping with a crisis of a different sort—one that put his solo career woes in perspective. While filming her TV show *SuperPop* in São Paolo, Luciana Morad collapsed on the set and was rushed to the hospital. Tests revealed she had contracted viral meningitis.

Mick, concerned that the potentially fatal disease might have been spread to their son Lucas, was on the phone to the toddler and Luciana asking if there was anything he could do. As it turned out, Lucas felt fine and was even chattier than usual with "Daddy." After three days, Luciana was given a clean bill of health and released from the hospital.

"I was terrified," Mick conceded. "This is the kind of thing that really makes you appreciate what is truly important in life."

So did George Harrison's death from cancer just days later. Jagger described himself as Harrison's onetime "drinking buddy" and claimed that George was more than just "'the quiet Beatle.' Oh, yeah, okay, he sits in the corner. But he wasn't really that. He was very complex, and he was very charming and friendly."

Harrison's death rocked both Mick and Keith in much the way that Lennon's did. "Really, whatever I say about my feelings is ridiculous and inadequate," Jagger mused. "I was very sad . . . But that's probably what most people think. Because the Beatles were a big part of one's life. And when someone like that dies, in a way, a part of your own life is gone."

Mick was not prepared to say good-bye to rock stardom. Scrambling to put the disastrous *Goddess* behind him, he began laying the groundwork for a Rolling Stones greatest hits album and the world tour to go with it. "I sing in a rock-and-roll band, so I go on the road," Mick said. "It's not much more complicated than that. That's what my life is."

For Keith, who had recorded solo albums of his own in the wake of Mick's decision to try going it alone, there was no question of where his friend's loyalties should lie. "The Stones are numero uno," he said. "The Stones are the reason I'm here. They are my whole working life. We all went out there and tried the solo thing on, but we all come back to the Rolling Stones. And what better occasion to mark with a tour than the Stones' fortieth anniversary?"

There were other nagging questions they were now forced to confront. Mick, Keith, and Ronnie were all pushing sixty; Charlie Watts was already there. Would they look ridiculous out there on the stage at this age? Could they even do it? During meetings in London and Paris to talk over a new tour, Mick and Keith were adamant. "Why? What's wrong? Of course we can do it," Mick insisted.

At these key planning sessions, Watts said, "You feel like you're a sissy if you say no."

On May 7, 2002, a yellow blimp emblazoned with the Stones' lips-and-tongue logo set down in the Bronx's Van Cortlandt Park and disgorged Mick and his bandmates. "It's getting to be a habit," a newly sober Ron Wood told the horde of reporters who had gathered in the spring sunshine to hear the tour details. "We've done the train, the boat, and the bridge," Wood continued. "We'll probably do a submarine next time."

As usual, Mick trained like an Olympic athlete for months, spending hours lifting weights, running, and doing calisthenics with the single-minded discipline that his father had drilled into him as a boy. To crack the proverbial whip, Mick brought his longtime personal trainer, Norwegian fitness guru Torje Eike.

"It's hell, pure hell," allowed Jagger, who now eschewed all alcohol on tour and stuck to a runner's low-fat, high-carbohydrate diet heavy in whole wheat bread, pasta, brown rice, and fruit. Thanks to his rigid diet and exercise regimen, Mick felt that he was more than up to tearing up concert stages from New York to Tokyo. "I keep waiting for it to get hard, I'm ready for it, prepared for it," he said. "But no, I don't find it hard at all."

There was ample evidence, however, that Mick was concerned about whether or not he could pull it off yet again. During the Bridges to Babylon tour, laryngitis had forced Mick to cancel three shows. Even when he was able to sing, he was "always on the edge—a nightmare, really." This time he worked with a voice coach named Don Lawrence to discover "a more scientific way," Mick explained, "of doing a proper warm-up routine for your voice, in the same way you need one for your body."

As for the body, this time Mick also took ballet lessons from Stephen Galloway, a dancer with the Frankfurt Ballet. "I came away," he said, "with a much larger movement vocabulary."

"Oh God, what's that bitch Brenda up to now?" Keith joked, employing one of his favorite nicknames for Mick. ("Her Majesty" was another.) Richards could not figure out why his friend would hire someone to teach him the moves that *he* had invented forty years earlier. "It's fascinating. I can't figure it out," Keith said. "It's almost as if Mick was aspiring to be Mick Jagger, chasing his own phantom. And getting design consultants to help him do it." As for the ballet lessons: "Shit, Charlie and I have been watching that ass for forty-odd years. We know when the moneymaker's shaking and when it's being told what to do."

And what did Keith Richards do to prepare for what they now called the Licks tour? He smiled and took another drag on an ever-present cigarette. "I show up," he said.

The Stones continued their recent practice of mixing stadiums for audiences of up to one hundred thousand with smaller arena, theater, and even club venues. Keith would call it the "Underwear tour" because it came in "small, medium, and large. But for the band, it makes it far more interesting." Mick agreed. "It's fun for us," he said, "a challenge to jump from one type of show to another. Keeps us on our toes."

Mick and Keith wanted to keep on their toes as songwriters as well. The Licks tour was, as always, designed to hype an accompanying CD: this time the *Forty Licks* double album containing forty of the Stones' greatest hits from all phases of their career. But Keith "didn't want it to be all just nostalgia," and so the retrospective included four new Jagger-Richards compositions. "It's important to me that I'm still writing songs," Mick added, "whether they're good or bad is another matter. I love working really, really hard. In the last five years, I've been working like a dog."

Even Mick conceded that the new material was a hard sell. "There's no point pretending the Rolling Stones is a new band," he said. "There's an old-fashioned idea you can only be good while you're unknown, and, hopefully, poor, and even better, slightly mentally ill . . . *and* a drug addict—always helpful. That makes you more interesting. It doesn't necessarily make your *work* more interesting."

Once again, Mick teamed up with Charlie Watts and designers Mark Fisher and Patrick Woodroffe to create a breathtaking set that could be adapted to both large and medium-sized venues. In addition to a striking two-hundred-foot-wide digital mural created by artist Jeff Koons (a bizarre hodgepodge including a woman's mouth, an inflatable dog, and trash), an animated video played while Mick belted out "Honky Tonk Women." It depicted a bare-breasted woman riding the lips-and-tongue logo before being devoured by it. "Not kiddie fare, exactly," Jagger cracked.

Although Mick and Keith no longer enjoyed the closeness they'd once shared (on tour, neither had visited the other's dressing room in years), the Glimmer Twins were back together and working harmoniously as a team. However, that came to an abrupt end on June 14, 2002—just two months before the start of the tour—when Buckingham Palace announced that Mick Jagger was included on the Queen's Birthday Honors List.

Concerned about how Richards might react, Mick had warned his partner earlier that Tony Blair had mentioned a knighthood. Now that it was a reality, however, Keith was indeed furious. He screamed at Mick for betraying him and the group, and threatened to pull out of the tour. Three weeks later, Keith had calmed down a bit, but he still admitted to feeling "cold, cold rage" over Mick's knighthood. "I went berserk, bananas! But quite honestly, Mick's fucked up so many times, what's another fuckup?"

With the Stones' tour plans back on track, Mick took his friend's reaction in stride. "Keith has his own personality," he said, "and he likes to make his own noise. I think Keith feels it's mandatory to keep his image by doing that." With a few glaring exceptions, Mick described their relationship as "mature . . . otherwise we wouldn't be working almost every day together."

Keith wasn't alone in his outrage over Mick's knighthood. Dub-bing Jagger the "Black Knight," one journalist joined a chorus of critics who argued that the world's number one hedonist wasn't worthy of the honor. "Serial womanizing and sexual profligacy," wrote James Reynolds in Edinburgh's *Scotsman,* "large quantities of drugs and alcohol, a short spell in jail followed by . . . tax exile. And there was some singing and making records along the way."

Mick took the more good-natured ribbing from family, friends, and fans in stride. Strangers now knelt before him in mock submission, while others waved plastic swords at him. "I've been teased," he said, "but I'm very happy. Delighted." At school, five-year-old Gabriel told his classmates that his father was going to be knighted.

"And what does that mean?" asked the teacher.

"Well," Gabriel replied, "he goes to the castle to see the king and get to be a knight, and from then on gets to wear armor all the time."

Afterward, Mick told the teacher, "Maybe after what's been written about me, that's not such a bad idea."

On July 16, 2002, the Stones returned to Toronto to start rehearsals at the same private boys' school where they had prepared for Bridges to Babylon. Two days later, the Stones' longtime road crew chief, Royden "Chuch" Magee, was looking over the soundboard while Mick practiced a new single, "Don't Stop." Suddenly Magee collapsed, the victim of a massive heart attack.

Fitness trainer Torje Eike performed CPR on Magee, but it was too late. "Mick and the other band members," said Alan Dunn, the Rolling Stones' logistics director, "couldn't do anything but watch. It was terrible."

Chuch Magee had been more than just the Stones' chief roadie; since signing on with the band in 1976, he had been a combination therapist, mentor, and guide to the Stones, particularly Mick. "He was," Jagger said, "that rare thing: a true friend."

Numb from having witnessed Magee's death (at fifty-four, he was five years younger than Jagger), Mick nevertheless went ahead with his plans. The day Magee died, the Stones moved to a new rehearsal space in Toronto's Old Masonic Temple. The next night, Jagger dined with three young women at one of the city's most fashionable restaurants, and a few days later, he danced the night away at a club called Revival. At a party to celebrate Jagger's fifty-ninth birthday, he toasted Chuch more than once and pointed out that Magee would have wanted his friends to "go on enjoying things. Life goes on. You know," he said in a rare introspective moment over his chilled cranberry juice, "it all goes by so fast . . ."

More than seven hundred people crowded into the Messiah Lutheran church in Marquette, Michigan, for Magee's funeral. Halfway through the service, Mick, Keith, and then Ronnie Wood rose from their front-row pew to take a seat by the altar. Strumming his guitar, Mick sang "Amazing Grace" and then joined Richards and Wood in performing "Rivers of Babylon," a reggae song with lyrics based on Psalm 137. As the trio of rock titans ended in perfect harmony and returned to their pew, Mick—along with the rest of the congregation—struggled to control his emotions.

Two weeks later, the Stones kicked off the Licks tour with their usual intimate warm-up concert at Toronto's Palais Royale ballroom. It was the first time in three years that all the Rolling Stones had performed together onstage, and their first appearance in the new millennium. It showed. "The rest of the Rolling Stones," Mick recalled, "were incredibly nervous. I had never seen them so nervous. I tried to calm them down because they were so intense: 'It's going to be great, guys, we sound great.'"

But they didn't. "They made tons of mistakes, tempos flying everywhere," Mick said. "You're thinking, 'How many times have we rehearsed this tune?' It was very ragged, but I guess that Keith and the rest of them hadn't been onstage in a long while."

They managed to pull everything together in time for the official launch of the tour on September 3, 2002, at Boston's Fleet Center, followed by performances at nearby Gillette Stadium and the city's Orpheum Theatre. The small (in Boston's case the Orpheum)/medium (Fleet Center)/large (Gillette Stadium) approach made Mick feel more in touch with the Stones' audience. "You're in town for a full week," he said, "you get into the swing of the city."

Yet when it came to the experience of being Mick onstage, nothing had really changed. Only now he took breaths from an oxygen mask during breaks, and a cardiac defibrillator sat backstage—just in case.

As the Stones barnstormed across the globe over the next fourteen months, performing 117 shows in 73 cities, Jagger's mind raced as it always had when he shot out onto the stage as if he'd been fired from a cannon. "There's certain feelings you get, you know: *'Jesus, all those people!'* There's a few empty seats sometimes I see, and you say, 'Oh God . . .'" There was the self-awareness: "'Oh, I'm doing this, and I'm doing that,' and you're sort of watching yourself doing it. 'Oh God, look at that girl! She's rather pretty. Don't concentrate on her!' But it's good to concentrate on her, she's good to contact one-on-one . . ."

In the end, he said, "It's very high adrenalin. Like driving a car very fast or being on a championship basketball team in the finals . . ." There was also the occasional "transcendent moment. I don't know whether you can say it's joyful. Sometimes it can be joyful. Sometimes it's just crazy."

One of those "just crazy" moments had nothing to do with the tour itself but with an eccentric American billionaire who happened to be looking for a memorable way to celebrate his birthday. As a cofounder of Texas Pacific Group, David Bonderman amassed a fortune of $5 billion buying and selling stakes in three airlines—Continental, Ryanair, and US Airways—as well as Burger King.

Now that Bonderman was turning sixty, as Mick would be doing in eight short months, the billionaire invited 1,500 of his nearest and dearest friends to the Hard Rock Hotel and Casino in Las Vegas. Since the Stones were winding up the 2002 leg of their Licks tour in Las Vegas anyway, they accepted the gig—for $6 million, easily making the Stones the most expensive party band in history. As if the Stones weren't enough, Bonderman hired heartland rocker John Mellencamp to open the show, and Robin Williams to perform his comedy act in between. Total cost to Bonderman for the evening: a reported $7.5 million.

Not that the Stones needed the money. According to *Fortune* magazine, their gross earnings for the previous ten years topped $1.7 billion, easily beating out Michael Jackson, U2, and Madonna. "I'm not first and foremost a business person," Mick said coyly. "I'm a creative artist. All I know about business is what I've managed to pick up along the way."

That, and his training at the London School of Economics. With Prince Rupert's expert assistance, Mick was still very much the sophisticated business brain behind the Stones' massive financial success. In addition to overseeing their cash-churning tours down to the tiniest detail, Jagger helped set up the labyrinth of corporations into which the money flowed. Many of these companies, wholly owned by the Stones, were based in the Netherlands for tax reasons.

Before the band embarked on the second half of the tour, Mick found the time to take L'Wren on a Caribbean cruise aboard Revlon chief Ron Perelman's 188-foot, $70 million yacht *Ultima III*. Jagger also checked up on his children, one of whom had placed him in a particularly awkward position.

When Jerry called Mick with the news that nineteen-year-old Lizzy was dating a forty-four-year-old Canadian actor named Michael Wincott, Dad went, in Lizzy's words, "ballistic." Wincott was known for playing villains in dark movies such as *The Crow* and *Along Came a Spider,* and offscreen he had already built a reputation as a hard-partying lady-killer.

As perhaps the world's most high-profile cradle robber, Mick knew that he was not exactly in a position to warn his daughter against older men. So he told Jerry to do it. "I don't like it," he told Hall. "You know she isn't going to listen to me."

"And why, *dahlin*'," Jerry drawled in reply, "would you suppose that is?" Her advice to Mick: "Keep your mouth shut."

Over the early months of 2003, as Lizzy and Wincott dated, broke up, and reconciled, Mick fumed on the sidelines. Dad soon took it upon himself to plead with his daughter to dump her boyfriend. "He is too old for you," Mick told Lizzy, "and too boring."

Lizzy eventually heeded her father's advice, although not before Mick admitted that the press had succeeded in making him look like "a fucking hypocrite." On the subject of his own behavior, Mick declared himself to be "a moral person. But as with most people, my moral values tend to be pretty fuzzy."

His daughter's dating habits seemed trivial indeed compared to the next family emergency that Mick faced. The Stones were in Singapore when a sobbing Luciana Morad called Mick with the terrifying news that their son, Lucas, had fallen and struck his head on the pavement while playing at school. Bleeding from a massive gash in his skull, the three-year-old was rushed by ambulance to a local hospital and wheeled immediately into the operating room. The doctors, concerned that the boy may have suffered brain damage, told Lucas's panic-stricken mother ("She was pulling her hair out and crying," a nurse said) that the situation was "touch and go."

Mick was preparing to board a plane for Brazil when Luciana called back hours later with an update. After closing the wound with twenty-four stitches, doctors were encouraged by the results of two brain scans. Lucas stayed an extra night in intensive care and, to Mick's relief, was well enough to go home the next day.

It was a side of Jagger—as caring father and grandfather—that the public rarely saw, and with reason. Mick had no intention of showing it to them. He had no desire to act his age—not with women, not in the press, and certainly not onstage.

Midway through the Asian leg of the tour, Mick reverted to his old ways when he rendezvoused with an old flame in Bangkok. Angelina Jolie had just signed on to play the lead opposite Brad Pitt in *Mr. and Mrs. Smith,* but before filming began, she was meeting with officials in Thailand in her new role as goodwill ambassador for the Office of the United Nations High Commissioner for Refugees. She was also there, she told Mick, to get an elaborate new tattoo.

Newly divorced from actor Billy Bob Thornton, Jolie also told her old paramour that she was excited about the chance to work with Pitt, who still happened to be married to actress Jennifer Aniston—though not for long. Mick and Angelina spent the night together in his suite at Bangkok's premier hotel, The Oriental—for old times' sake.

Jagger turned sixty on July 26, 2003—and the world was not about to let him forget it. "Sympathy for the Senior: Mick Turns 60" blared the headline in the *Boston Herald,* while Britain's the *Sun* led with "Not Fade Away—Jagger, 60 Today." The London *Sunday Times* proclaimed Mick to be "Satanic at Sixty"; the *Independent on Sunday* offered "Sympathy for the Old Devil"; and, of course, dozens of outlets, from the Associated Press, to the *New York Post,* to *Time* couldn't resist some variation on the "Mother's Little Helper" lyric "What a drag it is getting old."

Not, apparently, if you were Mick Jagger. The man who had once proclaimed that he would "rather be dead" than singing "Satisfaction" when he was forty-five now promised to go on indefinitely. "I will compose, sing, and play as long as I can—I hope even in my seventies," he told a reporter in Prague, one of the stops on the European leg of the Licks tour. "I said a long time ago that we were a symbol of eternity. Millions of our fans have convinced us of that."

That evening he joined a select group of guests for a candlelit dinner in his honor—served with a Bordeaux from the year of his birth, 1943—at the Four Seasons Hotel Prague, near the historic Charles Bridge. Actor Matt Damon, Bob Geldof (made an honorary knight by Queen Elizabeth in 1986, a year after Live Aid), and film director Terry Gilliam were there, along with Mick's eighty-nine-year-old father, five of his children, two grandchildren, and his new love L'Wren. Upstaging everyone but Mick, however, was former Czech president and ardent Jagger fan Vaclav Havel, who in 1990 had personally invited the Stones to perform before 110,000 of his newly liberated countrymen following the collapse of Czechoslovakia's old Communist government.

After midnight, the party—which now included the Stones and members of their entourage—moved on to Wenceslas Square and the Duplex, a retro nightclub with a purple VW bug parked on its roof. Actor Jeremy Piven, who later starred in the HBO series *Entourage,* stumbled into the party in the early morning hours. "Mick and I have the same birthday, just different decades!" Piven said. "I witnessed him dance for five hours straight. He was dancing exactly the way you'd think he would, like a chicken on meth. It was awesome."

Age, Mick stressed repeatedly, was now just a number. "When you're twenty-one, you can't believe you're twenty-one," he reflected. "When you're thirty, you can't believe you're thirty. You start getting a bit better at this as you go on, because you've already done forty—now, *that* was big, difficult, incredulous. So you just have to accept it."

On the tour, Mick proved night after night that he could still—as he was so fond of saying—deliver the goods. There was, of course, the occasional minor health setback; notwithstanding tips from his new vocal coach, Mick was again sidelined by laryngitis more than once. But the major changes in the Licks schedule had nothing to do with the health of any band member. An outbreak of SARS (severe acute respiratory syndrome) that had started in Asia the previous November swept into North America, forcing the rescheduling of several concerts in 2003. Toronto, in particular, had been hit hard, and four days after Mick's birthday, the Stones did what they could to help out. They headlined the July 30 Rolling Stones SARS benefit concert, which was attended by 490,000—technically, their largest audience to date—and raised millions of dollars for the beleaguered city.

In true Stones fashion, however, all was not goodwill and harmony—not even when the concert was for charity. Hard rock fans were incensed when Justin Timberlake took the stage, and hurled bottles and food at his feet while he performed. Later Timberlake gamely returned with Mick to sing "Miss You," winning back the crowd and earning the Stones' respect in the process.

The Licks tour ended on November 9 with another SARS benefit concert, this time joining Prince, Santana, and Neil Young as part of Hong Kong's Harbor Fest series. It marked the first time the Stones had ever appeared on mainland China.

Once the receipts were all in, Prince Rupert called Mick with the final tally. With official ticket prices hovering in the $350 range and Internet prices soaring to around $5,000, the gross for Licks— their least ambitious tour in over a decade—was a little over $300 million. This did not include merchandising revenues or, of course, record sales.

Still, no amount of money could purchase the honor that Mick had coveted his entire adult life. On December 12, 2003, after postponing the ceremony several times so as not to be overshadowed by any other celebrity recipients, Mick was knighted by Prince Charles at Buckingham Palace. Her Majesty's decision not to be present was not lost on Sir Mick. "I'm sure," he cracked, "the Queen prefers the Beatles because they're such nice, upstanding fellows. If only she knew the truth!"

All jesting aside, security surrounding Buckingham Palace that day was even tighter than usual. London's Metropolitan Police had received a threat to Jagger's life that, given John Lennon's murder and the near-fatal knife attack on George Harrison in 1999, authorities were not about to disregard.

At this stage in his long career, Mick took such threats in stride. His family was another matter. In early January, police on Ibiza were tipped off to a $5 million plot to kidnap Jade's daughters Assisi, ten, and Amba, seven. At the time Jade, hired in 2002 as creative director of "jewelers to the Crown" Garrard and Co., lived with the girls and nightclub DJ Dan Williams in the picturesque village of San Juan Bautista. Mick wasted no time in hiring bodyguards at a reported cost of $40,000 a week to watch his daughter and granddaughters around the clock. For the long term, Mick wanted Jade and her family to move back to the house he bought for her in Kensal Rise, Northwest London—and not just because of the kidnap threat. Ibiza, notorious for its unbridled hedonism and vibrant drug trade, had never impressed Mick as the sort of place to bring up a family.

Jerry Hall shared Mick's concern for the safety of Jade and her children, and urged Mick to buy a big house for himself in London where they could join him. Of course, Jerry had her own reasons for wanting Mick out of the house next door to hers in Richmond. "It's not a good long-term setup—it kind of cramps your style," Jerry said. "He hates me dating, but he can't say much about it, can he?"

Nor was Hall thrilled by the fact that her hard-to-miss replacement was now showing up next door. L'Wren's attempts at being inconspicuous verged on the comical. When paparazzi caught her emerging from Mick's house in Richmond, L'Wren turned around and marched back up the front steps—only to find the door shut and locked behind her. "So there she stood, ringing the bell," a photographer said, "trying to get back in. Finally, a Mercedes came to her rescue, and she was driven away."

Jerry, informed that Mick had sneaked his girlfriend into the house when she was on the road in *The Graduate*, called Mick from San Francisco with an ultimatum: either he moved out of the house next door, or she would sell the house in Richmond, pack up the kids, and leave.

Later that year, Mick did move, into a $35,000-a-week three-bedroom penthouse suite at Claridge's in Mayfair as a "permanent guest" of the hotel. He did not, however, sell his Richmond property next door to Jerry. Quite the opposite: he purchased an additional ground-floor flat for $800,000 and began renovating it for his life there with L'Wren.

In order to make the new flat suitable for his six-foot-four Mormon girlfriend, Mick lowered the floor ten inches. "Apparently," a member of the local planning council said, "he didn't want her bumping her head on the ceiling."

Mick's intentions were obvious to Jerry: he wanted L'Wren, who had already spent time with Georgia May and Gabriel while their mother was out of town, to play a bigger role in the youngest Jaggers' lives. Hall berated Mick yet again, claiming that his girlfriend's visits constituted a "bad influence" on the children. Equally important to Jerry, Mick's habit of popping through the door that connected the two dwellings at any time of the day or night continued to have a chilling effect on her romantic life. "He can't stand being alone even for a few minutes," Jerry said, "and it's driving me nuts."

The tensions between Mick and Jerry continued through 2004, as they bickered over whether she had the right to sell off the furniture and art from the Richmond house—including a million-dollar painting by Roy Lichtenstein—while the Stones were on tour. She called him "mean" and "petty"; he insisted that their settlement did not include the furnishings, and he wanted them back. In the end, Hall prevailed. "Too late, Mick," she said. "Too late."

One thing they could agree on was the blossoming romance between Lizzy, who had just renewed her $1 million contract with Lancôme cosmetics, and Sean Lennon. The only son of John and Yoko was dating actress Leelee Sobieski when Keith Richards introduced him to Lizzy at the Rock and Roll Hall of Fame ceremonies in New York.

Days later, the scions of two rock dynasties had their first date at a vegetarian restaurant in New York's Soho district. Neither was about to be intimidated by the other's father—a stumbling block for both Sean and Lizzy in past relationships. "It's hard to find someone," she said, "who isn't overwhelmed by my family." Twenty-eight-year-old Sean, with an impressive pedigree of his own, appeared to be that someone.

"They are so in love, and he's adorable," Jerry gushed. "He looks so like John now, and he writes beautiful poetry." Sean also charmed Jerry by sitting down at the piano in Richmond and serenading her with his father's song "Imagine." Mick was more muted in his approval, although he was grateful that, at twenty-eight, Sean was only seven-and-a-half years older than his daughter.

Mick was growing restless, and in March he called a summit of the Stones in Paris. It had only been four months since the Licks tour ended, but already all four band members were eager to get back onstage.

One of them, however, soon faced a life-and-death crisis that threatened not just the tour but the group's very existence. The Glimmer Twins were back at work writing songs and recording demos at La Fourchette when Charlie Watts called to tell them that he had been diagnosed with throat cancer. "I went to bed and cried," Charlie said later. "I thought that was it, that I'd only have another three months."

Doctors actually told Watts there was a 90 percent chance he would survive. "If I were him," Mick conceded, "I would have been in such a state. If Charlie had said, 'I can't do this tour, I've faced mortality,' we would have had to change our minds about touring. No one pressured him."

Watts underwent radiation therapy that summer, and Mick called several times to check up on him. "You have to get well," he told Charlie. "Don't worry about us." In reality, Mick was "terrified. I kept worrying, 'Is he eating?'" In that way, Mick allowed, "I'm like a nanny."

Charlie returned five months later, said Keith, "looking exactly the same, like he hadn't done anything more than comb his hair." It was the thought of going back out on tour with the Stones, Watts said, that kept him going. "I've seen forty years of Mick's bum running around in front of me—that's all I can see when I'm at the back of the stage!" he said. "But I'm not complaining. One of the biggest compliments I can have as a drummer is that someone is dancing to you."

Jagger was also "champing at the bit" to get back on the road. "I am addicted to late-night repeats on television," claimed Mick, suddenly sounding every bit his age. "I watch Turner Classic Movies until dawn." Unless he was watching cricket; an avid fan of the game, Mick founded Jagged Internetworks just so that he could get live coverage of cricket matches from around the world.

Even then, he was never really idle. Mick had previously worked on the soundtrack for the hit comedy *Ruthless People,* and now he was collaborating with former Eurythmics star Dave Stewart on the score for *Alfie,* a remake of the 1966 film starring Michael Caine. This time, Jude Law played the title role of a smooth-talking womanizer.

"If anybody was going to write the lyrics," said Stewart, a friend of Mick's for twenty years, "it had to be Mick. Mick *is* Alfie." Jagger agreed, sort of. "There's a lot of Alfie in everyone," he said. "Most men have had an Alfie moment." But so many Alfie moments? "All right," he allowed with a wry grin, "if you must, if you must." Later, after picking up a Golden Globe for the film's new theme "Old Habits Die Hard" (and thanking L'Wren from the stage for "not wearing heels"), Mick was ready when the comparison was made again. "Any vague resemblance between my life and a playboy's," he quipped, "is merely coincidental."

That Christmas, Mick once again slipped effortlessly into his family man persona. Unbeknownst to Jerry, Mick had invited L'Wren along when he took twelve-year-old Georgia May and Gabriel, six, on vacation to Rome a few weeks earlier. Around the same time, L'Wren had also attended Jade's thirty-third birthday in London and, significantly, spent time with Mick's grandchildren.

Now the holidays provided an opportunity for L'Wren to get to know the littlest Jagger, five-year-old Lucas. His mother, Luciana Morad, was nowhere in sight as L'Wren led the boy—now the spitting image of Mick—into the lobby of Claridge's and up to Jagger's palatial suite. For Mick, who divided Christmas among Karis,

Jade, Jerry and their children, Lucas, and his ninety-year-old father, L'Wren was proving to be a valuable helpmate. "I love Mick's children and the grandkids," L'Wren told her mother. "Everybody treats me like family. It's wonderful."

Jerry seemed anything but thrilled. Just before Christmas, she placed all the jewelry Jagger had bought her in a bank vault. Mick "would give me diamonds when he needed to atone for some misdeed, so, as you can imagine, I amassed quite a collection of 'guilt jewelry,'" Hall explained. "I don't wear them because there are too many bad memories attached to them."

Adding insult to injury, Jerry now wore the simple diamond-and-ruby engagement ring that Bryan Ferry had given her when she was nineteen—before Mick stole her away. "I offered to give it back when we broke off the engagement," she said, "but Bryan very gallantly allowed me to keep it. And now I've started wearing it again. This ring, I treasure."

Jerry didn't stop there. While Mick and L'Wren spent New Year's on Mustique, Jerry made her recording debut with a song called "Around This Table," a transparent attack on Mick's philandering: "Then you bring other women, while I'm out of town / And I can always sense when a stranger has sat down."

It may have been the unlikeliest setting of all for a Rolling Stones concert. After arriving by train, boat, bridge, and balloon, the band had chosen to announce its next tour with a performance outside New York's prestigious music and arts conservatory the Juilliard School.

The Stones' combined age was now 245, but Mick insisted that their new world tour—tentatively titled A Bigger Bang—would not be their last. It was a question, he liked to point out, that had first been asked him in 1966. ("I distinctly remember that.") There would be future tours and future records as long as the public wanted to hear the Rolling Stones. "If the demand's there, we'll supply." How long can the Stones go on? a reporter asked. "Forever," Keith answered. "We'll let you know when we keel over."

Just as important was the new CD, their first studio album in eight years and the longest since their landmark *Exile on Main St.* "If we go out on tour, we gotta do a record," Mick explained. "People say, 'I much prefer to hear "Brown Sugar" than some new song.' Well, I don't give a shit what you prefer. We're not just an oldies band."

Perhaps because Charlie Watts's bout with cancer had put things in perspective, Mick and Keith quarreled little during the making of *A Bigger Bang.* There was a time, Richards allowed, when he and Mick "argued forever over the most mundane things. The color of the album cover could turn into a life-and-death debate . . . We're like quarrelsome brothers. It's sibling rivalry."

This time, however, the Glimmer Twins took a different approach to songwriting. Richards pushed Mick to dig deep, to reveal more of himself in his lyrics. "I thought it was about time Mick stepped out of that closed shell," Keith said.

"Of course I'm as vulnerable as anyone else," Mick said. "It's crazy to think someone can't be hurt just because he's famous or he struts across a stage." This time, with Keith's help, Mick did not pull back from exposing his feelings as he had in the past.

Once in the studio, it was up to Mick to deliver the goods—but not before undergoing a transformation that always left producer Don Was speechless. In order to move about undetected in the real world of cineplexes and shopping malls, said Was, Mick had learned to "conceal his huge, charismatic persona." It took a while for Mick the shopper to become Mick Jagger the character. "He'll take his white shirt off, strip down to his tank top," Was said. "His whole musculature changes, and his lips get bigger. Suddenly he looks forty years younger. It is so intense that I feel I'm gawping at him the way a tourist would, and I get so embarrassed that I can't even look."

There were some tender, bluesy moments on *A Bigger Bang*. But critics were struck by the fact that anger, not pathos, dominated Jagger's lyrics. In "Oh No, Not You Again," Mick got back at Jerry for "Around This Table." ("Oh no! Not you again, fucking up my life," Mick sings. "It was bad the first time around, better take my own advice.")

The most provocative cut on the album turned out to be political, not personal. "Sweet Neo Con" was a scathing indictment of President George W. Bush and US foreign policy. "You call yourself a Christian, I think that you're a hypocrite," Jagger shouted. "You say you are a patriot, I think that you're a crock of shit." The song goes on to slam the Pentagon, the rising price of oil, and Vice President Dick Cheney's onetime employer, Halliburton.

Mick was equally critical of the man who proposed him for a knighthood: British prime minister Tony Blair. Jagger had actually been ambivalent about the 2003 invasion of Iraq, conceding that getting rid of dictator Saddam Hussein "was a gift for humanity." But when he came to decide that "Blair already knew the weapons of mass destruction were simply an excuse" and that there was no "coherent plan to put Iraq back on its feet," Mick was "shocked."

Richards initially voiced his concern about "Sweet Neo Con," pointing out that many of their fans were behind the war in Iraq. "Do we really want to distract attention from the rest of the album?" he asked. "I mean, it's not really metaphorical." No, Mick acknowledged that, if anything, the song was "very direct. I think Keith's a bit worried because he lives in the US," Mick surmised. "But *I* don't." Besides, Jagger added, the Stones had been rattling political cages ever since "Street Fighting Man." The new song was "a bit of a finger-pointer," he conceded, "but what's wrong with a poke in the eye?"

A poke in the eye, as it turned out, is exactly what Mick got next from Keith. Just as the Rolling Stones prepared to kick off the Bigger Bang tour at Boston's Fenway Park on August 21, 2005, a Boston paper ran an interview with Richards. In it, Keith made his first disparaging remark about Mick's manhood. "His cock's on the end of his nose," he sniped. "Big balls. Small cock." As soon as he read the story, Mick sprinted from his suite at the Four Seasons Hotel to Keith's. "What the fuck is *this*?" he demanded, waving the newspaper in the air.

Keith, who would repeat the claim six years later in his autobiography, seemed surprised at Mick's reaction. "Oh come *on*, Brenda," he said. "Can't take a fucking joke?"

Relations between the two men thawed out several weeks into the tour. The same could not be said for Mick and Jerry, whose new VH1 reality show, *Kept*, featured a dozen young men vying to be her boy toy. "Well," Mick fumed, "I'm going to do a show where I date thirty sixteen-year-olds!"

Hall was unimpressed. "Mick did that kind of research," she shot back, "for about twenty years."

Actually, much longer. But at sixty-two, there was now persistent speculation that rock's legendary Lothario could not possibly keep it up without pharmaceutical help. "You can only go so far being very charming and funny," he told *GQ* magazine. "Then," he added, looking down toward his crotch, "you have to have something else as well, don't you?" Had he ever taken Viagra? "Never!" Mick replied unequivocally. "I don't need that."

It was around this time that Bayer HealthCare announced that Jerry Hall was to be the spokesman for Levitra, its erectile dysfunction drug. Dr. Christa Kreuzburg, president of the company's pharmacology division in Europe and Japan, called Jerry "the perfect ambassador" for Levitra because she was "a global icon who embodies an open, confident, and bold approach to sex and relationships."

Given what the middle-aged Mick had put her through, Jerry's own explanation for becoming Levitra's spokesperson seemed, well, charitable: "A healthy love life is not and should not be the preserve of those in their twenties and thirties. It's important at all ages." She would get no argument from Jagger—or from L'Wren.

Whether or not Mick took potency-enhancing drugs seemed increasingly beside the point. His lusty image was taking a beating in the press, which now dubbed L'Wren "the Loin Tamer" for having seemingly curtailed Mick's philandering ways. Just how much influence Mick's Mormon lover had over him, and the nature of that influence, was a matter of considerable debate.

There were rumblings that L'Wren, on the verge of launching her own clothing line, had angered the other Stones by offering them unsolicited advice about what to wear onstage. Worse, it was rumored that she had even tried to convince Keith Richards and Ronnie Wood to quit smoking. Inevitably, L'Wren, accused of stirring up trouble within the band, was labeled the Stones' answer to Yoko Ono.

In a rare step, Mick actually issued a public statement addressing the issue. "It is completely untrue to say L'Wren has caused a rift between myself and the rest of the band," he said. "This is all nonsense. Everyone has their own style. We have not had any disagreements about clothes, smoking, or L'Wren, and this is all very hurtful for her. L'Wren," he continued, "would not dream of interfering with a band who have been on the road for forty years."

While Mick was on location in Australia playing a bandit in the cringe-inducing *Ned Kelly,* Marianne became the second woman in Mick's life to attempt suicide. Bianca (below, with Mick) was not the self-destructive type, and once became so enraged over his affairs that, according to Mick, she once pulled a gun on him.

14

15

After years of legal wrangling, Marsha Hunt, by then living on welfare, finally got Mick to admit that he was the father of their daughter, Karis. At London's Cafe Royale in 1973 (below), Mick, wearing nail polish, shared an androgynous moment with Lou Reed and David Bowie.

16

17

Mick's longtime friendship with the Queen's only sibling, Princess Margaret (above), raised eyebrows inside and outside palace walls. In 1976 Mick conferred with music industry legend Ahmet Ertegun; thirty years later, Mick was shattered when his friend and mentor died after a backstage fall.

20

21

Mick and Jerry Hall surveyed the scene from their balcony perch at New York's Studio 54. "Nobody knows more about fashion and beauty," Jerry once said of Mick, who tended to her tresses before hitting the red carpet.

22

23

Paul McCartney and wife, Linda (both at right in top photo), visit Mick backstage in 1978. Jagger remained friendly with all the Beatles, but was closest to John Lennon. The two men chatted at a gala honoring James Cagney in 1974.

Mick and Tina stole the show with their torrid rendition of "It's Only Rock 'n Roll" at 1985's Live Aid concert. That same year, Jagger's "Dancing in the Street" duet with David Bowie was such a hit that they considered donning dresses to film a remake of *Some Like It Hot.* Mick jammed with George Harrison and Bruce Springsteen at the Rock and Roll Hall of Fame ceremonies in 1988.

24

25

26

Just a few of the four-thousand-plus women Mick has slept with
(clockwise from top left): Janice Dickinson, Angelina Jolie, Brazilian
bombshell Luciana Morad, and Sophie Dahl.

Eric Clapton (above with Carla Bruni, holding cigarette) begged his friend Mick not to steal Bruni away from him, but Jagger did anyway. After an on-again, off-again affair with Mick that lasted for years, she finally married French president Nicolas Sarkozy (at left with Bruni) in 2008.

33

Family man. Even as his
having an out-of-wedlock
child with Luciana Morad
finally ended Mick and
Jerry's twenty-two-year
relationship, Jagger and Hall
were all smiles during an
outing with the kids (above).
Not long after, Mick joined
Luciana and their son,
Lucas, for a stroll near the
home he still shared with
Jerry in Richmond, Surrey.

35

Mick and younger brother Chris with Eva and Joe Jagger in 1999 (above). Mick would credit his parents with instilling in him the discipline needed for success. After Eva died the following year at age eighty-seven, Mick wept openly at her funeral.

36

Daughter Lizzy looked on respectfully as Dad chatted with Prince Charles at the royal premiere of *Enigma,* which Mick coproduced. On December 12, 2003, Joe, Karis, and Lizzy posed with Sir Mick minutes after he was knighted at Buckingham Palace. The Queen, never a Jagger fan, was conspicuous by her absence.

Network censors bleeped
some Stones lyrics, but
Mick still thrilled the TV
audience of 111 million
that tuned in to watch
the Super Bowl in 2006
(above). The following
year, Mick sang "Ain't
Too Proud to Beg" with
Amy Winehouse. He
predicted then that she
was headed for an early
death.

41

Mick, Ronnie Wood, Charlie Watts, and Keith together again at the London premiere of Martin Scorsese's Stones rockumentary *Shine a Light* in 2008. Jagger was less cheerful watching the World Cup soccer finals in South Africa in the company of a friend and fan three years his junior, Bill Clinton.

Moves like Jagger. Paying tribute to his late friend, blues great Solomon Burke, Mick tore up the stage at the 2011 Grammys.

With the exception of his children, the two most important people in Mick's life: L'Wren Scott and, of course, Keith.

44

There was, in fact, tangible evidence that the couple had taken a step toward some sort of commitment. In January 2006, while attending a Paris fashion show with her friend Victoria Beckham, L'Wren flashed a ten-carat sapphire-and-diamond ring on her left hand. It was, she confessed coyly, a gift from Mick.

Like so many women during so many tours before her, L'Wren was summoned periodically to join Mick on the road during A Bigger Bang. But she wasn't about to let her obligation to Mick get in the way of her own career. "L'Wren is very ambitious," a friend from her styling days pointed out. "She is focused, smart, and set on making a name for herself apart from Mick or any man."

Complaining that she had trouble finding the perfect "little black dress" that supposedly every fashion-conscious woman needs in her closet, L'Wren created an entire "Little Black Dress" collection. Her new line's biggest hit was what she called the "Headmistress Dress": a just-below-the-knee-length black wool dress with three-quarter-length sleeves and a wide white collar. The dress, fashioned partly on Mick's memory of what English girls' school headmistresses wore in the 1950s, was an instant success. Eventually L'Wren's trademark Headmistress Dress would be worn by, among others, Madonna, Sarah Jessica Parker, Amy Adams, Demi Moore, Reese Witherspoon, Jennifer Lopez, Oprah Winfrey, Renée Zellweger, Sandra Bullock—and First Lady Michelle Obama. L'Wren also had no qualms about dressing several famous women—Carla Bruni, Uma Thurman, Angelina Jolie—with whom she had one thing in common: Mick.

He had always shown a keen interest in clothing design, but now Mick was a fixture on the fashion scene. At runway shows in New York, London, Paris, and Milan, he was invariably seated in the front row next to L'Wren. At those times when L'Wren's designs were being shown—her empire expanded quickly to include handbags, shoes, jewelry, and makeup—Mick was always there to cheer her on, occasionally hopping up to snap photos or to get a closer look. "Mick always has something to say about what I wear and what I design," L'Wren said. "Look at the way he dresses! I don't think there's a more fashion-conscious man in the world."

L'Wren was equally loyal and attentive to Mick's career, routinely hopping planes to join him wherever he was in the world. On February 5, 2006, she was on hand at Super Bowl XL in Detroit when Mick, getting ready to perform the Stones' new song "Rough Justice" during the band's three-song halftime performance, was told that ABC network censors had a problem with one of the lyrics: "Once upon a time I was your little rooster / but now I'm just one of your cocks." That last word was cut from the broadcast. "It is hilarious to think about these very serious men sitting around," Jagger said, "discussing whether the word *cocks* could be broadcast or not."

A television audience of 89.9 million watched the Stones' Super Bowl performance, an experience that Mick described as "fantastically mad—you had to be so *on* immediately. Then as soon as you're on, you're off." Two weeks later, they experienced a different sort of thrill when an astounding 1.5 million people—far and away their largest live audience ever—mobbed Rio de Janeiro's Copacabana beach to hear the band for free.

A special bridge was constructed from the Stones' hotel to the stage, enabling them to get to and from the stage over the heads of the crowd. "You have to sort of pinch yourself," Mick recalled. "You couldn't really see the crowd at Rio—it was too big. But the sound of them was like hundreds of hives of bees; the buzz was really loud."

The buzz also signified a major windfall for the group, since the Brazilian government had in essence paid for the concert. When worldwide broadcast rights and merchandise sales were factored in, the take for this one night in Rio topped $17 million.

As if the Rio experience wasn't sufficiently surreal, Luciana Morad's new TV tycoon boyfriend, Marcelo de Carvalho, proposed to her at the Stones concert. After the show, a breathless Luciana rushed backstage with her new fiancé to break the news to Mick. "He was happy for me, of course," said Luciana. "But it was hilarious watching him standing there talking to Marcelo."

Once the Stones ended the Asian leg of A Bigger Bang, Mick and Charlie returned to London while Keith and Ronnie flew off to a private island retreat in Fiji. After a swim, Keith climbed up six feet onto the low-hanging branch of a gnarled palm tree to dry off. As he climbed down, his hand slipped, and he fell to the ground, hitting the back of his head on the trunk.

"He thought he was Tarzan and lost his grip," Wood said. "I spun around, and there he was on the ground. He was very bloody, and clutching his head."

Still, once he'd cleaned up, Keith felt fine. Two days later, however, he was out on a boat when he was suddenly struck by a blinding headache. The pain persisted and worsened until one night Richards suffered two seizures in his sleep.

Suffering from a large blood clot on the brain, Keith was flown to a hospital in Auckland, New Zealand, for emergency surgery. "He wouldn't have survived if he hadn't had it removed," said Andrew Law, the neurosurgeon who operated on Keith. It was only after the surgery that Dr. Law told Richards that, as a boy, he had a picture of Keith at the foot of his bed. "Luckily," Keith quipped, "he was a fan of mine!"

Mick, who was called the minute Keith was strapped into the plane bound for Auckland, appeared shaken by the prospect of losing his closest friend. "He was very upset, obviously," L'Wren said. "They love each other." But there were also decisions to be made. At first the press was told only that Keith had suffered a minor concussion and was recuperating. Second, the rest of the tour would have to be put on hold so that Keith could recuperate. Mick was informed that could be as long as six months—if, in fact, Keith did make a full recovery.

Astoundingly, just six weeks later, Keith was back playing with the Stones in Milan. "Six weeks!" he proclaimed in a masterpiece of understatement. "I mean, not bad for a brain job."

No one was more relieved than Mick, now confident that much of the Bigger Bang tour could be resumed as originally planned. "We were all holding our breath," Mick said, "and there he was, playing as good as he ever has." But in the future, Jagger cautioned, "Keith should never go up in anything without a parachute."

As it happened, Keith's brush with death was only the first in a series of blows that in the coming months would leave Mick reeling. In late August, Mick learned that Marianne Faithfull, a sometime film actress and a consistent presence in the music world since the release of her album *Broken English* in 1979, had been diagnosed with breast cancer and had just undergone surgery at a clinic in Paris.

Faithfull was asleep when the phone rang. "'Ello, Marian darling," Mick said. "How are you?" He was calling from Miami.

"He didn't say who he was," she recalled. "He didn't need to. No one else in the world calls me Marian—as in Maid Marian."

It was the first time they had spoken in thirty-five years. "And here he was on the phone," Marianne said, "making sure I was okay." Faithfull found out later that Mick had phoned agents and friends for hours trying to track down her number at the clinic. "All the time we were talking, I was thinking, 'This is so kind' . . . He went to a lot of trouble. I was extremely touched. He's a good man, a classy guy. If you love someone, you love each other forever. It never stops."

One of the subjects that the former lovers touched on during their chat was the state of Mick's voice. She had read that Jagger had once again been plagued by laryngitis on the road, forcing the cancellation of shows.

Mick somehow managed to pull it together on October 29 for a special concert at New York's comparatively intimate Beacon Theater. Part of Bill Clinton's belated three-day-long sixtieth birthday bash, the star-studded benefit for the former president's Clinton Foundation was also being filmed by Martin Scorsese for a documentary on the Stones.

Just before the group was set to go on, Mick's mentor and friend Ahmet Ertegun joined celebrities gathered backstage in the VIP lounge area band members called "the Rattlesnake Inn." In the commotion and excitement, the eighty-three-year-old Atlantic Records founder and music industry titan lost his balance, fell, and struck his head on the concrete floor.

Unaware of what had happened, the Stones went on with the show as an ambulance pulled up behind the theater and whisked Ertegun to the hospital. "Where's Ahmet?" a nonplused Jagger asked once the concert was over. "What the fuck happened?"

Distraught, Mick contacted the hospital to check on Ertegun's condition. At first the news was grim. He was unconscious in the intensive care unit, and doctors gave him little chance of pulling through. After less than a week, however, Ertegun was off the respirator and breathing on his own; his condition was upgraded to stable.

Jagger was still trying to make sense of it all when, just two days after Ertegun's tragic accident, ninety-three-year-old Joe Jagger fell at his home in Richmond, fracturing two ribs and puncturing a lung. Over the next twelve days, Jagger would rack up sixteen thousand miles shuttling back and forth across the Atlantic to be with his father. "He was very red eyed and emotional," a nurse said. "He talked to his dad even when he wasn't conscious. He told him how much he loved him. It wasn't something we associated with Mick Jagger. We were all very moved."

Mick and L'Wren spent eight hours by Joe's bedside at Kingston Hospital in Surrey, then boarded a plane for the Stones' next concert date, in Las Vegas. Just before going onstage at the MGM Grand Garden Arena, Mick was told that his father had died of pneumonia. Rather than cancel, Mick chose to go on. "Mick was shattered and obviously in shock," a Stones staffer said. "You could see it in his face. But you sort of go out there on automatic pilot and just do it."

It was impossible to overstate how attached Mick was to both of his parents and how much Mick the ageless rock star owed to Joe in particular. "The whole athleticism thing, which has been Mick's strength down through the years, is entirely Joe's influence," said Jagger's Dartford schoolmate and early Stone Dick Taylor. Ray Connolly, a British journalist who attended the London School of Economics at the same time as Jagger, agreed. "Discipline is something Mick always had," he said. "The Rolling Stones would have achieved nothing without Mick's work ethic. And that came from his dad."

There was something else. "We all hanker for the security of our childhoods," Dick Taylor observed, "and Mick is no different. He was just so close to his mum and dad."

This was a watershed moment in Mick's life, and those who knew him well understood the depth of his grief. This time, L'Wren, Jerry Hall, Bianca (who by now had earned high praise for her humanitarian works around the globe), and Marsha Hunt were all present to comfort Mick at his father's funeral. All of the Jagger children attended the services at St. Mary's College Chapel in Twickenham as well—with the exception of Lucas, who remained in Brazil with his mother, Luciana.

Mick was even more emotional than he had been at his mother's funeral. Tears rolled down his cheeks as the congregation sang his father's favorite hymn, "Morning Has Broken"—one of the songs also performed at Eva Jagger's funeral—and he had to be comforted by L'Wren and his daughters. "He was a very good father to me," Mick told the mourners. "A very good father to me."

The year's horrible events were not yet over, however. Sadly, after lingering in a coma for six weeks, Ahmet Ertegun died of the injuries he had sustained backstage at the Stones' concert for Bill Clinton.

The series of tragedies and near tragedies that had struck in rapid succession—especially Charlie's throat cancer, Keith's brain injury, Marianne's breast cancer, and the deaths of Ahmet Ertegun and Joe Jagger—left Mick reeling.

On Christmas Day, James Brown, the Godfather of Soul and one of Mick's early influences, also died. "What did the Queen call the year Windsor Castle almost burnt down? An *annus horribilis*?" Mick mused. "Well, we've just had ours."

When I started, it was a different century, and it seems like it. You move on.

—MICK

10

◆ ◆ ◆

Hanging with William and Kate/
The President of France Is Jealous/
Revenge of the Tiny Todger

*T*he president of France was jealous—jealous of Mick Jagger. Nicolas Sarkozy had thought that his wife's eight-year love affair with Mick was over, but there in the apartment she still kept at Villa Montmorency in Paris's chic Sixteenth Arrondissement was a silver-framed photograph of her and Mick embracing on the beach. Did she still love him? he wanted to know. Did he love her?

The two men had much in common. Each was a compact, charismatic dynamo, a fitness fanatic, and, in his own way, a sex symbol. Each defied convention and courted controversy. Once viewed as renegades, they now operated at the pinnacle of power and prestige. They were household names, known in every corner of the globe. Their misadventures with members of the opposite sex made headlines. And, after two failed marriages and countless affairs (Sarkozy's second wife, Cecilia, also a former model, had branded him a "womanizer" and "cheap"), they both had fallen in love with the same woman.

The object of their affection had not exactly been standing still in the few years since she'd last traded insults with Jerry Hall. Encouraged by Mick, Carla embarked on a career as a smokey-voiced chanteuse in 1997. Her first album was a hit in French-speaking countries, and she went on to sell more than two million records in Europe.

Bruni's private life, meanwhile, had all the twists and turns of the Monte Carlo Grand Prix. Since the early part of the decade, Carla had been involved with actors Vincent Perez and Charles Berling, French director Leos Carax, Nazi hunter Arno Klarsfeld (who had actually worked with the future French president when Sarkozy was interior minister), and even former French prime minister Laurent Fabius.

In 2001 she moved in with noted French intellectual Jean-Paul Enthoven and fell in love with his son, philosophy professor Raphael Enthoven. The younger Enthoven was married at the time to French novelist Justine Levy. The affair ended Raphael's marriage, and in 2001 Carla gave birth to his son, Aurelien. In her 2004 novel *Nothing Serious,* Levy recounts the tale of "Paula," a "praying mantis" with a "Terminator smile" who absconds with the main character's husband.

Through it all, Carla was unapologetic about Mick, and the role she may or may not have played in his breakup with Jerry Hall. "There are so many other women with Mick," she said. "I was one of the four thousand other women, but I never really felt responsible . . . He is, I think, like Don Juan. I am used to that because in Italy, the men like women very much."

Just months before she was to meet her future husband, Carla admitted that she and Mick were at the very least "close friends," and that she never felt her affair with Jagger had been harmful to her reputation. "I'd be proud to be known as that," she said. "It's not like I had an affair with General Pinochet or Mussolini." Besides, she added, "when you have a relationship with someone, they become only a man. If they are talented, of course, it's better. But still, a man is only a man."

In November 2007, not long after Carla broke up with Raphael and only one month after Sarkozy's second marriage ended in divorce, French advertising mogul Jacques Seguela introduced Bruni to the French president during a dinner party at Seguela's Paris home. According to Seguela, Bruni and Sarkozy chatted about Mick during that first meeting. "When it comes to the celebrity press, you are an amateur," Carla chided Sarkozy. "My time with Mick was secret for eight years. We went to all the world capitals, and we were never photographed once."

Sarkozy, pretending to be unimpressed, took aim at Mick's slight physique. "How could you have stayed eight years," he asked Bruni, "with a man who has such ridiculous calves?"

It was not long before Sarkozy took the stunning Carla on a stroll through the Elysée Palace gardens. "He kept giving me all these flowers' names—he knows all the Latin names, all these details about tulips and roses," she recalled. "I said to myself, 'My God, I must marry this man. He's the president, and he knows everything about flowers as well. This is incredible.'"

Soon Sarkozy was pursuing Bruni in earnest—and she him. "When my sister wants someone," Carla's sister, actress Valeria Bruni-Tedeschi, observed, "she takes him."

As the presidential romance turned serious, Mick contacted Carla and quizzed her on Sarkozy. "It's that old rivalry that drives him," one of Mick's former girlfriends said. "Competing with another rock star is one thing, but the *president of France*?"

Bruni was torn. After years spent alternating between blanket denials and fervent declarations of love for Jagger, Carla now publicly referred to their relationship as nothing more than a "fling." Friends knew otherwise. They had heard Carla describe only one man as "the love of my life": Mick.

Sarkozy and Bruni were married at the Elysée Palace on February 2, 2008. Andrée Sarkozy, the mother of the groom, was less than enthusiastic. "I," she said, "have had enough of brides." A few weeks later, just before embarking on a state visit to the United Kingdom, a nude photograph of Bruni was put up for auction at Christie's. It went for $91,000.

As she went about her duties as France's impossibly glamourous first lady, Carla Bruni-Sarkozy remained in touch with that other iconic figure she had once wanted to marry. Carla and Mick continued to talk on the phone—Bruni's personal assistant Franck Demules insisted that she still regarded him as "God"—and Sarkozy continued to fume.

The French president had another reason to be jealous when Carla, whose inheritance from her industrialist father put her net worth at more than $35 million, decided to look for a new apartment to replace her townhouse in the Sixteenth Arrondissement. The Sarkozys' official residence was the Elysée Palace, of course, but she had always maintained a place of her own—a sanctuary for herself outside palace walls.

She finally settled on the spectacular $15 million Left Bank garden duplex at 55 Rue de Babylone that had once been home to the late designer Yves Saint Laurent and his partner, Pierre Bergé. The three-story apartment had housed the Saint Laurent–Bergé art collection, which had been auctioned off only weeks earlier for more than $600 million.

At first glance, the apartment seemed perfect. It was situated on a broad street in the Seventh Arrondissement, near parliament and directly across the Seine River from the Elysée Palace. Sarkozy approved—until he was informed that Jagger owned the penthouse just two floors above. The president, not surprisingly, nixed the deal.

It was not the only time Sarkozy appeared to have cause for concern. In the summer months, Carla shuttled back and forth by boat between Fort de Brégançon, the official presidential summer home, and Château Faraghi at Cap Nègre, the opulent seafront estate owned by Carla's family. Faraghi Castle just happened to be a stone's throw from Jerry Hall's Mediterranean villa, where Mick still spent time with his children.

When he realized that Jagger was nearby, Sarkozy started spending more time with Carla at Castle Faraghi—"apparently," said a friend of Bruni's, "to keep an eye on her." For Carla, who still wanted to pursue her singing career once her husband left office, maintaining her close relationship with Mick made sense. But in the meantime, speculation concerning a possible Sarkozy-Bruni-Jagger triangle provided grist for the rumor mill. "Carla is typically Italian," said Sarah Doukas, whose Paris model agency once represented Bruni. "Very theatrical. She's the kind of girl who likes to create a disturbance."

Mick understood all too well. With him as the group's mastermind, the Rolling Stones had already blown away the competition as they barreled across the globe, leaving attendance records shattered in their wake. By the time they took their last bows at London's O2 Arena, A Bigger Bang had played 147 shows with such lead acts as Maroon 5, the Black Eyed Peas, John Mayer, Christina Aguilera, Beck, Smashing Pumpkins, Pearl Jam, Metallica, Alice Cooper, Mötley Crüe, and the Dave Matthews Band. Total gross: $558.3 million, making A Bigger Bang easily the highest-grossing tour of all time.

The rigors of the road behind him, Mick could concentrate on film projects—his Jagged Films was producing a remake of Clare Boothe Luce's classic 1939 motion picture comedy *The Women*— and spending time with L'Wren and his family. *The Women,* which starred Eva Mendes, Annette Bening, and Meg Ryan in place of original screen legends Norma Shearer, Rosalind Russell, and Joan Crawford, misfired with the critics upon its 2008 release. A. O.

Scott of the *New York Times* called it a "witless, straining mess," and *Time*'s Richard Schickel said it was simply "one of the worst movies I've ever seen."

Even worse was the ill-conceived *The Knights of Prosperity*, a cringe-inducing ABC sitcom about a bunch of bumbling crooks who attempt to rob assorted celebrities—beginning with one of the show's own executive producers: namely, Mick. In fact, at one point, the series was titled *Let's Rob Mick Jagger*. In a scene that may have hit a little too close to home, Mick gives the viewing audience a tour of his ersatz $25 million New York residence. "Hi, I'm Mick," he says. "Welcome to my apartment. It's so nice, I never want to go out." Among the over-the-top features are a solid gold fountain shaped like the Stones' lips-and-tongue logo, a hat room kept at sixty-two degrees ("about the right temperature to keep a really good hat"), and an indoor pool solely for the use of his four dogs, because Mick "hates getting wet." ABC pulled the plug after nine weeks.

Martin Scorsese's *Shine a Light* documentary, filmed close up with eighteen cameras at the Beacon Theater concert honoring Bill Clinton two years earlier, made up for these misses. Showing backstage squabbles and preshow jitters as well as the powerful performances fans had come to expect, *Shine a Light* offered a look at the Stones that was unprecedented in its intimacy. With the group's tacit consent, Scorsese made no attempt in either the filming or the editing to conceal anyone's age. "Their lined faces, ravages, and scars are plain to see," wrote David Gritten in London's *Daily Telegraph*, "and lend the band a leonine nobility."

As he turned sixty-five in July 2008, Mick, like the rest of the Stones, expressed no interest in erasing those deep grooves, crow's feet, and wrinkles with plastic surgery. A facelift was out of the question, as was one plastic surgeon's bizarre suggestion that Mick get his lips plumped even further with collagen. (Joe Jagger, who once said that his son inherited the "big Jagger mouth" from him, had warned that Mick's lips would get smaller with age.) Nevertheless, Mick stood his ground. "You can only be so vain," he said, "and then it gets a bit ridiculous."

For now, Mick held off on all cosmetic surgery procedures, including Botox. Beauty treatments were an entirely different matter. Mick had never stopped experimenting with creams, moisturizers, and ointments of all kinds, and that only intensified as he crept into his midsixties. A regular at Claridge's Olympus Health and Fitness suite in London, he preferred La Prairie's pricey line of skin care products—especially its caviar facial line containing wheat germ and seaweed. The cost: $390 for a 5.2-ounce jar.

With age came the inevitable speculation that Mick might finally settle down. L'Wren was flashing her sapphire-and-diamond ring with abandon, refusing to comment on whether it was or wasn't an engagement ring. "It's a beautiful ring," she stated, "and that's all I'm going to say about it." Mick, however, wasn't budging from his "Monogamy is not for me" mantra.

Still, after six years, Mick and his Utah-raised girlfriend were closer than ever. "They scream with laughter at the same things," said their friend Nicky Haslam, the designer. "They like the same food, the same decor, the same people. Of all his partners, she's the one who seems nearest to him and his tastes and the way he likes to live . . . She's very observant and witty, and he adores that."

In the wake of his father's death, Mick was, for the first time, taking a serious look at his spiritual side, and in L'Wren he found a willing partner. The couple made the usual pilgrimage to India, staying at the 374-room palace of the Maharaja of Jodhpur as they visited ashrams and folk music festivals. Before they left, Mick told Maharaja Gaj Singh II that he would be the patron of Jodhpur's international folk festival. Praising Indian music as a "huge mosaic of styles," Mick said that he was struck most by the contrasts in India—"a guy with a camel cart in front of a shopping mall. Just amazing."

Jagger returned with a red-string bracelet on his right wrist— not a Kabbalah band like the one worn by Jerry, but a Rajasthani holy thread intended to ward off evil spirits. Now Mick incorporated yoga, meditation, and Buddhist prayer in his morning routine.

Mick was making changes of a more concrete nature as well. Much to Jerry's relief, he was finally moving out of the house next to hers in Richmond. In 2008 Mick bought a seventeenth-century Chelsea mansion overlooking the Thames for $18 million and then poured millions more into renovating it. Among the new features: a Georgian orangery housing a swimming pool, solar panels on the roof, and separate his-and-hers dressing rooms, with his more than twice the size of hers.

While work was being done on the new Chelsea mansion, Mick also expanded his holdings on Mustique, buying the villa next door to Stargroves and christening it Pelican Beach. Never one to pass up an opportunity to make money, Mick rented out Stargroves ($22,000 per week) and Pelican Beach (a mere $7,000 weekly) when he wasn't in residence.

Mick and L'Wren were among the one hundred–plus VIPs who showed up in August 2008 to celebrate the fortieth anniversary of the Mustique Company, the firm set up by landowners to run the island. Outshining all other guests at the affair ("Dress: Silver and White") were Prince William and his girlfriend Kate Middleton. William had been away at sea with the Royal Navy for five weeks—the longest that he and Kate had ever been apart—and the couple was staying at Villa Hibiscus, a stone-walled hilltop estate overlooking Mustique's Macaroni Beach.

At Basil's Bar that night, Sir Mick sang "Satisfaction," "Jumpin'

Jack Flash," and "Brown Sugar" while the future king and queen rocked out on the dance floor. Jagger hit the dance floor with Kate, but even he was not about to make moves on the woman who had captured William's heart.

Kate's attractive younger sister, Pippa, may have been another matter. Over the next two years, all the Middletons—Kate's parents, Carole and Michael, as well as Pippa and their younger brother, James—visited the island frequently, ultimately making Mustique their vacation home. As all the Middletons and Kate's prince became fixtures on Mustique, islanders claimed to have spotted Mick and Pippa together, inevitably giving rise to rumors that he was at it again. Ironically Pippa, whose derriere would have its own international fan club after she almost upstaged Kate at the wedding, would later be touted to replace Mick's daughter Georgia May as the face of the British brand Hudson Jeans.

A number of the Middletons' Mustique neighbors would be among the chosen few invited to the royal wedding of William and Kate, but not Mick. "Elton and not me?" Mick joked when he realized that he would not be on the guest list. Mick was disappointed, although, said a friend, "It would have been much worse if they'd invited Paul McCartney." They didn't.

The British press took special delight in pointing out that, as a British subject over the age of sixty-five, Mick was now technically a pensioner entitled, among other things, to a free bus pass. Yet the reports (some more credible than others) of dalliances with much younger women persisted.

At the Isle of Wight Festival the previous summer, Mick performed a duet for the first time with Amy Winehouse. They bumped and ground and slithered their way through the Temptations' classic "Ain't Too Proud to Beg," fueling speculation over the next few months that Mick and the equally libidinous Winehouse had a brief offstage fling. "Amy worshiped Mick," a musician friend said. "She was completely over the moon just being in his presence." For his part, Mick was already predicting the tragic end that awaited Winehouse. "Amy is a brilliant artist," he said. "But I'm worried she might die if she goes down the road that she has taken." He spoke from experience. "I could have ended up like Amy years ago," Jagger said. "In the end, I realized I didn't want to die young."

There were other rumored relationships, including one with a beautiful aristocrat named Molly Miller Mundy. The daughter of an old friend, Molly was just twenty-three.

Nevertheless, L'Wren remained the most important woman in Mick's life—although even the preternaturally calm L'Wren was anxious when her predecessor crashed the Jaggers' 2010 Christmas cocktail party at Mick's new riverside mansion in Chelsea.

On the pretext of picking up their now thirteen-year-old son, Gabriel, Jerry Hall barged in the front door and made a beeline for L'Wren. A hush fell over the room: it was the first time that the two women had met, and, said one guest, "knowing Jerry we had no idea if she would kick L'Wren in the shins." Thankfully, Hall introduced herself warmly, telling L'Wren how much she admired her designs. Mick, who had been watching warily from the sidelines, then wished Jerry a Merry Christmas—and with that, the other thirty guests, very much relieved, burst into applause.

Jerry was in a conciliatory mood, stressing that she still regarded Mick as a "good man" and a "wonderful father." The problem, she never failed to add, was that Mick "just slept with every single girl that came around. It was quite tiring rushing home making sure he wasn't sleeping with someone."

L'Wren seemed up to the task, although Mick showed no signs of caving in on the issue of marriage. On the very day of their fateful Christmas party, Mick was quoted in the *New York Times* as not believing in marriage. "I'm not saying it's not a wonderful thing and people shouldn't do it," he explained, "but it's not for me . . . I just think it's perhaps not quite what it's cracked up to be. I know it's an elaborate fantasy."

Mick may have felt that he could manage only one spouse at a time, and from the beginning that spouse had been Keith. For all the ego-blistering quarrels, the slammed doors and hurled insults, the Glimmer Twins had always somehow managed to patch up their differences and return to the business of making music. Now, in the wake of the publication of Richards's blockbuster memoir, *Life*, their union was in serious trouble.

Prior to the book's release, Mick gave only a cursory glance to the advance unbound galley proofs provided by Keith. He took special notice of the fact that Keith had mentioned his use of a vocal coach and asked that the reference be taken out. Richards refused. "Funnily enough," Keith said later, "it was the weirdest thing he wanted taken out . . . Everyone knew it anyway!"

It was only when portions of Keith's book were leaked to the press in late October 2010 that Mick realized he had been savaged by his friend. Not only was Mick "unbearable" and "insufferable," but Keith relished calling his friend and creative partner for nearly a half century "Brenda" and "Her Majesty." Richards also likened Mick to an "annoying mynah bird" and claimed that he no longer really knew his friend. "Sometimes I think, 'I miss my friend.' I wonder, 'Where did he go?'"

Not surprisingly, even these nasty bits were drowned out by Keith's claim—originally made in 2005 but repeated in the book— that Mick was marginally endowed. According to Keith, when Marianne Faithfull slept with Mick, "she had no fun with his tiny todger. I know he's got an enormous pair of balls—but it doesn't quite fill the gap."

"R.I.P. the Rolling Stones, Killed by One Man's Jealousy," proclaimed the *Daily Mail*'s Ray Connolly. "Keith Richards' Memoirs, Published Tomorrow, Humiliate Jagger with Sexual Taunts." Jerry leapt to Mick's defense. "Keith has penis envy," she said. "There's not an ounce of truth in it. They're always shagging each other off. They're like adolescents. Mick is very well endowed, and I should know because I was with him for twenty-three years. Keith is just jealous."

Pamela Des Barres also stood up for Jagger. "I beg to differ with Keith on the sexual prowess of his lead singer," the supergroupie chimed in. "In all ways—including size—and on several occasions, I got plenty of satisfaction." Even Mick's old chum Pete Townshend had something to say on the subject. "I think it's sad that we will only remember Keith's book because of what he said about the size of Mick's genitals," Townshend said. "Which, by the way, to use an apt term, is bollocks. I've seen them, and it's not just the balls that are big."

In the book, however, Keith had only referred to whether or not Marianne had been satisfied with Mick's "todger." Was Richards's observation true? "Not quite," Marianne said, "but nearly."

Faithfull also said, however, that she wished Keith "hadn't said those awful things about Mick. I think that was a bit much." Marianne went on to claim that editors had been "trying to get someone to say that for years," and that she had refused, even though it would have meant "a lot more money" when it came to negotiating the advances for her own two autobiographies.

There was no telling how much money the Stones stood to make from a fiftieth-anniversary world tour already being talked about for the summer of 2012. It would, without a doubt, be the biggest in history. For the first time, salivating promoters whispered that, following U2's $720 million–grossing 2009–2011 tour, a Stones tour could conceivably break the $1 billion barrier.

All the Stones had privately expressed interest in going ahead with a 2012 fiftieth-anniversary tour. Now, because Keith had held Mick up to ridicule, all that was in jeopardy.

Keith began to backpedal—and furiously. "He was a bit peeved about this and that," Richards said, "but Mick and I are still great friends and still want to work together. I love the man dearly. I'm still his mate."

Understandably, Mick was not feeling quite so warm and fuzzy. To L'Wren and his tight circle of friends in London and New York, Jagger expressed genuine hurt and dismay over the book's many nasty remarks aimed squarely at him. He found Keith's oft-repeated explanation—"I thought Mick would have no problem with the truth"—less than adequate.

For weeks, Mick employed the one tactic that always succeeded in driving Keith up the wall: he ignored Richards, refusing to take his calls or say anything about the book. For two months, Mick maintained his silence before making any comment at all, and then in only the most oblique way. "Personally," Jagger sniffed, "I think it's really quite tedious raking over the past. Mostly, people only do it for the money." In 1980, Mick almost did just that, accepting what was then a record $5 million from British publisher Lord Weidenfeld to write his memoirs. Eight years later Jagger returned the money, vowing never to write his own life story. "You don't want to end up like some old footballer in a pub," he now said in reference to Keith's book, "talking about how he made the Cup final in 1964."

That was not about to happen to Mick, who was happy to let Keith stew about whether he had scuttled any chance for a fiftieth anniversary world tour. In the meantime, the name Jagger seemed to be on everyone's lips.

With a full mane of dark hair and the same 27-inch waist, Jagger still managed to evoke a youthful vitality and stamina that rockers one-third his age found daunting. And if there was any doubt that even the vast teenage audience still revered Mick as a rock god, it vanished with the release of Ke$ha's debut single, "TiK ToK." Featuring the lyric "We kick 'em to the curb unless they look like Mick Jagger," the dance-pop record was nothing short of a global phenomenon; sales for 2010 alone topped 12.8 million copies, making it that year's top-selling record worldwide.

Similarly, British singer Cher Lloyd would release a number one party single entitled "Swagger Jagger," further popularizing a new term that *Urban Dictionary* defined as "the confident, cocky attitude Mick Jagger emits when he struts his stuff."

Mick gave a live television audience a master class in Jagger swagger when he showed up at the 2011 Grammy Awards on February 13 to pay tribute to the late blues great Solomon Burke. It was the first time a member of the Rolling Stones had ever performed at the Grammys.

Standing with his back to the audience, Jagger spun around and flung off the cape he was wearing while the crowd at LA's Staples Center cheered wildly. Mick's rendition of Burke's "Everybody Needs Somebody to Love" was nothing less than electrifying, and when it was over the star-packed throng leapt to its feet.

For Maroon 5 lead singer Adam Levine and Christina Aguilera, paying homage to Mick also turned out to be a shrewd career move. Their chart-topping "Moves Like Jagger" was Maroon 5's first Top Ten single in four years, and Aguilera's first number one single since "Lady Marmalade" a decade earlier. "Moves Like Jagger" dominated the airwaves for months and would also be nominated for a Grammy.

There would be other sly references to Mick in modern music, made all the easier by the ability to rhyme Jagger with *swagger*: in "Heart and Soul" by the Jonas Brothers ("That won't matter if you can swagger like old Mick Jagger"), in the Black Eyed Peas' "The Time" ("All these girls, they like my swagger, they callin' me Mick

Jagger"), and by Kanye West on T.I.'s "Swagger Like Us," boasting "My swagger is Mick Jagger."

Conscious of the need to remain relevant, Jagger was careful not to offend younger fans by publicly criticizing their favorites. For years, he had privately decried most hard-core rap and hip-hop as "not really music." But now that Kanye West was lauding Mick as "crazy fresh," Jagger eagerly embraced him as a friend, along with P. Diddy and Jay-Z.

Another unexpected fan was preteen heartthrob Justin Bieber, who Tweeted to his fifteen million followers online: "Mick Jagger is a trending topic. Why? Mick Jagger is The Man and was trending long before Twitter came along. True Legend."

Jagger let the praise wash over him. "I don't think he has the heart to say something mean to a sweet kid like Justin," said a record company executive who knew them both, "but I'm sure Mick finds his stuff absolutely nauseating. Big surprise!"

Jagger was genuinely enthusiastic in his praise for Beyoncé, claiming that he was "impressed, really impressed. She's a very up-to-date, very modern version of Tina Turner." Mick also had what, for him, were words of high praise for Lady Gaga: "a good musician, good songwriter, good piano player."

For her part, Lady Gaga admitted that Jagger had been one of her role models. She decided that since she had experienced a normal, happy upbringing, she would have to take a walk on the wild side if she was going to make it as a performer. It was part of her "quest for an artistic journey," she said, to "fuck myself up like Warhol and Bowie and Mick, and just go for it."

Jagger never stopped going for it. After decades of being spied on by Fleet Street—most notably by reporters for *News of the World*—Mick hatched plans to produce and star in *Tabloid*, an "adult thriller" about "a global media mogul with dubious morality."

Musically, he struck out in an entirely new direction, teaming up with his old friend Dave Stewart, British soul singer Joss Stone, Bob Marley's youngest son Damian Marley, and Oscar-winning *Slumdog Millionaire* composer A. R. Rahman to form a supergroup Mick devoutly hoped would live up to its name: SuperHeavy.

So that the new group could record in total secrecy, Microsoft cofounder Paul Allen lent Jagger his 414-foot yacht *Octopus,* which boasted two helicopters, two submarines, and a Jet Ski dock. With Mick registered on board under the alias "Mr. Gibson 3.3," Super-Heavy recorded its first album as the yacht sailed to Jamaica, California, Turkey, Italy, Greece, India, and Florida.

Stone, like the others, was sworn to a vow of silence. "I didn't tell Prince William or Kate about it either," she said of her two good friends. "They are lovely people and they are interested in what I do, but I didn't mention it."

SuperHeavy's eponymous first album ran the gamut from soulful ballads to reggae to Indian songs in Urdu. Critics raved and Mick, always eager to achieve something outside the orbit of the Stones, was delighted. "This band, this project," he mused, "it's all good."

Unavoidably, the music world was paying far more attention to that other band Mick belonged to, and the drama that swirled around it. "The Stones are iconic figures in Western society," said Sting, echoing the sentiments of millions. "I hope they'll stop bickering. I'd like to see them doing what they do."

With the Stones' fiftieth anniversary weighing heavily on his mind, Keith flew to London on December 1, 2011 to jam in the recording studio with Ronnie Wood and Charlie Watts—long a part of the Stones' creative process. They were soon joined by former Stone Mick Taylor, and there was talk that Bill Wyman would also come aboard.

The real purpose of all this, of course, was to persuade Mick to let bygones be bygones. "Mick is welcome," Keith said. "I'm sure he'll turn up." On the third day, Mick did—"which," admitted Keith, "was a real joy. Because I set it up really as a magnet, you know . . ."

"There's a healing process waiting to take place," added Wood, who had witnessed similar rifts in the past—though perhaps none, he would admit, as serious as this. "I think it's happening now as we speak, but it has to be resolved. Something has to be resolved there . . . Charlie and I will help make that happen. Wish me luck!"

To be sure, Mick had more than his share of distractions in early 2012, including his first-ever concert at the White House on February 21. Following such blues greats as B. B. King and Buddy Guy—and with L'Wren looking on—Jagger had the president and First Lady Michelle Obama up out of their chairs and swaying as he belted out "I Can't Turn You Loose" and "Miss You." It was, Mick said, "a surreal gig experience"—particularly when he handed the microphone over to the president, who then sang a few bars of "Sweet Home Chicago."

Weeks later, at a star-packed Carnegie Hall tribute concert honoring the Rolling Stones, speculation raged on and off stage about the relationship between Mick and Keith, and what the future held. But fans needn't have worried. As they had always done, the Glimmer Twins fought bitterly, went to their separate corners, and came back together for the sake of the band.

The Stones went ahead with plans to record a new album and announced the fall 2012 release of yet another behind-the-scenes Stones documentary—this one directed by Brett Morgen, who had received an Academy Award nomination for his film on the life of flamboyant Hollywood producer Robert Evans, *The Kid Stays in the Picture*. The new documentary would, Morgen promised, "defy convention and create a sonic tapestry to transport viewers into the world of the Rolling Stones."

For now, fans would have to settle for Morgen's cinematic "sonic tapestry." After much deliberation, plans were scrapped for a full-blown 2012 tour. "You can't just walk up there and do it," Mick said after the White House concert. "You've got to practice. I feel very confident. I don't want to sound cocky, but it's just part of what you do. If you prepare, then you can be cocky."

In the end, Jagger's petulance over Richards's wounding remarks had nothing to do with the Stones' ultimate decision to postpone their fiftieth anniversary tour until 2013. On the contrary, perpetually fit Mick was more than ready to hit the road. It was reportedly out of concern for Keith's health—not only the effects of his 2006 brain injury but also the severe arthritis that appeared to have settled in Richards's hands—that the decision was made not to rush into the sort of punishing multicontinent tour they had undertaken before.

Although there was no question that the Rolling Stones first performed on stage at London's Marquee Club on July 12, 1962, Richards now claimed that he personally regarded 1963 as the band's real birth year because it was then that Charlie Watts came aboard. According to Keith, 1962 was "really the year of the Stones' conception. Next year will really mark the fiftieth birthday."

As with everything he undertook, Mick pressed forward, refusing to look back. "I live in the now," he said. "I don't ever think, 'This is amazing, I can't believe I'm still doing this.' I *am* doing it. I'm just doing it. And I don't think, 'It's all gone so fast,' because for me it's still happening."

It's still happening, indeed.

ACKNOWLEDGMENTS

♦ ♦ ' ♦

"*I* think," Mick said when asked about my 1993 biography, *Jagger Unauthorized,* "that my reputation has remained unsullied." No doubt he will say the same about *Mick,* which does even more to confirm the reputation of a life spent pushing the proverbial envelope—and, at times, gleefully ripping it to shreds.

Along the way, I was accorded a kind of fly-on-the-wall status—first covering the notorious Altamont Rock Festival in 1969 as a young reporter for *Time,* then during the surreal Studio 54 days, when I was a senior editor of *People,* right up through Mick's 2003 investiture as a knight of the realm—an event that, given my five *New York Times* best-selling books on the royal family, I felt particularly well qualified to write about.

A tremendous amount of research is essential for any comprehensive biography, and this was particularly true for *Mick.* In essence, work began on the book when I stood on a brown Northern California hillside watching Jumpin' Jack Flash hold nearly a half million people spellbound—a day chronicled in the landmark documentary *Gimme Shelter* and by Don McLean in his song "American Pie."

Years were spent interviewing friends, family members, fellow musicians, producers, industry figures and colleagues, former teachers, classmates, neighbors, mentors, protégés, employees, photographers and journalists who covered Mick over the years, and, of course, the wives—and lovers. A few of these sources insisted that they not be identified, and I have respected their wishes.

A number of people particularly close to Jagger—Atlantic Records founder Ahmet Ertegun, for example—were originally asked by Mick not to speak with me. He eventually did anyway, only not for attribution. Hundreds of others talked candidly and on the record, without ever bothering to seek Jagger's approval.

I am once again indebted to my Gallery editor, the talented and consummately professional Mitchell Ivers. I'm grateful, as well, to the dedicated Simon & Schuster team, especially Louise Burke, Carolyn Reidy, Jennifer Bergstrom, Jennifer Robinson, Eric Rayman, Felice Javit, Jean Anne Rose, Lisa Keim, Jessica Chin, Philip Bashe, and Natasha Simons.

For the twenty-eighth time in as many years, I thank Ellen Levine for her wise counsel and friendship. I also wish to thank all the folks at the Trident Media Group, especially Ellen's colleagues Claire Roberts, Monika Woods, and Alanna Ramirez.

For the encouragement, support, and loving patience that she has lavished on me for more than forty years, I thank my wife, Valerie. Our daughters, Kate and Kelly, smart and accomplished women in their own right, provided a more youthful perspective on the subject of this book, proving beyond doubt that Mick Jagger's influence spans the generations.

Additional thanks to Chrissie Shrimpton Messenger, Andrew Oldham, Bianca Jagger, Gered Mankowitz, Bebe Buell, Angela Bowie, Ahmet Ertegun, Christopher Gibbs, Marianne Faithfull, Keith Altham, John Dunbar, Dick Taylor, Dick Cavett, May Pang, Barry Miles ("Miles"), Phil May, Peter Jones, Dick Clark, Earl McGrath, Brian Knight, Sam Cutler, Greg Phillinganes, Geoff Bradford, Carlo Little, Leee Black Childers, Rodney Bingenheimer, Nicolas Roeg, Jerry Schatzberg, Tom McGuinness, Victor Bockris, Steve Turner, Harold Pendleton, John Michel, Sandy Lieberson, Arthur Collins, Trevor Churchill, Chris O'Donnell, Stephanie Bluestone, Giorgio Gomelsky, David McGough, Christopher Makos, Danny Fields, Pat Hackett, Patricia Lawford Stewart, Allie Willis, Daniel Stewart, Kevin Kahn, Alan Hamilton, Valerie Watson Dunn, Tony Brenna, Norah Darwen, Wayne Darwen, Fred Hauptfuhrer, Richard Kay, Fred Hughes, Stephanie Mansfield, Rita Jenrette, Victoria Balfour, Jouet Moreau, Elena Brenna, Lance Loud, Ruby Mazur, Michael Gross, Gael Love, Brian Morris, Chuckie Starr, Kenny Valente, Tom Freeman, Hazel Southam, Joyce Wansley, Peter Gillman, Leni Gillman, Peter Frame, Wendy Leigh, Steven Karten, William Wilkinson, Dick Allen, Walter Bennett, Arthur Page, David Herrington, John Wilkinson, Tony Smith, Vinnie Zuffante, Russell Turiak, Mary Boone, Michael Horowitz, Robert Littman, Erika Bell, the late Truman Capote, Halston, Marvin Mitchelson, Steve Rubell, Roy Cohn, Cranston Jones, Malcolm Forbes, Jesse Birnbaum, Bill Graham, Donna Miller, Bobby Zarem, Susan Crimp, Peter Archer, Barbara Levine, Baird Jones, April Todd, Rosemary McClure, Wendi Rothman, Peter Newcomb, Mary Vespa, Mary Beth Whelan, Brooke Mason, Kendra Kabasele, Chris DiNenna, Shantel Burgess, Anne Di Pasquale, Lindzee Smith, the staffs of Dartford Grammar School in Dartford, Kent, and the London School of Economics, the Lincoln Center Library for the Performing Arts, the National Academy of Recording Arts and Sciences, the Rock and Roll Hall of Fame, the New York Public Library, the Silas Bronson Library, the Litchfield Library, the Gunn Memorial Library; the Lansdowne Club, Garrick Club, Reform Club, and Lotos Club; Sotheby's, *The Times* of London, *The Daily Mail, The New York Times,* Reuters, Bloomberg, Associated Press, Rex USA, BEImages, Retna, Getty Images, Alpha Photos, and Globe Photos.

SOURCES AND CHAPTER NOTES

◆　◆　◆

*T*he following chapter notes are designed to give a general view of the sources drawn upon in preparing *Mick,* but they are by no means all-inclusive. The author has respected the wishes of many interview subjects to remain anonymous and therefore has agreed not to list them here or elsewhere in the text. Obviously, there were thousands of news reports and articles on Mick Jagger and the Rolling Stones over the course of the last half century that serve as source materials for this book. These reports have appeared in such wide-ranging publications as the *Times* of London, *The New York Times, Time, Newsweek, Life, Vanity Fair, People, Rolling Stone, The New Yorker, The Los Angeles Times, Paris Match, The Guardian, The Daily Mail, Le Monde, Esquire, Entertainment Weekly, Spin, USA Today, Forbes, The Economist,* and *The Wall Street Journal,* and have been carried over Reuters, Bloomberg, Gannett, United Press International, and Associated Press wires as well as every major news Web site from Yahoo! News and Google News to the Huffington Post.

CHAPTERS 1–3

For these chapters, the author drew on conversations with, among others, Chrissie Shrimpton, Andrew Oldham, Marianne Faithfull,

John Dunbar, Dick Taylor, Keith Altham, Phil May, Carlo Little, Christopher Gibbs, Brian Morris, William Wilkinson, Dick Allen, Walter Bennett, Arthur Page, John Wilkinson, David Herrington, Tony Smith, Valerie Watson Dunn, Giorgio Gomelsky, Chris O'Donnell, Victor Bockris, Paul Jones, Geoff Bradford, Brian Knight, Peter Jones, Harold Pendleton, Tom McGuinness, Michael Horovitz, John Mayall, and Steve Turner. Published sources included Andrew Pierce, "Jagger's Hard Day's Knight," *Times* of London, November 16, 2001; Matthew Fearn, "That's *Sir* Street Fighting Man to You," Associated Press, December 12, 2005; Leah McLaren, "Knight in Black Armor?" Toronto *Globe & Mail,* June 12, 2002; Aly Sujo, "Nice Shoes, Sir Mick," *New York Post,* December 13, 2005; "Official Announcement of Knighthood," London *Gazette,* August 24, 2004; "Jagger Knighted by the Queen," *Guardian,* June 15, 2002; "Sir Mick Enters the World of the Establishment," *Times* of London, December 13, 2003; "Stones Frontman Becomes Sir Mick," BBC, December 12, 2003; Philip Norman, "Who'd Make This Man a Knight?" *Daily Mail,* December 7, 2005; Sally Brompton, "I'm an Ordinary Mum, Says Mrs. Jagger," *London Sunday Express,* May 16, 1971; Danny Danziger, *Eton Voices* (London: Viking Penguin, 1978); Henrietta Knight, "Mick Jagger's Mum Shares Their Secrets," *TV Times,* July 7, 1990; "Everyone Has to Be Tied Down to Something . . ." *Radio Times,* April 5, 1973; John Salmon, "Mick Jagger as a Schoolboy Rebel?" *Today,* May 8, 1992; John Carpenter, "Mick Jagger Raps," *Eye,* November 1968; "Introducing the Rolling Stones," *Rave,* July 1964; Robert Greenfield, "The Rolling Stone Interview: Keith Richards," *Rolling Stone,* August 19, 1971; G. R., "Can Rolling Stones Crush the Beatles?" *Chronicle,* November 29, 1963; Anthony Carthew, "Shaggy Englishman Story," *New York Times,* September 6, 1964; Denna Allen and Matthew Norman, "Darling Cleo," *Mail on Sunday,* August 16, 1992; Michael

Iachetta, "They Wouldn't Dare!" *Sunday News,* January 5, 1969; Unity Hall, "What Makes Mick Tick," *Sun,* March 11, 1970; David Dalton, *The Rolling Stones: The First 20 Years* (London: Thames and Hudson, 1981); Bill Wyman with Ray Coleman, *Stone Alone* (New York: Viking Penguin, 1991); Ian Dickson, "Marianne Faithfull," *Vox* (1974); Al Aronowitz, "Brian Jones," *New York Post,* July 10, 1969; A. E. Hotchner, *Blown Away* (New York: Simon & Schuster, 1990); Tina Turner and Kurt Loder, *I, Tina* (New York: William Morrow, 1986); Anthony Haden-Guest, "She Devil," *Sunday Correspondent,* February 11, 1990; Mandy Aftel, *Death of a Rolling Stone* (London: Sidgwick & Jackson, 1982); Keith Richards, *Life* (New York: Little, Brown, 2010); Chrissy Iley, "I Should Have Chosen Keith Instead of Mick: Life for Marianne Faithfull Hasn't Exactly Gone as Planned," London *Sunday Telegraph,* March 6, 2011. The Redlands scandal ranks as one of the most widely covered drug cases in history, written about in every major news publication, including the *Times* of London, *The Guardian, The New York Times, Time, Newsweek, Der Spiegel, Paris Match,* and even *Pravda,* in what was then the Soviet Union. The author also consulted the trial transcripts. The diaries of Cecil Beaton were a major source for accounts of Jagger's escapades in Morocco.

CHAPTERS 4–6

Information for these chapters was based in part on conversations with Nicolas Roeg, Bebe Buell, Grace Slick, Gram Parsons, Dick Carter, Bill Graham, Sam Cutler, Sandy Lieberson, Barry Miles, Stephanie Bluestone, Gered Mankowitz, John Dunbar, Lindzee Smith, Allie Willis, Greg Phillinganes, Earl McGrath, Rodney Bingenheimer, Robert Littman, Keith Altham, Jerry Schatzberg, Pete Frame, Trevor Churchill, Ruby Mazur, Lance Loud, Christopher

Makos, John Marion, Arthur Collins, Pat Hackett, Gael Love, Truman Capote, Mary Boone, Halston, Kenny Valente, Melvin Belli, Wendy Leigh, Joanne Bobrowicz, Fred Hughes, and Rosemary McClure. Among the published sources consulted were Nik Cohn, "A Briton Blasts the Beatles," *New York Times,* December 15, 1968; Ronald Maxwell, "Marianne Faithfull," *Sunday Mirror,* December 5, 1971; Martin Elliott, *Rolling Stones: The Complete Recording Sessions* (London: Blandford, 1990); Barry Norman, "Mick Jagger Talking as Never Before," *Daily Mail,* August 19, 1970; "No, the Rolling Stones Are Not Fascists," *New York Times,* December 28, 1969; James Fox, "Madame Sex," *Vanity Fair,* May 1987; "Mick Jagger and the Future of Rock," *Newsweek,* January 4, 1971; "Prince Rupert Loewenstein Is the Man," *Independent on Sunday,* August 23, 1992; Marsha Hunt, *Real Life* (London: Chatto & Windus, 1986); "Eclectic, Reminiscent, Amused, Fickle, Perverse," *The New Yorker,* May 29, 1978; Robert Greenfield, "Prodigal Sons Tour Mother Country," *Rolling Stone,* April 15, 1971; Martha Smilgis, "Bianca Is Tired of Playing Zelda to Jagger's Scott," *People,* May 2, 1977; Fredric Dannen, *Hit Men* (New York: Random House, 1990); Tony Scadutto, "Everybody's Lucifer," *New York Post,* August 1, 1974; Pamela Des Barres, *I'm with the Band* (New York: William Morrow, 1987); Carey Schofield, *Jagger* (New York: Beaufort Books, 1985); Don Heckman, "Feeling . . ." *New York Times Magazine,* July 16, 1972; Thomas Thompson, "The Stones Blast Through the Land," *Life,* July 14, 1972; Robert Greenfield, "Stones Tour: Rock & Roll on the Road Again," *Rolling Stone,* July 6, 1972; Jack Lewis, "Mick Jagger Shocks Lady X on Jumbo Jet," *Daily Mirror,* December 1, 1971; Harriet Van Horne, "The Rolling Stones Party," *New York Post,* July 29, 1972; Kenneth Eastaugh, "Ask a Silly Question," *Sun,* January 23, 1971; Grace Lichtenstein, "Jagger and Stones Whip 20,000 into Frenzy at Garden," *New York Times,* July 25, 1972;

Judith Martin, "Jagger Stones 'Em in D.C.," *Washington Post,* May 3, 1973; Don Short, "When I'm 33—That's When I'll Quit!" *Daily Mirror,* August 5, 1972; Andrew Loog Oldham, *Stoned* (New York: Vintage, 2004); David Wigg, "Baby, That's the Way It's Going to Be," *Daily Express,* August 24, 1973; Anthea Disney, "There's a Certain Singer I'd Like to Tear into Pieces," *Daily Mail,* November 1973; Rosemary Kent, "Bianca Jagger's Interview," *Viva,* November 1973; Stanley Booth, *True Adventures of the Rolling Stones* (Chicago: Chicago Review Press, 2000); Sheila Weller, *Girls Like Us: Carole King, Joni Mitchell, Carly Simon, and the Journey of a Generation* (New York: Atria/Simon & Schuster, 2008); John Rockwell, "The Pragmatic Jagger: Planning Stones Onslaught," *New York Times,* May 15, 1975; Mary Campbell, "Jagger Talks of Latest Tour," Associated Press, May 29, 1975; Marian McEvoy, "Mick Rolls On," *Women's Wear Daily,* June 24, 1975; Steve Lawrence, "Moving Mick Jagger," *New York Post,* June 7, 1975; Roderick Gilchrist, "Mick and Marsha End Baby Row," *Daily Mail,* February 12, 1975; "Mick Jagger Had Drug Overdose," *Evening Standard,* February 27, 1976; Ian Ball, "Canada Agog over Stones and Mrs. Trudeau," *Daily Telegraph,* March 10, 1977; James Johnson, "'Mrs. Trudeau? I Wouldn't Go Near Her with a Barge Pole,'" *Evening Standard,* September 14, 1977; Robin Denselow, "People Like Bing Crosby . . ." *Guardian,* October 10, 1977; David Felton, "Absolute, Ultimate Fantasy," *Washington Post,* June 16, 1978; Gordon Burn, "Mick Jagger Holds Court in New York," *Sunday Times,* June 25, 1978; Pauline McLeod, "Money, Women, and Me!" *Daily Mirror,* August 29, 1978; Jonathan Cott, "Mick Jagger: The King Bee Talks About Rock's Longest Running Soap Opera," *Rolling Stone,* June 29, 1978; "Jaggers Divorced," *New York Times,* November 3, 1979; Marsha Hunt, "Mick Made Me Beg for Money," *London Star,* October 14, 1986; Liz Derringer, "Mick Jagger: The Man Behind the Mascara," *High Times,* June 1980; Maureen Cleave, "Confessions of a Dilettante Englishman," *Observer,* August 30, 1981; Carl Arrington, "Mr. Rolling Stone Finds Sweet Satisfaction with Rock's Richest Tour Ever," *People,* December 28, 1981; "Mick Jagger: Cocktails with Jerry Hall, Charlie Watts, Bob Colacello & Andy Warhol," *Interview,* August 1981; Rick Sky, "Mick Jagger: 'What I Want from a Woman,'" *London Daily Star,* June 16, 1982; "The Rolling Stones: Once Adolescent, They've Grown Up," *New York Times,* August 26, 1981; "Mick Jagger and Model Jerry Hall Call It Quits," *People,* November 22, 1982; Lauren McKay, "There's a Gun in My Bag and I Know How to Use It," Glasgow *Sunday Mail,* August 11, 2002; Julian Brouwer, "My Romps," *Daily Record,* February 7, 2002; Mick Jagger, "When He Was the Young Man About Town . . ." *Rolling Stone,* January 17, 2002. The author reviewed more than 130 legal documents, including court transcripts and affidavits regarding the divorce case of Bianca and Michael Philip Jagger filed in Los Angeles Superior Court (Case No. D 985 336).

CHAPTERS 7–10

Dick Cavett, Angela Bowie, May Pang, Truman Capote, Liz Derringer, Ahmet Ertegun, Marvin Mitchelson, Malcolm Forbes, Steve Rubell, George Plimpton, Ruby Mazur, Allen Klein, Patricia Neal, Leee Black Childers, Kevin Kahn, Richard Kay, Rita Jenrette, Barbara Levine, Susan Crimp, Peter Archer, Jouet Moreau, Guy Pelly, Patricia Lawford, Fred Hauptfuhrer, Stephanie Mansfield, April Todd, Roy Cohn, Andrew Hamilton, Keith Altham, Alan Hamilton, Victor Bockris, Bobby Zarem, David McGough, Russell Turiak, Pat Hackett, Daniel Stewart, Lee Wohlfert, Vinnie Zuffante, Victoria Balfour, and Bebe Buell. Among articles and other published material consulted: Pete Townshend, "Jagger: A Butterfly Reaches 40," *Times* of

London, July 25, 1983; Vincent Coppola with Nancy Cooper, "Rock Grows Up," *Newsweek,* December 19, 1983; "Why I Want Babies with Jerry—by Jagger," *Sun,* July 3, 1983; Lisa Robinson, "Mick Jagger," *Interview,* February 1985; Bill Flanagan, "Mick Musically," *Musician,* April 1985; Jay McInerney, "Jagger-Watching," *Esquire,* May 1985; Jay Cocks, "Roll Them Bones," *Time,* September 4, 1989; Christopher Connelly, "Stepping Out," *Rolling Stone,* February 14, 1985; David Gates, "The Stones Start It Up," *Newsweek,* September 11, 1989; Peter Newcomb, "Satisfaction Guaranteed," *Forbes,* October 2, 1989; Anthony DeCurtis, "The Rolling Stones: Artists of the Year," *Rolling Stone,* March 8, 1990; Stephanie Mansfield, "The Jagger Mystique," *Vogue,* May 1991; Stephen Schiff, "Mick's Moves," *Vanity Fair,* February 1992; Edna Gundersen, "Mick Jagger's Hard Rock Life," *USA Today,* February 9, 1993; Danae Brook, "Marriage, Jagger, Babies and Me," *Daily Mail,* January 21, 1996; Richie Taylor, "Mick's Out of My Life, Says Model Lover Jana," *Mirror,* October 19, 1996; Rachael Bletchley and Nigel Bowden, "Exposed: Jagger's Daughter Jade in Sex Film Scandal," *The People,* July 12, 1998; Tracy Connor, "Paint It Green: Furious Jerry Hall Wants $50 Million Divorce from Mick," *New York Post,* January 16, 1999; Brian Degen Leitch, "Jumpin' Jade Flash," *New York Times,* January 24, 1999; Jane Mayer, "Bianca Jagger Lobbies Her Black Book," June 7, 1999; Peter Allen and Jane Kerr, "Jagger the Lover," *Mirror,* October 17, 1996; Sarah Hall, "The End of the Affair: After 22 Years Together and a Marriage That Never Was, Jagger and Hall Split Up," *Guardian,* July 10, 1999; Anne Shooter, "Has Jagger Met His Match in Daughter Elizabeth?" *Daily Mail,* June 24, 1999; Maria Croce, "I Pity Mick," *Daily Record,* June 26, 2000; Thomas Whitaker, "Jagger Mourns Mum He Adored," *Sun,* May 19, 2000; Alan Rimmer, "Mick Walked Naked from the Shower . . ." *Sunday Mirror,* May 19, 2002; Jane Moore, "Hall Together: Interview," *Sunday Times,* December

24, 2000; Doug Sanders, "Mogul Mick," Toronto *Globe & Mail,* January 24, 2001; Geoffrey Levy, "Mick Jagger Really Has Fallen for Miss Dahl," *Daily Mail,* June 30, 2001; James Dohert, "Jagger's Girls Disgusted by His Exploits," Edinburgh *Scotsman,* March 4, 2002; David Wilkes, "The Night Jagger's Limo Was Rocking," *Daily Mail,* May 6, 2002; Bernard Weinraub, "Half a Lifetime on the Road," *New York Times,* September 26, 2002; Nick Parker, "Hey You, Get Off My Child," *Sun,* November 15, 2002; Kira Cochrane, "Old Father Jagger's Piece of Cheek," *Sunday Times* of London, January 26, 2003; Leigh-Ann Jackson, "Jerry Hall Bares Some," *Austin American-Statesman,* September 14, 2003; Anna Hunt, "Mick Was a Womanizer," *Mail on Sunday,* May 11, 2003; Adam Sherwin, "World Tour Triumph Sees Stones Earnings Roll Past One Million Pounds," *Times* of London, November 28, 2003; Robin Eggar, "Most Men Have Had an Alfie Moment," *Daily Telegraph,* October 6, 2004; Anthony Barnes, "Jerry Hall's Single . . ." *Independent on Sunday,* March 20, 2005; Casper Llewellyn Smith, "The Observer Profiles Mick Jagger," *Observer,* August 28, 2005; Nicholas Wapshott, "It's *Not* Only Rock and Roll," *Sunday Telegraph,* September 11, 2005; Michael Hainey, "What a Drag It Is Getting Old—Unless You're Mick Jagger," *GQ,* October 2005; Eric Gillin, "Mick Jagger at 62," Maximonline.com, October 2005; Natalie Clarke, "The Loin Tamer," *Daily Mail,* January 2, 2006; Reuters, "Joe Jagger, Fitness Expert 1913–2006," November 14, 2006; Tom Pettifor, "Jagger's Women Turn Out for Dad's Funeral," *Daily Record,* November 29, 2006; Jane Wheatley, "Sir Mick's Gazelle, L'Wren Scott," *Times,* May 17, 2007; *The Rolling Stone Interviews* (New York: Little, Brown, 2007); Charles Bremner, "Bonjour, Madame le President?" *Times,* December 18, 2007; John Dingwall, "I Used to Be One of Jagger's 4,000 Other Women," *Daily Record,* June 4, 2007; Oliver Harvey, "Ooh Carla La," *Sun,* December 19, 2007; Simon Mills,

"The Day Carla Bruni Opened the Door to Me Topless," *Mail Online,* January 24, 2008; James Kaplan, "Mick Jagger Is Still Ready to Party," *Parade,* March 30, 2008; David Fricke, "Blues Brothers," *Rolling Stone,* April 17, 2008; Jancee Dunn, "Icon: Mick Jagger," *Maxim,* April 2008; Maureen Orth, "Carla Bruni: The New Jackie O?" *Vanity Fair,* September 2008; Todd Venezia, "Wild Mackenzie: Papa's Old Pal Mick Bedded Me," *New York Post,* September 25, 2009; John Robinson, "The House of the Unholy," *Guardian,* May 15, 2010; William Norwich, "A Day in the Life of L'Wren Scott," *Vogue Daily,* June 9, 2011; Mick Jagger Interview, *Larry King Live,* CNN, June 21, 2010; Jerry Hall, *My Life in Pictures* (London: Quadrille, 2010); Robert Crampton, "I Never Really Felt Confident Because of Mick's Infidelity," *Times,* October 2, 2010; Christine Lennon, "Georgia Girl," *Harpers Bazaar,* November 2010; Mackenzie Phillips, *High on Arrival* (New York: Gallery Books, 2009); Nandini D'Souza, "L'Wren Takes Flight," *W,* January 2010; Bridget Foley, "L'Wren Scott: Fearlessly Chic," *WWD,* April 12, 2010; Zoe Heller, "Mick Without Moss," *New York Times,* December 5, 2010; Phoebe Eaton, "L'Wren Scott Interview," *Harpers Bazaar,* March 23, 2011; "Mick Jagger Forms New Group SuperHeavy," *Financial Times,* May 23, 2011; Gavin Edwards, "Lizzy Jagger: Between the Sheets with Mick's Daughter," *Playboy,* June 2011; Louise Gannon, "SuperHeavy—It Was All Very Secret . . ." *Mail Online,* September 10, 2011; Nate Chinen, "SuperHeavy: A New Album from Mick Jagger and Friends," *New York Times,* September 19, 2011; Christine Ockrent, "Carla Bruni: My Love for Sarkozy the Gardener," *BBC News Magazine,* September 25, 2011.

BIBLIOGRAPHY

◆　◆　◆

Aftel, Mandy. *Death of a Rolling Stone*. London: Sidgwick & Jackson, 1982.

Aldridge, John. *Satisfaction*. London: Proteus Publishing, 1984.

Altham, Keith. *The PR Strikes Back*. London: John Blake, 2001.

Andersen, Christopher. *Jagger Unauthorized*. New York: Delacorte Press, 1993.

———. *Jackie After Jack: Portrait of the Lady*. New York: William Morrow, 1998.

———. *William and Kate: A Royal Love Story*. New York: Gallery Books, 2010.

Balfour, Victoria. *Rock Wives*. New York: William Morrow, 1986.

Bockris, Victor. *Keith Richards*. New York: Poseidon Press, 1992.

———. *The Life and Death of Andy Warhol*. New York: Bantam, 1989.

Booth, Stanley. *The True Adventures of the Rolling Stones*. London: Sphere Books Ltd., 1985.

Bowie, Angela, with Patrick Carr. *Backstage Passes*. New York: G. P. Putnam's Sons, 1993.

Clapton, Eric. *Clapton: The Autobiography*. New York: Broadway Books, 2007.

Clarke, Gerald. *Capote: A Biography*. New York: Carroll and Graf, 1988.

BIBLIOGRAPHY

Cohn, Nik. *Rock: From the Beginning*. New York: Stein and Day, 1969.

Coleman, Ray. *Clapton!* New York: Warner, 1985.

Cooper, Michael. *Blinds and Shutters*. London: Genesis, 1990.

Cutler, Sam. *You Can't Always Get What You Want*. New York: Random House, 2010.

Dalton, David. *The Rolling Stones*. London: Rogner & Bernhard, 1981.

Dannen, Fredric. *Hit Men*. New York: Random House, 1990.

Danzier, Danny. *Eton Voices*. New York: Viking, 1988.

Des Barres, Pamela. *I'm with the Band*. New York: William Morrow, 1987.

Edwards, Henry, and Tony Zanetta. *Stardust: The David Bowie Story*. New York: McGraw-Hill, 1986.

Elliott, Martin. *The Rolling Stones: The Complete Recording Sessions*. London: Blandford, 1990.

Faithfull, Marianne, with David Dalton. *Faithfull: An Autobiography*. New York: Little, Brown, 1994.

Flippo, Chet. *On the Road with the Rolling Stones*. New York: Doubleday, 1985.

Frame, Pete. *Rock Family Trees*. London: Omnibus Press, 1980.

Goodman, Pete. *Our Own Story by the Rolling Stones*. New York: Bantam, 1965.

Graham, Bill, and Robert Greenfield. *Bill Graham Presents*. New York: Doubleday, 1992.

Greenfield, Robert. *S.T.P.: A Journey Through America with the Rolling Stones*. New York: Dutton, 1974.

Hackett, Pat, ed. *The Andy Warhol Diaries*. New York: Warner, 1989.

Hall, Jerry. *Jerry Hall: My Life in Pictures*. London: Quadrille Publishing, 2010.

Hall, Jerry, and Christopher Hemphill. *Jerry Hall's Tall Tales*. New York: Pocket Books, 1985.

Hebel, Francois. *Mick Jagger: The Photo Book*. Rome: Contrasto, 2011.

Hoffman, Dezo. *The Rolling Stones*. New York: Vermillion, 1984.

Holt, Georgia, and Phyllis Quinn with Sue Russell. *Star Mothers*. New York: Simon & Schuster, 1988.

Hotchner, A. E. *Blown Away: The Rolling Stones and the Death of the Sixties*. New York: Simon & Schuster, 1990.

Hunt, Marsha. *Real Life*. London: Chatto & Windus, 1986.

Mankowitz, Gered. *Satisfaction*. New York: St. Martin's Press, 1984.

Miles, Barry. *Mick Jagger in His Own Words*. London: Omnibus, 1982.

Morton, Andrew. *Angelina: An Unauthorized Biography*. New York: St. Martin's Press, 2010.

Norman, Philip. *Symphony for the Devil: The Rolling Stones Story*. London: Linden Press, 1984.

Oldham, Andrew Loog. *Stoned*. New York: Vintage, 2004.

Pang, May, and Henry Edwards. *Loving John*. New York: Warner, 1983.

Philips, Julia. *You'll Never Eat Lunch in This Town Again*. New York: Signet, 1992.

Phillips, Mackenzie. *High on Arrival*. New York: Gallery Books, 2009.

Richards, Keith. *Life*. New York: Little, Brown, 2010.

Rivera, Geraldo, with Daniel Paisner. *Exposing Myself*. New York: Bantam, 1991.

Sanchez, Tony. *Up and Down with the Rolling Stones*. New York: William Morrow, 1979.

Scaduto, Tony. *Mick Jagger: Everybody's Lucifer*. New York: David McKay, 1974.

Schofield, Carey. *Jagger*. New York: Beaufort Books, 1985.

Turner, Tina, and Kurt Loder. *I, Tina*. New York: William Morrow, 1986.

Weller, Sheila. *Girls Like Us: Carole King, Joni Mitchell, Carly Simon, and the Journey of a Generation*. New York: Atria/ Simon & Schuster, 2008.

Wheen, Francis. *Tom Driberg: His Life and Indiscretions*. London: Pan, 1990.

Wood, Ronnie. *Ronnie*. New York: St. Martin's, 2007.

Wyman, Bill, with Ray Coleman. *Stone Alone*. New York: Viking Penguin, 1991.

Wyman, Bill, with Richard Havers. *Rolling with the Stones*. London: DK Publishing, 2002.

INDEX

INDEX